D1065609

VISION AND DESIGN

⁂

ROGER FRY

Edited by J. B. Bullen

DOVER PUBLICATIONS, INC.
Mineola, New York

Bibliographical Note

This Dover edition, first published in 1998, is an unabridged republication of the work originally issued by Chatto & Windus in 1920, then reprinted as an Oxford University Press paperback in 1981. Its present republication is made possible through special arrangement with Oxford University Press, 198 Madison Avenue, New York, N.Y. 10016.

Library of Congress Cataloging-in-Publication Data

Fry, Roger Eliot, 1866–1934.
Vision and design / Roger Fry ; edited by J. B. Bullen.
p. cm.
Originally published: London ; New York : Oxford University Press, 1981, in series: Oxford paperbacks
Includes bibliographical references and index.
ISBN-13: 978-0-486-40087-7 (pbk.)
ISBN-10: 0-486-40087-5 (pbk.)
1. Art. I. Bullen, J. B. II. Title.
N7445.2.F78 1998
700—dc21 98-26347
CIP

Manufactured in the United States by LSC Communications
40087505 2020
www.doverpublications.com

DEDICATED TO

MY SISTER MARGERY

WITHOUT WHOSE GENTLE BUT PERSISTENT PRESSURE

THIS BOOK WOULD NEVER HAVE BEEN MADE

PREFACE

This book contains a selection from my writings on Art extending over a period of twenty years. Some essays have never before been published in England; and I have also added a good deal of new matter and made slight corrections throughout. In the laborious work of hunting up lost and forgotten publications, and in the work of selection, revision, and arrangement I owe everything to Mr R. R. Tatlock's devoted and patient labour.*

* Robert Tatlock was the editor of the *Burlington Magazine*.

CONTENTS

✱

LIST OF PLATES

✱

INTRODUCTION

✱

WHAT do we see when we look at a picture? Do we see the objects painted in pictures in the same way as we see them in real life? How is it that the calm passivity of a still life can stir us more deeply than all the noisy action of a battle-piece? How do we respond to the works of art from cultures about which we know nothing? When Roger Fry asked himself questions like this he was not posing academic puzzles. All through his life he thought of himself as a painter first and and as a critic second, so every time he picked up his brush he was faced, as generations of painters before him had been faced, with the curious and paradoxical relationship between art and life.

The fact that Fry was a painter explains a great deal about *Vision and Design*. The essays that make it up were written between 1900 and 1920, covering roughly the first half of Fry's critical career, and all of them have some bearing on the practice of art. There is plenty of theory in them and a great deal of argumentative, controversial writing, but the important thing for Fry was how sculpture and painting looked. He writes fluently using abstract ideas or historical facts, but his starting-point is always in the realm of appearances. The underlying assumption of many essays in this volume is that a work of art is primarily a configuration of lines, shapes, and colours and must be judged as such. The psychology of the artist fascinated him, as did the physiology of vision. Inevitably he was preoccupied with the problems of art-history, but art-history was most valuable in what it said about the work and achievement of his contemporaries. Foreign art forms interested him, too, but not in a random eclectic way. Fry was selective and he chose those exotic forms which seemed to him to have a bearing on the visual sensibility of the modern mind.

The 'Essay in Aesthetics' comes exactly half-way through the period covered by *Vision and Design* and it is Fry's most import-tant theoretical statement. It is easy to find fault with the logic of the argument but in the course of attempting to rationalise intuitive, powerful feelings about visual experience Fry described clearly why he thought form in art was of primary significance. In order to appreciate a picture, said Fry, the mind had to be cleared of debris. All the sentimental clutter of emotional or literary association had to be discarded. All the puzzles that the image might provide for the mind, all the talk of whether the picture was or was not like nature had to be forgotten if any just evaluation of its aesthetic merit was to be arrived at. As early as 1877 Walter Pater in his essay on the school of Giorgione had drawn attention to the fact that pictures were pictures before they were illustrations or reminders of natural appearances. He wrote that 'essentially pictorial qualities must first of all delight the sense, delight it as directly and sensuously as a fragment of Venetian glass', and that in its primary aspect 'a great picture has no more definite meaning for us than an accidental play of sun and shadow for a few moments on the wall or floor'.[1] When Fry took up this idea and applied it to all kinds of art, ancient and modern, familiar and unfamiliar, it appeared to his critics that either he was another mutation of late-nineteenth-century decadence or he was a blinkered formalist. In fact, Fry was waging a personal war. He was striking out against an effete critical tradition which tried to explain works of art in terms of some abstract notion of 'Beauty' or the degree to which they stimulated a sentimental response in the beholder. As he wryly commented in 'Art and Science': 'Without some previous knowledge of Caligula or Mary Queen of Scots we are likely to miss our way in a great deal of what passes for art today' (p.56). There is no doubt, however, that Fry's formalism imposed limitations on his taste. He never cared much for the 'coarse, turbulent, clumsy' art of the nineteenth century (p.40) and he was always suspicious of the operatic gestures of the Baroque. But what he did was to bring certain important areas of artistic experience into extremely

[1] 'The School of Giorgione', in *The Renaissance*, ed. Donald L. Hill (California, 1980), p.104.

sharp focus. He went straight to the heart of Florentine art and its preoccupation with the third dimension, he argued persuasively for Cézanne and the Post-Impressionists, and he was eloquent about South American sculpture and Negro art, both of which struck the sentimental critic dumb.

The cardinal point in Fry's aesthetic is the radical distinction between art and nature. The similarities between art objects and natural effects, said Fry, were merely superficial. In reality they presented the human mind with experiences of quite different orders. Nature offers the mind a mass of undifferentiated stimuli with no purpose attached. Art, however, is organised, structured and purposive. Of course Fry was restating in a subdued and rational way one of the central themes of Whistler's flamboyant *Ten O'Clock Lecture* of 1885. 'To say to the painter, that Nature is to be taken as she is', said Whistler, 'is to say to the player, that he may sit on the piano ... Nature is very rarely right.' Closer to home, Fry's first art teacher, Francis Bate, insisted on the independence of art from moral considerations[2] and in the works of both George Santayana and Denman Waldo Ross (with which Fry was familiar) there is an attempt to formulate theories which locate aesthetic satisfaction within the work of art itself. It was Bernard Berenson's description of Florentine painting, however, and his account of the work of Giotto in particular, that encouraged Fry in his analysis of the formal properties of art. According to Berenson the early Florentines created a kind of super-realism in their pictures. Giotto, said Berenson, conveys 'a keener sense of reality, of life-likeness than the objects themselves'.[3] This was achieved not by illusionist tricks or by slavish imitation of natural effects, but rather by the careful selection of telling formal relationships. It was, he said, 'upon form and form alone, that the great Florentine masters concentrated their efforts' so that 'finally we are forced to the belief that, in their pictures at least, form is the principal source of aesthetic enjoyment'.[4]

[2] *The Naturalistic School of Painting*, 2nd. ed. (1877), p.92.

[3] 'The Florentine Painters of the Renaissance' in *Italian Painters of the Renaissance*, new ed. (1952), p.41.

[4] Ibid., p.42.

Once again Fry's response was to try to expand Berenson's theory to account for a much wider compass of aesthetic experience and to make formal considerations the basis for the criticism of modern as well as ancient art. Fry also tried to find a psychological explanation for the appeal of form in art. The sharp distinction he made between what he called the 'instinctive life' and the 'imaginative life' of the mind may now seem to be too cut-and-dried for plausibility (as it seemed to critics like I.A. Richards at the time),[5] but it must be grasped if we are to understand why Fry felt that some types of art were superior to others. For Fry, the 'instinctive life' is the life of practicalities, of doing, being, and striving. It is bound up with ideas of right and wrong and consequently with the moral side of our nature. By contrast the 'imaginative life', he said, is contemplative, objective, withdrawn from the pressures of everyday existence and remote from issues of morality. Both aspects of the mind have their own way of apprehending the external world. The instinctive life relies upon a utilitarian, analytical vision which is dominated by concepts. The imaginative life, however, operates according to a system of aesthetic values and is associated with an intuitive, creative, synthesising view of the physical world. Both aspects of our mental life have their characteristic means of expression. The instinctive life is promoted through action and doing, whereas art, as Fry puts it, 'is the chief organ of the imaginative life' (p.17).

It was Tolstoy's book *What is Art?* (1898) that helped Fry in the next stage of his theory. Though Tolstoy's judgments of specific works of art are extraordinarily perverse,[6] his idea about the nature of art itself was invaluable to Fry. All previous aesthetic theories, Tolstoy pointed out, assumed that aesthetic value was an abstract notion – that 'Beauty' was a condition to which all art aspired. In actual fact '"Beauty" "Truth" and "Goodness"', said Tolstoy, 'not only have no definite meaning, but

[5] In his *The Principles of Literary Criticism* (1924).

[6] According to Tolstoy, folk and peasant art had a more profound and more widespread effect than the work of Michelangelo, Raphael, Titian and Beethoven which, as Fry points out (p.20), Tolstoy was forced to condemn as being 'bad or false art'.

they hinder us in attaching any definite meaning to existing art.'[7] So Tolstoy developed an expressive theory of art. He put it like this: 'To evoke in oneself a feeling one has once experienced and, having evoked it in oneself, then by means of movements, lines, colours, sounds or forms expressed in words, so to transmit that feeling that others experience the same feeling – this is the activity of art.'[8] In other words, for Tolstoy, art is not the creation of beauty, it is the generation of expressive forms which communicate emotion. When Tolstoy went on to insist that the power of art was to be measured by its effect on the instinctive life, Fry disagreed. For Fry art could not be measured by moral criteria, but he transferred Tolstoy's expressive theory to the context of the imaginative life. Art, said Fry, was to be judged by the subtlety and power with which it communicated the emotions of the imaginative life. The means by which it did this were formal – movements, lines, and colours. Form in the graphic arts, he concluded, was the expressive medium of the imaginative life.

Fry's explanation of how form affects the contemplative mind is probably the least satisfactory part of his theory and is based largely on another idea suggested by Berenson. In *The Florentine Painters of the Renaissance,* Berenson developed the notion of what he called 'tactile values'. Speaking about figure painting, he claimed that for it to be really effective it must create 'the illusion of being able to touch the figure'. He elaborated: 'I must have the illusion of varying muscular sensations inside my palm and fingers corresponding to the various projections of this figure, before I shall take it for granted as real, and let it affect me lastingly.'[9] Similarly Fry resorted to a physiological explanation of the power of form. In 'An Essay on Aesthetics' he tried to show how by manipulating rhythm and mass, space, chiaroscuro, and colour the artist manages to evoke physical responses through retinal impressions. Fry's explanation of the effects of form on the central nervous system might not be convincing, but his understanding of the function

[7] *Tolstoy on Art,* ed. and trans. Aylmer Maude (Oxford, 1925), p.189.
[8] Ibid., p.173.
[9] *Italian Painters of the Renaissance,* p.40.

of the imaginative life was crucial to his interpretation of the works of specific artists.

As Fry saw it, the tendency of western art since the High Renaissance (with some notable and important exceptions) had been to forget that the artist's primary function was to give expression to the imaginative life. Instead art had gradually slipped into a series of brilliant but superficial tricks to entertain the mind. The 'Kodak Company method',[10] as he once called it, reached its apogee in the Impressionist pursuit of fleeting images (about which he had ambivalent feelings) and reached its nadir in what Fry considered to be Alma-Tadema's painful attempt to paint all the spectators in his reconstruction of Roman games at the Colosseum. It is strange to find Sir Joshua Reynolds in the vanguard of modernism, but in 1905 when Fry edited the *Discourses* he felt more in sympathy with Reynolds's views than with those of most of his English contemporaries. Both Fry and Reynolds believed in classical values and in the power of tradition in art. Fry, like Reynolds before him, stressed the notion that art was primarily concerned with the selection of types and not with imitation and that a painting was a structured artefact and not a random impression. It was not long after 1905, however, that Fry was using similar terms to support modern art. In the work of the Frenchman Maurice Denis and the German Julius Meier-Graefe[11] Fry discovered a defence of Post-Impressionism which contained echoes of Reynolds's wise remarks to the students of the Royal Academy. The Post-Impressionists looked upon 'woods and meadows' as 'no more than a purely mechanical medium such as ... brushes or ... palette'[12] said Meier-Graefe, and Cézanne was a modern classic who painstakingly constructed his works in a manner similar to that of the 'art of museums'. Byzantine work was

[10]'The Case of the late Sir Lawrence Alma-Tadema, O.M.', *Athenaeum*, 18 Jan. 1913, p.667.

[11]Maurice Denis, 'Cézanne', *L'Occident*, Sept. 1907. Translated by Fry in the *Burlington Magazine*, Jan. – Feb. 1910. Denis's writings on art were collected together in *Théories* (Paris, 1912). Julius Meier-Graefe, *Modern Art*, trans. F. Simmonds and G. Chrystal (1908).

[12]*Modern Art*, p.3.

invoked to describe the hieratic dignity of Cézanne's pictures whose 'magical mosaic of colour ... expresses only exact realities'.[13] In his introduction to the catalogue of the second Post-Impressionist exhibition (reprinted in *Vision and Design* as 'The French Post-Impressionists') Fry summed up the connection between art as the formal expression of the imaginative life and the work of the moderns. 'These artists', he wrote, referring to the followers of Cézanne,

> do not seek to give what can, after all, be but a pale reflex of actual appearance, but to arouse the conviction of a new and definite reality. They do not seek to imitate form, but to create form; not to imitate life, but to find an equivalent for life. By that I mean that they wish to make images which by the clearness of their logical structure, and by their closely-knit unity of texture, shall appeal to our disinterested and contemplative imagination with something of the same vividness as the things of actual life appeal to our practical activities. In fact, they aim not at illusion but at reality. (p.167)

In his two roles as painter and as critic, Fry inevitably developed an interest in what he called 'the handling of natural appearances' – how we perceive the world around us. Most of the time, said Fry, we do not actually look at anything. The objects of our everyday existence take the form of so many ideas in our mind. The chairs and tables around us are used in a practical way, discarded and rarely looked at. In 'The Ottoman and the Whatnot' Fry shows how some objects acquire sentimental or romantic associations connected with the period in which they were made. The curios which fill antique shops are seen in a different way from everyday objects because of the associations which cluster about them. Consequently many antiques go in or out of fashion according to current attitudes to the period which produced them. In 'The Artist's Vision' Fry continues this theme and suggests two further categories of vision even more removed from practical life – aesthetic vision and creative vision. Aesthetic vision is connected with a true appraisal of the retinal impression. When we look at something not for its practical value but for its formal uniqueness we

[13]Ibid., p.267.

employ aesthetic vision. The aesthetic critic and the modern Impressionist use this mode – the one to give an account of works of art, the other to capture the effects of light and atmosphere. In his essay on Bushman art Fry suggested that some primitive tribes also shared this ability to respond to the forms of nature in a visual and non-conceptual way. Impressed by Helen Tongue's copies of Bushman paintings, Fry noticed the way in which the primitive African tribesmen managed to capture the fleeting movements of animals and the foreshortening of figures with an even greater facility than the Impressionists. Why, he wondered, had the civilising process dimmed our ability to apprehend true formal relationships but enhanced our tendency to see things as concepts? More sophisticated cultures perceive the world in a way not unlike that of the modern child. Objects are ideas first and images only second. Aesthetic vision, Fry implies, might with effort be achieved to some extent by all, but the more sophisticated creative vision is the prerogative of the artist alone. While aesthetic vision is passive and self-conscious, creative vision is active and curiously undiscriminating. It searches out new and remote visual experiences. It obeys no conventional laws of correctness or propriety. It refuses to accept what is ordinarily considered tasteful. In fact taste, says Fry, is created by the artist and for this he must have freedom.In order that the artistic sensibility might operate freely it must be released from psychological pressures and from financial restraints, and in 'Art and Socialism' Fry proposes the ideal conditions for the creation of art.

When Fry wrote his contribution to H.G. Wells's anthology of essays *Socialism and the Great State* (1912) he was about to set up the Omega Workshop. The story that Duncan Grant could not take up Fry's invitation to visit him in Guildford for want of the train fare is probably apocryphal but it points up Fry's concern for the financial state of young artists. In 'Art and Socialism' Fry expresses distrust for both aristocratic and plutocratic patronage since both limit the freedom of the artist. The howls of derision which greeted the two Post-Impressionist exhibitions made Fry suspicious of any corporate response to works of art and elsewhere he mentions with approval

Cézanne's private income, El Greco's obscurity and Blake's eccentricity, all of which helped to insulate them from the pressures of public and private opinion. Nevertheless, the artist must live, and in 'Art and Socialism' Fry suggested that in a more perfect world 'the artist would naturally turn to one of the applied arts as his means of livelihood; and we should get the artist coming out of the *bottéga,* as he did in fifteenth-century Florence' (p.53). This activity he says 'would leave him to pursue other callings in his leisure'. Fry's own *bottéga* – the Omega Workshop – invited artists to contribute designs for chairs, tables, trays, rugs, ceramics and so on in return for a small but regular income. The venture ran well for a time producing sometimes striking, sometimes bizarre household objects and fabrics from ideas devised by Duncan Grant, Vanessa Bell, Wyndham Lewis, Fry himself, and a number of other artists. It failed, not because the theory was necessarily unsound, but because Fry lacked any real business sense and the personal rivalry among members of the group became quite venomous.

When Fry reviewed George Moore's *Modern Painting* in 1893 he used a sentence to describe Moore which would have been equally applicable to Fry himself. Moore, said Fry, 'looks upon modern painting with eyes that have grown accustomed to the old masters and selects for his admiration those modern painters whom he conceives to have inherited the great artistic traditions of the past'.[14] We have seen how Roger Fry shared Reynolds's respect for artistic traditions but where Reynolds admired the achievements of the High Renaissance it was Fry's love of early Italian art which was so important in conditioning his view of Post-Impressionism. In 'The Art of Florence' he explains the appeal for him of this 'intellectual' school of painting. Giotto, Bernardo Daddi and Masaccio all 'refused to admit the given facts of nature except in so far as they could become amenable to the generalising power of their art' (p.125). And elaborating on the theme, Fry explores the balance between vision and design in the work of three pictures from the Jacquemart-André collec-

[14]'George Moore and Modern Art', *Cambridge Review,* 22 June 1893. Reprinted in *The Cambridge Mind,* ed. Eric Homberger, William Janeway and Simon Schama (1970), p.211.

tion in Paris – one by Uccello, one by Baldovinetti and one by Signorelli. He scotches the myth that Uccello's passion for representational devices in any way anticipated the illusionism of Van Eyck or the naturalism of William Powell Frith. Uccello, said Fry, created an 'abstract art' of rhythmic forms and if his *St George* is judged as illustration it is merely 'quaint, innocent and slightly childish'. Judged as design, however, 'it must rank among the great masterpieces' (p.133). The creative impulse behind much Florentine art seemed to Fry to resemble the creativity of science. Fry himself had received a fine scientific education at Cambridge[15] and was always fascinated by the links between the methods of science and those of art. In the case of the Florentines, they resemble the scientists in their preoccupation with 'the discovery of fundamental relations between . . . objects' and by 'the construction of a synthetic system which satisfies the mind, both for its truth to facts and its logical coherence' (p.124). The emphasis on construction and logical coherence is central to all that Fry has to say about art. He was brought up in the techniques of Impressionism in the school of Francis Bate, but he rebelled against what he felt to be its formlessness when he discovered the 'logical coherence' of early Italian art. In 1894 he despaired of ever finding in modern art the same tightly-knit massive simplicity of earlier work and wrote to his father: 'the more I study the Old Masters the more terrible does the chaos of modern art seem to me.'[16] The change came in 1906 when he found what he was looking for in the work of Cézanne. He suddenly realised that a revolution had been going on in art – 'the greatest revolution in art that had taken place since Graeco-Roman impressionism became converted into Byzantine formalism' (p.8). Cézanne, said Fry, followed by Gauguin and Van Gogh, and at a greater distance by Matisse and Picasso, had created a new pictorial language in which form and structure had taken precedence over imitation, symbolism and sentiment.

[15]In 1885 Fry went up to King's College to read natural sciences. He obtained a first-class degree in the Tripos.

[16]Letter of 27 Sept. 1894 in *Letters of Roger Fry*, ed. Denys Sutton (1972), p.159.

This discovery meant that in Fry's view the early Italians now had worthy modern counterparts and most of the essays in *Vision and Design* were written with this understanding. By 1910 his art-historical ideas moved easily between the two poles of Byzantium and Post-Impressionism and the success of other artists could be measured by their relationship to these antipodes. William Blake, for example, looked back to the Byzantines while El Greco anticipated Cézanne. In his essay on Blake, Fry points out how, like the mosaics of Ravenna, Blake's tempera paintings are quite removed from the stress of the immediate. They give us 'an experience freed from the disturbing conditions of actual life' (p.153) and in his account of the El Greco acquired in 1919 for the National Gallery, Fry develops Maurice Denis's idea that Cézanne 'a du Greco en lui'.[17] Both artists, says Fry, adopted the same uncompromising directness in their rendering of natural forms. 'Nowhere', says Fry, 'is a violent form softened, nowhere is the expressive quality of brushwork blurred in order to give verisimilitude of texture' (p.146). Elsewhere Fry adopts similar historical comparisons. The firm sense of structure in the drawing of Ingres looks back to the Italian primitives ('Drawings at Burlington') while some of Claude's effects anticipate those of the Impressionists ('Claude').

Once Fry had established his ideas about expressive form in Western art he turned his attention to non-European cultures whose art until recently had been seen as the object of only anthropological research. The exhibition of Negro art at the Chelsea Book Club, for example, was one of the first of its kind in this country and on 15 April 1919 Fry took Virginia Woolf to see the sculpture. She found it 'dismal and impressive' and confessed to her sister, Vanessa Bell, that 'heaven knows what real feeling I have about anything after hearing Roger discourse'.[18] On the following day Fry's review appeared in the *Athenaeum* and the essay 'Negro Art' must contain the substance of the lecture which he read to Virginia Woolf. It is probable that the enormous enthusiasm which Fry had for Negro art

[17]'Cézanne', *L'Occident*, Sept. 1907.

[18]Virginia Woolf, *The Question of Things Happening: The Letters of Virginia Woolf 1912–1922*, ed. Nigel Nicolson and Joanne Trautmann (1976), p.429.

stemmed originally from Matisse. In 1905 Matisse already had some interest in African art. He showed some to Picasso and the influence can be seen in the famous *Les Demoiselles d'Avignon* of 1907.[19] In 1909 Fry visited Matisse in his studio at Issy where he saw Matisse's sculptured piece *La Serpentine* which was based upon African forms. Fry then arranged that it should be shown at the second Post-Impressionist exhibition in London in 1910. Both Fry and Clive Bell admired Negro Art:[20] it seemed to them to represent perfect mastery over the medium, and it also came very close to what Fry in his introduction to the catalogue of the second Post-Impressionist exhibition called 'pure art'. It was quite free from the 'practical responses to sensations of ordinary life' and was completely without any 'romantic associations' (p.169). The very remoteness of the culture was a positive advantage for Fry's method. The only possible approach to the sculpture was through the formal relations – the way in which mass and volume was created in each piece – and though Fry does not mention the modernist connection in his essay, there is no doubt that the resemblance between the plastic sense of Negro art and the solid geometry of Cubism brought the sculpture alive for him. Fry describes the way in which the African conceives the neck and torso 'as cylinders, not as masses with a square section' and the head as 'a pear-shaped mass' (p.71) with the same relish that he suggested Uccello's simplification of the form 'anticipates in a curious way that of the modern cubists' (p.131).

There is a modernist connection with yet another of Fry's excursions into the art of a remote culture – this time the art of Islam. When Fry visited the huge and much publicised[21] exhibition of Mohammedan art at Munich he probably knew that

[19]See Alfred H. Barr, *Matisse, His Art and His Public* (1951, repr. 1966), p.85.

[20]In 'Negro Sculpture', *Athenaeum*, 20 Aug. 1920, Bell expressed his enthusiasm for African art, but in more cautious terms than Fry. He wrote: 'Though the capital achievements of the greatest schools do seem to me to have an absolute superiority over anything Negro I have seen, yet the finest black sculpture is so rich in artistic qualities that it is entitled to a place beside them.'

[21]There were notices of the exhibition in *The Times* of 5 Jan., 27 Jan., 16 May, 19 Aug., 17 Oct. 1910.

it was stirring the imagination of a number of modern artists. In the summer of 1910 both Henri Matisse and Albert Marquet visited the exhibition and met Hugo von Tschudi, the director of the Staatsgalerie there. Von Tschudi was one of Germany's best known collectors of Impressionist and Post-Impressionist art and he was forced to move from Berlin for trying to introduce modern works into the Kaiser-Friedrich-Museum (see note 8, p.227). Fry, who recalls a conversation he had with von Tschudi in his essay on El Greco, probably met him on his trip to Munich. His task was to review the Mohammedan exhibition for the *Burlington Magazine* and the *Morning Post,* but with the Post-Impressionist exhibition to take place in November of that year his head was also filled with new ideas about modern art. The essay is not one of his most successful. Both the scholarship and the speculative interpretation is now well out of date, but it does preserve the freshness of one of the earliest aesthetic responses to the art of Islam.

Though the formalist criticism of art in *Vision and Design* was extremely adventurous in its own day and still retains a great deal that is of interest to the modern reader, one primary difficulty remains. D.H. Lawrence's satirical portrait of Fry as the high priest of abstraction is wilful and unfair but it does have a grain of truth in it. In 'An Introduction to These Pictures' (1927) Lawrence put his finger on one of the limitations of Fry's method. He lampooned the new aesthetic treatment of art thus:

> But let scoffers scoff, the aesthetic ecstasy was vouchsafed only to the few, the elect, and even then only when they had freed their minds of false doctrine. They had renounced the mammon of 'subject' in pictures, they went whoring no more after the Babylon of painted 'interest', nor did they hanker after the flesh-pots of artistic 'representation'. Oh purify yourselves, ye who would know aesthetic ecstasy, and be lifted up to the 'white peaks of artistic inspiration'. Purify yourselves of all base hankering for a tale that is told, and of all low lust for likeness.[22]

Fry of course did not encourage and promote the worship of

[22] *Phoenix*, ed. Edward D. MacDonald, new ed. (1961), p.565. Lawrence's essay formed the preface to the catalogue of an exhibition of his own pictures at the Warren Gallery in 1927.

pure abstraction as Lawrence suggests, but he never really solved the problem of representation in art. Indeed Fry himself said that he had 'never denied the existence of some amount of representation in all pictorial art' and that he had 'always admitted the purely representational nature of the presentiment of the third dimension on the flat surface of a picture';[23] yet much of his criticism fails to make any allowance for what is actually depicted in that third dimension. For example, when he says that in a painting by Renoir 'the planes recede by insensible gradations towards the contour, which generally remains the vaguest, least ascertained part of the modelling' and contrasts this with Cézanne's 'method of suggesting endless recessions of planes' (p.189), he makes nothing of the important fact that Renoir's study is of an extremely voluptuous nude and Cézanne's is not. There are two places in *Vision and Design* where Fry recognises this difficulty. The first is in a note which he added to his essay on Giotto and the other is in the last essay in the book, 'Retrospect'. When Fry first wrote his account of Giotto's frescoes at Assisi he assumed the formal power of the painting to be a direct result of Giotto's psychological response to the legend of St Francis. In other words he felt that the subject had inspired the form. By 1920 he had changed his mind. He had come to the conclusion that the responsiveness to form and interpretation of drama were quite separate emotional experiences and should not be confused. He dealt with the problem again in his discussion of Raphael's *The Transfiguration* in 'Retrospect'. The peculiar treatment of the subject in this picture, says Fry, can produce a number of feelings in us, but those feelings have nothing to do with the unity of the painting as a configuration of shapes and colours. How, then, is our emotional reaction to the subject of a work of art related to our comprehension of line, mass and shape? To this question Fry has no answer. He knew that it was an important one, however, and decided to include the essay on Giotto in *Vision and Design* even though the ideas in it did not conform to his later views.

Fry was not an aesthetician nor a philosopher; nor was he a psychologist or an art-historian. He saw prehistoric art not as an archaeologist would see it but as someone intimately concerned with the problems of vision. Similarly, his view of Negro art is not that of the anthropologist, nor his interpretation of El Greco or Claude that of the scholar. He once claimed that he was 'a middleman between the art-historian and the amateur'[24] and his intense empiricism reminds one of Ruskin. Like Ruskin he was a great talker and many of his friends – E.M. Forster, Clive Bell and Virginia Woolf in particular – recall the delight and perplexity of being marched around exhibitions by him. The essays in *Vision and Design* preserve something of the quality of highly informed and original conversation. They are experimental and tentative. They are not theoretical statement, they are points of view. Their unity comes from Fry's curiosity about how art is made, how a piece of sculpture or a picture is constructed. He was well informed about the history of the art of a number of cultures, but the vitality of his point of view always comes from his subtle and close acquaintance with the creative process itself.

J. B. Bullen

[23]'Mr MacColl and Drawing', *Burlington Magazine,* 35 (Aug. 1919), p.84.
[24]'Art Before Giotto', *Monthly Review,* 1 (Oct. 1900), p.126.

ART AND LIFE

✷

WHEN we look at ancient works of art we habitually treat them not merely as objects of aesthetic enjoyment but also as successive deposits of the human imagination. It is indeed this view of works of art as crystallised history that accounts for much of the interest felt in ancient art by those who have but little aesthetic feeling and who find nothing to interest them in the work of their contemporaries, where the historical motive is lacking, and they are left face to face with bare aesthetic values.

I once knew an old gentleman who had retired from his city office to a country house – a fussy, feeble little being, who had cut no great figure in life. He had built himself a house which was preternaturally hideous; his taste was deplorable and his manners indifferent; but he had a dream, the dream of himself as an exquisite and refined intellectual dandy living in a society of elegant frivolity. To realise this dream he had spent large sums in buying up every scrap of eighteenth-century French furniture which he could lay hands on. These he stored in an immense upper floor in his house, which was always locked except when he went up to indulge in his dream and to become for a time a courtier at Versailles doing homage on the du Barry,[1] whose toilet-tables and whatnots were strewn pell-mell about the room without order or effect of any kind. Such is an extreme instance of the historical way of looking at works of art. For this old gentleman, as for how many an American millionaire,[2] art was merely a help to an imagined dream life.

To many people then it seems an easy thing to pass thus directly from the work of art to the life of the time which produced it. We all in fact weave an imagined Middle Ages around the parish church and an imagined Renaissance haunts us in the college courts of Oxford and Cambridge. We don't, I fancy, stop to consider very closely how true the imagined life is: we are satisfied with the prospect of another sort of life which we might have lived, which we often think we might have preferred to our actual life. We don't stop to consider much how far the pictured past corresponds to any reality, certainly not to consider what proportion of the whole reality of the past life gets itself embalmed in this way in works of art. Thus we picture our Middle Ages as almost entirely occupied with religion and war, our Renaissance as occupied in learning, and our eighteenth century as occupied in gallantry and wit. Whereas, as a matter of fact, all of these things were going on all the time while the art of each period has for some reason been mainly taken up with the expression of one or another activity. There is indeed a certain danger in accepting too naïvely the general atmosphere – the ethos, which the works of art of a period exhale. Thus when we look at the thirteenth-century sculpture of Chartres or Beauvais we feel at once the expression of a peculiar gracious piety, a smiling and gay devoutness which we are tempted to take for the prevailing mood of the time – and which we perhaps associate with the revelation of just such a type of character in S. Francis of Assisi. A study of Salimbeni's[3] chronicle with its interminable record of squalid avarice and meanness, or of the fierce brutalities of Dante's Inferno is a necessary corrective of such a pleasant dream.

It would seem then that the correspondence between art and life which we so habitually assume is not at all constant and requires much correction before it can be trusted. Let us approach the same question from another point and see what result we obtain. Let us consider the great revolutions in art and the revolutions in life and see if they coincide. And here let me try to say what I mean by life as contrasted with art. I mean the general intellectual and instinctive reaction to their surroundings of those men of any period whose lives rise to complete self-consciousness. Their view of the universe as a whole and their conception of their relations to their kind. Of course their conception of the nature and function of art will itself be one of the most varying aspects of life and may in any particular period profoundly modify the correspondence of art to life.

Perhaps the greatest revolution in life that we know of at all intimately was that which effected the change from Paganism to Christianity. That this was no mere accident is evident from the fact that Christianity was only one of many competing religions, all of which represented a closely similar direction of thought and feeling. Any one of these would have produced practically the same effect, that of focussing men's minds on the spiritual life as opposed to the material life which had preoccupied them for so long. One cannot doubt then that here was a change which denoted a long prepared and inevitable readjustment of men's attitude to their universe. Now the art of the Roman Empire showed no trace whatever of this influence; it went on with precisely the same motives and principles which had satisfied Paganism. The subjects changed and became mainly Christian, but the treatment was so exactly similar that it requires more than a cursory glance to say if the figure on a sarcophagus is Christ or Orpheus, Moses or Aesculapius.

The next great turning-point in history is that which marks the triumph of the forces of reaction towards the close of the twelfth century – a reaction which destroyed the promising hopes of freedom of thought and manners which make the twelfth century appear as a foretaste of modern enlightenment. Here undoubtedly the change in life corresponds very closely with a great change in art – the change from the Romanesque to the Gothic, and at first sight we might suppose a causal connection between the two. But when we consider the nature of the changes in the two sequences, this becomes very doubtful. For whereas in the life of the Middle Ages the change was one of reaction – the sharp repression by the reactionary forces of a gradual growth of freedom – the change in art is merely the efflorescence of certain long prepared and anticipated effects. The forms of Gothic architecture were merely the answer to certain engineering problems which had long occupied the inventive ingenuity of twelfth-century architects, while in the figurative arts the change merely showed a new self-confidence in the rendering of the human figure, a newly developed mastery in the handling of material. In short, the change in art was in the opposite direction to that in life. Whereas in life the direction of movement was sharply bent backwards, in art the direction followed on in a continuous straight line.

It is true that in one small particular the reaction did have a direct effect on art. The preaching of S. Bernard of Clairvaux[4] did impose on the architects who worked for the Cistercian order a peculiar architectural hypocrisy. They were bound by his traditional influence to make their churches have an appearance of extreme simplicity and austerity, but they wanted nevertheless to make them as magnificent and imposing as possible. The result was a peculiar style of ostentatious simplicity. Paray le Monial[5] is the only church left standing in which this curious and, in point of fact, depressing evidence of the direct influence of the religious reaction on art is to be seen, and, as a curiosity in psychological expression, it is well worth a visit. For the rest the movement of art went on entirely unaffected by the new orientation of thought.

We come now to the Renaissance, and here for the first time in our survey we may, I think, safely admit a true correspondence between the change in life and the change in art. The change in life, if one may generalise on such a vast subject, was towards the recognition of the rights of the individual, towards complete self-realisation and the recognition of the objective reality of the material universe which implied the whole scientific attitude – and in both these things the exemplar which men put before themselves was the civilisation of Greece and Rome. In art the change went *pari passu* with the change in life, each assisting and directing the other – the first men of science were artists like Brunelleschi, Uccello, Piero della Francesca and Leonardo da Vinci. The study of classical literature was followed in strict connection with the study of classical canons of art, and the greater sense of individual importance found its expression in the new naturalism which made portraiture in the modern sense possible.

For once then art and the other functions of the human spirit found themselves in perfect harmony and direct alliance, and to that harmony we may attribute much of the intensity and self-assurance of the work of the great Renaissance artists. It is one of the rarest of good fortunes for an artist to find himself actually understood and appreciated by the mass of his educated contemporaries, and not only that, but moving alongside of and in step with them towards a similar goal.

The Catholic reaction retarded and impeded the main movement of Renaissance thought, but it did not really succeed either in suppressing it or changing the main direction of its current. In art it undoubtedly had some direct effect, it created a new kind of insincerity of expression, a florid and sentimental religiosity – a new variety of bad taste, the rhetorical and over-emphatic. And I suspect that art was already prepared for this step by a certain exhaustion of the impulsive energy of the Renaissance – so that here too we may admit a correspondence.

The seventeenth century shows us no violent change in life, but rather the gradual working out of the principles implicit in the Renaissance and the Catholic reaction. But here we come to another curious want of correspondence between art and life, for in art we have a violent revolution, followed by a bitter internecine struggle among artists. This revolution was inaugurated by Caravaggio,[6] who first discovered the surprising emotional possibilities of chiaroscuro and who combined with this a new idea of realism – realism in the modern sense, viz., the literal acceptance of what is coarse, common, squalid or undistinguished in life – realism in the sense of the novelists of Zola's time. To Caravaggio's influence we might trace not only a great deal of Rembrandt's art but the whole of that movement in favour of the extravagantly impressive and picturesque, which culminated in the romantic movement of the nineteenth century. Here, then, is another surprising want of correspondence between art and life.

In the eighteenth century we get a curious phenomenon. Art goes to court, identifies itself closely with a small aristocratic clique, becomes the exponent of their manners and their tastes. It becomes a luxury. It is no longer in the main stream of spiritual and intellectual effort, and this seclusion of art may account for the fact that the next great change in life – the French Revolution and all its accompanying intellectual ferment – finds no serious correspondence in art. We get a change, it is true; the French Republicans believed they were the counterpart of the Romans, and so David[7] had to invent for them that peculiarly distressing type of the ancient Roman – always in heroic attitudes, always immaculate, spotless and with a highly polished 'Mme Tussaud' surface. By-the-by, I was almost forgetting that we do owe Mme Tussaud to the French Revolution. But the real movement of art in quite other directions to David – lay in the gradual unfolding of the Romanticist conception of the world – a world of violent emotional effects, of picturesque accidents, of wild nature, and this was a long prepared reaction from the complacent sophistication of eighteenth-century life. It is possible that one may associate this with the general state of mind that produced the Revolution, since both were a revolt against the established order of the eighteenth century; but curiously enough it found its chief ally in the reaction which followed the Revolution, in the neo-Christianism of Chateaubriand and the new sentimental respect for the age of faith – which, incidentally, appeared so much more picturesque than the age of reason.

It would be interesting at this point to consider how far during the nineteenth century reactionary political and religious thought was inspired primarily by aesthetic considerations – a curious instance of the counter-influence of art on life might perhaps be discovered in the devotees of the Oxford Movement. But this would take us too far afield.

The foregoing violently foreshortened view of history and art will show, I hope, that the usual assumption of a direct and decisive connection between life and art is by no means correct. It may, I hope, give pause to those numerous people who have already promised themselves a great new art as a result of the present war, though perhaps it is as well to let them enjoy it in anticipation, since it is, I fancy, the only way in which they are likely to enjoy a great art of any kind. What this survey suggests to me is that if we consider this special spiritual activity of art we find it no doubt open at times to influences from life, but in the main self-contained – we find the rhythmic sequences of change determined much more by its own internal forces – and by the readjustment within it, of its own elements – than by external forces. I admit, of course, that it is always conditioned more or less by economic changes, but these are rather conditions of its existence at all than directive influences. I also admit that under certain conditions the rhythms of life and of art may coincide with great effect on both; but in the main the two rhythms are distinct, and as often as not play against each other.

We have, I hope, gained some experience with which to handle the real subject of my inquiry, the relation of the modern movement in art to life. To understand it we must go back to the impressionist movement, which dates from about 1870. The artists who called themselves impressionists combined two distinct ideas. On the one hand they upheld, more categorically than ever before, the complete detachment of the artistic vision from the values imposed on vision by everyday life – they claimed, as Whistler did in his '10 o'clock',[8] to be pure artists. On the other hand a group of them used this freedom for the quasi-scientific description of new effects of atmospheric colour and atmospheric perspective, thereby endowing painting with a quite new series of colour harmonies, or at least of harmonies which had not been cultivated by European painters for many hundreds of years. They did more than this – the effects thus explored were completely unfamiliar to the ordinary man, whose vision is limited to the mere recognition of objects with a view to the uses of everyday life. He was forced, in looking at their pictures, to accept as artistic representation something very remote from all his previous expectations, and thereby he also acquired in time a new tolerance in his judgments on works of art, a tolerance which was destined to bear a still further strain in succeeding developments.

As against these great advantages which art owes to impressionism we must set the fact that the pseudo-scientific and analytic method of these painters forced artists to accept pictures which lacked design and formal co-ordination to a degree which had never before been permitted. They, or rather some of them, reduced the artistic vision to a continuous patchwork or mosaic of coloured patches without architectural framework or structural coherence. In this, impressionism marked the climax of a movement which had been going on more or less steadily from the thirteenth century – the tendency to approximate the forms of art more and more exactly to the representation of the totality of appearance. When once representation had been pushed to this point where further development was impossible, it was inevitable that artists should turn round and question the validity of the fundamental assumption that art aimed at representation; and the moment the question was fairly posed it became clear that the pseudo-scientific assumption that fidelity to appearance was the measure of art had no logical foundation. From that moment on it became evident that art had arrived at a critical point, and that the greatest revolution in art that had taken place since Graeco-Roman impressionism became converted into Byzantine formalism was inevitable. It was this revolution that Cézanne inaugurated and that Gauguin and van Gogh continued. There is no need here to give in detail the characteristics of this new movement: they are sufficiently familiar. But we may summarise them as the re-establishment of purely aesthetic criteria in place of the criterion of conformity to appearance – the rediscovery of the principles of structural design and harmony.

The new movement has also led to a new canon of criticism, and this has changed our attitude to the arts of other times and countries. So long as representation was regarded as the end of art, the skill of the artist and his proficiency in this particular feat of representation were regarded with an admiration which was in fact mainly non-aesthetic. With the new indifference to representation we have become much less interested in skill and not at all interested in knowledge. We are thus no longer cut off from a great deal of barbaric and primitive art the very meaning of which escaped the understanding of those who demanded a certain standard of skill in representation before they could give serious consideration to a work of art. In general the effect of the movement has been to render the artist intensely conscious of the aesthetic unity of the work of art, but singularly naïve and simple as regards other considerations.

It remains to be considered whether the life of the past fifty years has shown any such violent reorientation as we have found in the history of modern art. If we look back to the days of Herbert Spencer and Huxley, what changes are there in the general tendencies of life? The main ideas of rationalism seem to me to have steadily made way – there have been minor counter revolutions, it is true, but the main current of active thought has surely moved steadily along the lines already laid down. I mean that the scientific attitude is more and more widely accepted. The protests of organised religion and of various mysticisms seem to grow gradually weaker and to carry less weight. Hardly any writers or thinkers of first-rate calibre now appear in the reactionary camp. I see, in short, no big change in direction, no evident revulsion of feeling.

None the less I suppose that a Spencer would be impossible now, and that the materialism of today is recognisably different from the materialism of Spencer. It would be very much less naïvely self-confident. It would admit far greater difficulties in presenting its picture of the universe than would have occurred to Spencer. The fact is that scepticism has turned on itself and has gone behind a great many of the axioms that seemed self-evident to the earlier rationalists. I do not see that it has at any point threatened the superstructure of the rationalist position, but it has led us to recognise the necessity of a continual revision and reconstruction of these data. Rationalism has become less arrogant and less narrow in its vision. And this is partly due also to the adventure of the scientific spirit into new regions. I refer to all that immense body of study and speculation which starts from Robertson Smith's *Religion of the Israelites.*[9] The discovery of natural law in what seemed to earlier rationalists the chaotic fancies and caprices of the human imagination. The assumption that man is a mainly rational animal has given place to the discovery that he is, like other animals, mainly instinctive. This modifies immensely the attitude of the rationalist – it gives him a new charity and a new tolerance. What seemed like the wilful follies of mad or wicked men to the earlier rationalists are now seen to be inevitable responses to fundamental instinctive needs. By observing mankind the man of science has lost his contempt for him. Now this I think has had an important bearing on the new movement in art. In the first place I find something analogous in the new orientation of scientific and artistic endeavour. Science has turned its instruments in on human nature and begun to investigate its fundamental needs, and art has also turned its vision inwards, has begun to work upon the fundamental necessities of man's aesthetic functions.

But besides this analogy, which may be merely accidental and not causal, I think there can be little doubt that the new scientific development – for it is in no sense a revolution – has modified men's attitude to art. To Herbert Spencer, religion was primitive fear of the unknown and art was sexual attraction – he must have contemplated with perfect equanimity, almost with satisfaction, a world in which both these functions would disappear. I suppose that the scientific man of today would be much more ready to admit not only the necessity but the great importance of aesthetic feeling for the spiritual existence of man. The general conception of life in the mid-nineteenth century ruled out art as noxious, or at best, a useless frivolity, and above all as a mere survival of more primitive stages of evolution.

On the other hand, the artist of the new movement is moving into a sphere more and more remote from that of the ordinary man. In proportion as art becomes purer the number of people to whom it appeals gets less. It cuts out all the romantic overtones of life which are the usual bait by which men are induced to accept a work of art. It appeals only to the aesthetic sensibility, and that in most men is comparatively weak.

In the modern movement in art, then, as in so many cases in past history, the revolution in art seems to be out of all proportion to any corresponding change in life as a whole. It seems to find its sources, if at all, in what at present seem like minor movements. Whether the difference between the nineteenth and twentieth centuries will in retrospect seem as great in life as they already do in art I cannot guess – at least it is curious to note how much more conscious we are of the change in art than we are of the general change in thought and feeling.

NOTE – The original lecture was not illustrated, but the opportunity of publishing this summary of it has suggested the possibility of introducing a few examples to illustrate one point, viz., the extent to which the works of the new movement correspond in aim with the works of early art while being sharply contrasted with those of the penultimate period ... In Plate I I have placed Picasso beside Raphael. Here the obvious fact is the common pre-occupation of both artists with certain problems of plastic design and the similarity of their solutions. Had I had space to put a Sargent[10] beside these the same violent contrast would have been produced. [Fry's note to the first edition.]

AN ESSAY IN AESTHETICS

✱

A CERTAIN painter, not without some reputation at the present day, once wrote a little book on the art he practises, in which he gave a definition of that art so succinct that I take it as a point of departure for this essay.

'The art of painting', says that eminent authority, 'is the art of imitating solid objects upon a flat surface by means of pigments.'[1] It is delightfully simple, but prompts the question – Is that all? And, if so, what a deal of unnecessary fuss has been made about it. Now, it is useless to deny that our modern writer has some very respectable authorities behind him. Plato, indeed, gave a very similar account of the affair, and himself put the question – is it then worth while? And, being scrupulously and relentlessly logical, he decided that it was not worth while, and proceeded to turn the artists out of his ideal republic.[2] For all that, the world has continued obstinately to consider that painting was worth while, and though, indeed, it has never quite made up its mind as to what, exactly, the graphic arts did for it, has persisted in honouring and admiring its painters.

Can we arrive at any conclusions as to the nature of the graphic arts, which will at all explain our feelings about them, which will at least put them into some kind of relation with the other arts, and not leave us in the extreme perplexity, engendered by any theory of mere imitation? For, I suppose, it must be admitted that if imitation is the sole purpose of the graphic arts, it is surprising that the works of such arts are ever looked upon as more than curiosities, or ingenious toys, are ever taken seriously by grown-up people. Moreover, it will be surprising that they have no recognisable affinity with other arts, such as music or architecture, in which the imitation of actual objects is a negligible quantity. To form such conclusions is the aim I have put before myself in this essay. Even if the results are not decisive, the inquiry may lead us to a view of the graphic arts that will not be altogether unfruitful.

I must begin with some elementary psychology, with a consideration of the nature of instincts. A great many objects in the world, when presented to our senses, put in motion a complex nervous machinery, which ends in some instinctive appropriate action. We see a wild bull in a field; quite without our conscious interference a nervous process goes on, which, unless we interfere forcibly, ends in the appropriate reaction of flight. The nervous mechanism which results in flight causes a certain state of consciousness, which we call the emotion of fear. The whole of animal life, and a great part of human life, is made up of these instinctive reactions to sensible objects, and their accompanying emotions. But man has the peculiar faculty of calling up again in his mind the echo of past experiences of this kind, of going over it again, 'in imagination' as we say. He has, therefore, the possibility of a double life; one the actual life, the other the imaginative life. Between these two lives there is this great distinction, that in the actual life the processes of natural selection have brought it about that the instinctive reaction, such, for instance, as flight from danger, shall be the important part of the whole process, and it is towards this that the man bends his whole conscious endeavour. But in the imaginative life no such action is necessary, and, therefore, the whole consciousness may be focussed upon the perceptive and the emotional aspects of the experience. In this way we get, in the imaginative life, a different set of values, and a different kind of perception.

We can get a curious side glimpse of the nature of this imaginative life from the cinematograph. This resembles actual life in almost every respect, except that what the psychologists call the conative part of our reaction to sensations, that is to say, the appropriate resultant action is cut off. If, in a cinematograph, we see a runaway horse and cart, we do not have to think either of getting out of the way or heroically interposing ouselves. The result is that in the first place we *see* the event much more clearly; see a number of quite interesting but irrelevant things, which in real life could not struggle into our consciousness, bent, as it would be, entirely upon the problem of our appropriate reaction. I remember seeing in a cinematograph the arrival of a train at a foreign station and the people descending from the carriages; there was no platform, and to my intense surprise I saw several people turn right round after reaching the ground, as though to orientate themselves; an almost ridiculous performance, which I had never noticed in all the many hundred occasions on which such a scene had passed before my eyes in real life. The fact being that at a station one is never really a spectator of events, but an actor engaged in the drama of luggage or prospective seats, and one actually sees only so much as may help to the appropriate action.

In the second place, with regard to the visions of the cinematograph, one notices that whatever emotions are aroused by them, though they are likely to be weaker than those of ordinary life, are presented more clearly to the consciousness. If the scene presented be one of an accident, our pity and horror, though weak, since we know that no one is really hurt, are felt quite purely, since they cannot, as they would in life, pass at once into actions of assistance.

A somewhat similar effect to that of the cinematograph can be obtained by watching a mirror in which a street scene is reflected. If we look at the street itself we are almost sure to adjust ourselves in some way to its actual existence. We recognise an acquaintance, and wonder why he looks so dejected this morning, or become interested in a new fashion in hats – the moment we do that the spell is broken, we are reacting to life itself in however slight a degree, but, in the mirror, it is easier to abstract ourselves completely, and look upon the changing scene as a whole. It then, at once, takes on the visionary quality, and we become true spectators, not selecting what we will see, but seeing everything equally, and thereby we come to notice a number of appearances and relations of appearances, which would have escaped our notice before, owing to that perpetual economising by selection of what impressions we will assimilate, which in life we perform by unconscious processes. The frame of the mirror, then, does to some extent turn the reflected scene from one that belongs to our actual life into one that belongs rather to the imaginative life. The frame of the mirror makes its surface into a very rudimentary work of art, since it helps us to attain to the artistic vision. For that is what, as you will already have guessed, I have been coming to all this time, namely that the work of art is intimately connected with the secondary imaginative life, which all men live to a greater or less extent.

That the graphic arts are the expression of the imaginative life rather than a copy of actual life might be guessed from observing children. Children, if left to themselves, never, I believe, copy what they see, never, as we say, 'draw from nature', but express, with a delightful freedom and sincerity, the mental images which make up their own imaginative lives.

Art, then, is an expression and a stimulus of this imaginative life, which is separated from actual life by the absence of responsive action. Now this responsive action implies in actual life moral responsibility. In art we have no such moral responsibility – it presents a life freed from the binding necessities of our actual existence.

What then is the justification for this life of the imagination which all human beings live more or less fully? To the pure moralist, who accepts nothing but ethical values, in order to be justified, it must be shown not only *not* to hinder but actually to forward right action, otherwise it is not only useless but, since it absorbs our energies, positively harmful. To such a one two views are possible, one the Puritanical view at its narrowest, which regards the life of the imagination as no better or worse than a life of sensual pleasure, and therefore entirely reprehensible. The other view is to argue that the imaginative life does subserve morality. And this is inevitably the view taken by moralists like Ruskin, to whom the imaginative life is yet an absolute necessity. It is a view which leads to some very hard special pleading, even to a self-deception which is in itself morally undesirable.

But here comes in the question of religion, for religion is also an affair of the imaginative life, and, though it claims to have a direct effect upon conduct, I do not suppose that the religious person if he were wise would justify religion entirely by its effect on morality, since that, historically speaking, has not been by any means uniformly advantageous. He would probably say that the religious experience was one which corresponded to certain spiritual capacities of human nature, the exercise of which is in itself good and desirable apart from their effect upon actual life. And so, too, I think the artist might if he chose take a mystical attitude, and declare that the fullness and completeness of the imaginative life he leads may correspond to an existence more real and more important than any that we know of in mortal life.

And in saying that, his appeal would find a sympathetic echo in most minds, for most people would, I think, say that the pleasure derived from art were of an altogether different character and more fundamental than merely sensual pleasures, that they did exercise some faculties which are felt to belong to whatever part of us there may be which is not entirely ephemeral and material.

It might even be that from this point of view we should rather justify actual life by its relation to the imaginative, justify nature by its likeness to art. I mean this, that since the imaginative life comes in the course of time to represent more or less what mankind feels to be the completest expression of its own nature, the freest use of its innate capacities, the actual life may be explained and justified by its approximation here and there, however partially and inadequately, to that freer and fuller life.

Before leaving this question of the justification of art, let me put it in another way. The imaginative life of a people has very different levels at different times, and these levels do not always correspond with the general level of the morality of actual life. Thus in the thirteenth century we read of barbarity and cruelty which would shock even us; we may, I think, admit that our moral level, our general humanity is decidedly higher today, but the level of our imaginative life is incomparably lower; we are satisfied there with a grossness, a sheer barbarity and squalor which would have shocked the thirteenth century profoundly. Let us admit the moral gain gladly, but do we not also feel a loss; do we not feel that the average business man would be in every way a more admirable, more respectable being if his imaginative life were not so squalid and incoherent? And, if we admit any loss then, there is some function in human nature other than a purely ethical one, which is worthy of exercise.

Now the imaginative life has its own history both in the race and in the individual. In the individual life one of the first effects of freeing experience from the necessities of appropriate responsive action is to indulge recklessly the emotion of self-aggrandisement. The day-dreams of a child are filled with extravagant romances in which he is always the invincible hero. Music – which of all the arts supplies the strongest stimulus to the imaginative life, and at the same time has the least power of controlling its direction – music, at certain stages of people's lives, has the effect merely of arousing in an almost absurd degree this egoistic elation, and Tolstoy appears to believe that this is its only possible effect.[3] But with the teaching of experience and the growth of character the imaginative life comes to respond to other instincts and to satisfy other desires, until, indeed, it reflects the highest aspirations and the deepest aversions of which human nature is capable.

In dreams and when under the influence of drugs the imaginative life passes out of our own control, and in such cases its experiences may be highly undesirable, but whenever it remains under our own control it must always be on the whole a desirable life. That is not to say that it is always pleasant, for it is pretty clear that mankind is so constituted as to desire much besides pleasure, and we shall meet among the great artists, the great exponents, that is, of the imaginative life, many to whom the merely pleasant is very rarely a part of what is desirable. But this desirability of the imaginative life does distinguish it very sharply from actual life, and is the direct result of that first fundamental difference, its freedom from necessary external conditions. Art, then is, if I am right, the chief organ of the imaginative life; it is by art that it is stimulated and controlled within us, and, as we have seen, the imaginative life is distinguished by the greater clearness of its perception, and the greater purity and freedom of its emotion.

First with regard to the greater clearness of perception. The needs of our actual life are so imperative, that the sense of vision becomes highly specialised in their service. With an admirable economy we learn to see only so much as is needful for our purposes; but this is in fact very little, just enough to recognise and identify each object or person; that done, they go into an entry in our mental catalogue and are no more really seen. In actual life the normal person really only reads the labels as it were on the objects around him and troubles no further. Almost all the things which are useful in any way put on more or less this cap of invisibility. It is only when an object exists in our lives for no other purpose than to be seen that we really look at it, as for instance at a China ornament or a precious stone, and towards such even the most normal person adopts to some extent the artistic attitude of pure vision abstracted from necessity.

Now this specialisation of vision goes so far that ordinary people have almost no idea of what things really look like, so that oddly enough the one standard that popular criticism applies to painting, namely, whether it is like nature or not, is one which most people are, by the whole tenour of their lives, prevented from applying properly. The only things they have ever really *looked* at being other pictures; the moment an artist who has looked at nature brings to them a clear report of something definitely seen by him, they are wildly indignant at its untruth to nature. This has happened so constantly in our own time that there is no need to prove it. One instance will suffice. Monet is an artist whose chief claim to recognition lies in the fact of his astonishing power of faithfully reproducing certain aspects of nature, but his really naïve innocence and sincerity were taken by the public to be the most audacious humbug, and it required the teaching of men like Bastien-Lepage,[4] who cleverly compromised between the truth and an accepted convention of what things looked like, to bring the world gradually round to admitting truths which a single walk in the country with purely unbiassed vision would have established beyond doubt.

But though this clarified sense perception which we discover in the imaginative life is of great interest, and although it plays a larger part in the graphic arts than in any other, it might perhaps be doubted whether, interesting, curious, fascinating as it is, this aspect of the imaginative life would ever by itself make art of profound importance to mankind. But it is different, I think, with the emotional aspect. We have admitted that the emotions of the imaginative are generally weaker than those of actual life. The picture of a saint being slowly flayed alive, revolting as it is, will not produce the same physical sensations of sickening disgust that a modern man would feel if he could assist at the actual event; but they have a compensating clearness of presentment to the consciousness. The more poignant emotions of actual life have, I think, a kind of numbing effect analogous to the paralysing influence of fear in some animals; but even if this experience be not generally admitted, all will admit that the need for responsive action hurries us along and prevents us from ever realising fully what the emotion is that we feel, from co-ordinating it perfectly with other states. In short, the motives we actually experience are too close to us to enable us to feel them clearly. They are in a sense unintelligible. In the imaginative life, on the contrary, we can both feel the emotion and watch it. When we are really moved at the theatre we are always both on the stage and in the auditorium.

Yet another point about the emotions of the imaginative life – since they require no responsive action we can give them a new valuation. In real life we must to some extent cultivate those emotions which lead to useful action, and we are bound to appraise emotions according to the resultant action. So that, for instance, the feelings of rivalry and emulation do get an encouragement which perhaps they scarcely deserve, whereas certain feelings which appear to have a high intrinsic value get almost no stimulus in actual life. For instance, those feelings to which the name of the cosmic emotion has been somewhat unhappily given find almost no place in life, but, since they seem to belong to certain very deep springs of our nature, do become of great importance in the arts.

Morality, then, appreciates emotion by the standard of resultant action. Art appreciates emotion in and for itself.

This view of the essential importance in art of the expression of the emotions is the basis of Tolstoy's marvellously original and yet perverse and even exasperating book, *What is Art?* and

I willingly confess, while disagreeing with almost all his results, how much I owe to him.

He gives an example of what he means by calling art the means of communicating emotions. He says, let us suppose a boy to have been pursued in the forest by a bear.[5] If he returns to the village and merely states that he was pursued by a bear and escaped, that is ordinary language, the means of communicating facts or ideas; but if he describes his state first of heedlessness, then of sudden alarm and terror as the bear appears, and finally of relief when he gets away, and describes this so that his hearers share his emotions, then his description is a work of art.

Now in so far as the boy does this in order to urge the villagers to go out and kill the bear, though he may be using artistic methods, his speech is not a pure work of art; but if of a winter evening the boy relates his experience for the sake of the enjoyment of his adventure in retrospect, or better still, if he makes up the whole story for the sake of the imagined emotions, then his speech becomes a pure work of art. But Tolstoy takes the other view, and values the emotions aroused by art entirely for their reaction upon actual life, a view which he courageously maintains even when it leads him to condemn the whole of Michelangelo, Raphael and Titian, and most of Beethoven, not to mention nearly everything he himself has written, as bad or false art.

Such a view would, I think, give pause to any less heroic spirit. He would wonder whether mankind could have always been so radically wrong about a function that, whatever its value be, is almost universal. And in point of fact he will have to find some other word to denote what we now call art. Nor does Tolstoy's theory even carry him safely through his own book, since, in his examples of morally desirable and therefore good art, he has to admit that these are to be found, for the most part, among works of inferior quality. Here, then, is at once the tacit admission that another standard than morality is applicable. We must therefore give up the attempt to judge the work of art by its reaction on life, and consider it as an expression of emotions regarded as ends in themselves. And this brings us back to the idea we had already arrived at, of art as the expression of the imaginative life.

If, then, an object of any kind is created by man not for use, for its fitness to actual life, but as an object of art, an object subserving the imaginative life, what will its qualities be? It must in the first place be adapted to that disinterested intensity of contemplation, which we have found to be the effect of cutting off the responsive action. It must be suited to that heightened power of perception which we found to result therefrom.

And the first quality that we demand in our sensations will be order, without which our sensations will be troubled and perplexed, and the other quality will be variety, without which they will not be fully stimulated.

It may be objected that many things in nature, such as flowers, possess these two qualities of order and variety in a high degree, and these objects do undoubtedly stimulate and satisfy that clear disinterested contemplation which is characteristic of the aesthetic attitude. But in our reaction to a work of art there is something more – there is the consciousness of purpose, the consciousness of a peculiar relation of sympathy with the man who made this thing in order to arouse precisely the sensations we experience. And when we come to the higher works of art, where sensations are so arranged that they arouse in us deep emotions, this feeling of a special tie with the man who expressed them becomes very strong. We feel that he has expressed something which was latent in us all the time, but which we never realised, that he has revealed us to ourselves in revealing himself. And this recognition of purpose is, I believe, an essential part of the aesthetic judgment proper.

The perception of purposeful order and variety in an object gives us the feeling which we express by saying that it is beautiful, but when by means of sensations our emotions are aroused we demand purposeful order and variety in them also, and if this can only be brought about by the sacrifice of sensual beauty we willingly overlook its absence.

Thus, there is no excuse for a china pot being ugly, there is every reason why Rembrandt's and Degas' pictures should be, from the purely sensual point of view, supremely and magnificently ugly.

This, I think, will explain the apparent contradiction between two distinct uses of the word beauty, one for that which has sensuous charm, and one for the aesthetic approval of works of imaginative art where the objects presented to us are often of extreme ugliness. Beauty in the former sense belongs to works of art where only the perceptual aspect of the imaginative life is exercised, beauty in the second sense becomes as it were supersensual, and is concerned with the appropriateness and intensity of the emotions aroused. When these emotions are aroused in a way that satisfies fully the needs of the imaginative life we approve and delight in the sensations through which we enjoy the heightened experience because they possess purposeful order and variety in relation to those emotions.

One chief aspect of order in a work of art is unity; unity of some kind is necessary for our restful contemplation of the work of art as a whole, since if it lacks unity we cannot contemplate it in its entirety, but we shall pass outside it to other things necessary to complete its unity.

In a picture this unity is due to a balancing of the attractions of the eye about the central line of the picture. The result of this balance of attractions is that the eye rests willingly within the bounds of the picture. Dr Denman Ross of Harvard University has made a most valuable study of the elementary considerations upon which this balance is based in his *Theory of Pure Design*. He sums up his results in the formula that a composition is of value in proportion to the number of orderly connections which it displays.[6]

Dr Ross wisely restricts himself to the study of abstract and meaningless forms. The moment representation is introduced forms have an entirely new set of values. Thus a line which indicated the sudden bend of a head in a certain direction would have far more than its mere value as line in the composition because of the attraction which a marked gesture has for the eye. In almost all paintings this disturbance of the purely decorative values by reason of the representative effect takes place, and the problem becomes too complex for geometrical proof.

This merely decorative unity is, moreover, of very different degrees of intensity in different artists and in different periods. The necessity for a closely woven geometrical texture in the composition is much greater in heroic and monumental design than in genre pieces on a small scale.

It seems also probable that our appreciation of unity in pictorial design is of two kinds. We are so accustomed to consider only the unity which results from the balance of a number of attractions presented to the eye simultaneously in a framed picture that we forget the possibility of other pictorial forms. In certain Chinese paintings the length is so great that we cannot take in the whole picture at once, nor are we intended to do so. Sometimes a landscape is painted upon a roll of silk so long that we can only look at it in successive segments. As we unroll it at one end and roll it up at the other we traverse wide stretches of country, tracing, perhaps, all the vicissitudes of a river from its source to the sea, and yet, when this is well done, we have received a very keen impression of pictorial unity.

Such a successive unity is of course familiar to us in literature and music, and it plays its part in the graphic arts. It depends upon the forms being presented to us in such a sequence that each successive element is felt to have a fundamental and harmonious relation with that which preceded it. I suggest that in looking at drawings our sense of pictorial unity is largely of this nature; we feel, if the drawing be a good one, that each modulation of the line as our eye passes along it gives order and variety to our sensations. Such a drawing may be almost entirely lacking in the geometrical balance which we are accustomed to demand in paintings, and yet have, in a remarkable degree, unity.

Let us now see how the artist passes from the stage of merely gratifying our demand for sensuous order and variety to that where he arouses our emotions. I will call the various methods by which this is effected the emotional elements of designs.

The first element is that of the rhythm of the line with which the forms are delineated.

The drawn line is the record of a gesture, and that gesture is modified by the artist's feeling which is thus communicated to us directly.

The second element is mass. When an object is so represented that we recognise it as having inertia we feel its power of resisting movement, or communicating its own movement to other bodies, and our imaginative reaction to such an image is governed by our experience of mass in actual life.

The third element is space. The same-sized square on two pieces of paper can be made by very simple means to appear to represent either a cube two or three inches high, or a cube of hundreds of feet, and our reaction to it is proportionately changed.

The fourth element is that of light and shade. Our feelings towards the same object become totally different according as we see it strongly illuminated against a black background or dark against a light.

A fifth element is that of colour. That this has a direct emotional effect is evident from such words as gay, dull, melancholy in relation to colour.

I would suggest the possibility of another element, though perhaps it is only a compound of mass and space: it is that of the inclination to the eye of a plane, whether it is impending over or leaning away from us.

Now it will be noticed that nearly all these emotional elements of design are connected with essential conditions of our physical existence: rhythm appeals to all the sensations which accompany muscular activity; mass to all the infinite adaptations to the force of gravity which we are forced to make; the spatial judgment is equally profound and universal in its application to life; our feeling about inclined planes is connected with our necessary judgments about the conformation of the earth itself; light, again, is so necessary a condition of our existence that we become intensely sensitive to changes in its intensity. Colour is the only one of our elements which is not of critical or universal importance to life, and its emotional effect is neither so deep nor so clearly determined as the others. It will be seen, then, that the graphic arts arouse emotions in us by playing upon what one may call the overtones of some of our primary physical needs.

They have, indeed, this great advantage over poetry, that they can appeal more directly and immediately to the emotional accompaniments of our bare physical existence.

If we represent these various elements in simple diagrammatic terms, this effect upon the emotions is, it must be confessed, very weak. Rhythm of line, for instance, is incomparably weaker in its stimulus of the muscular sense than is rhythm addresed to the ear in music, and such diagrams can at best arouse only faint ghost-like echoes of emotions of differing qualities; but when these emotional elements are combined with the presentation of natural appearances, above all with the appearance of the human body, we find that this effect is indefinitely heightened.

When, for instance, we look at Michelangelo's *Jeremiah*,[7] and realise the irresistible momentum his movements would have, we experience powerful sentiments of reverence and awe. Or when we look at Michelangelo's *Tondo*[8] in the Uffizi, and find a group of figures so arranged that the planes have a sequence comparable in breadth and dignity to the mouldings of the earth mounting by clearly-felt gradations to an overtopping summit, innumerable instinctive reactions are brought into play.*

At this point the adversary (as Leonardo da Vinci calls him) is likely enough to retort, 'You have abstracted from natural forms a number of so-called emotional elements which you yourself admit are very weak when stated with diagrammatic purity; you then put them back, with the help of Michelangelo, into the natural forms whence they were derived, and at once they have value, so that after all it appears that the natural forms contain these emotional elements ready made up for us, and all that art need do is to imitate Nature.'

But, alas! Nature is heartlessly indifferent to the needs of the imaginative life; God causes His rain to fall upon the just and upon the unjust. The sun neglects to provide the appropriate limelight effect even upon a triumphant Napoleon or a dying

* Rodin is reported to have said 'A woman, a mountain, a horse – they are all the same thing; they are made on the same principles.'[9] That is to say, their forms, when viewed with the disinterested vision of the imaginative life, have similar emotional elements.

Caesar.* Assuredly we have no guarantee that in nature the emotional elements will be combined appropriately with the demands of the imaginative life, and it is, I think, the great occupation of the graphic arts to give us first of all order and variety in the sensuous plane, and then so to arrange the sensuous presentment of objects that the emotional elements are elicited with an order and appropriateness altogether beyond what Nature herself provides.

Let me sum up for a moment what I have said about the relation of art to Nature, which is, perhaps, the greatest stumbling-block to the understanding of the graphic arts.

I have admitted that there is beauty in Nature, that is to say, that certain objects constantly do, and perhaps any object may, compel us to regard it with that intense disinterested contemplation that belongs to the imaginative life, and which is impossible to the actual life of necessity and action; but that in objects created to arouse the aesthetic feeling we have an added conciousness of purpose on the part of the creator, that he made it on purpose not to be used but to be regarded and enjoyed; and that this feeling is characteristic of the aesthetic judgment proper.

When the artist passes from pure sensations to emotions aroused by means of sensations, he uses natural forms which, in themselves, are calculated to move our emotions, and he presents these in such a manner that the forms themselves generate in us emotional states, based upon the fundamental necessities of our physical and physiological nature. The artist's attitude to natural form is, therefore, infinitely various according to the emotions he wishes to arouse. He may require for his purpose the most complete representation of a figure, he may be intensely realistic, provided that his presentment, in spite of its closeness to natural appearance, disengages clearly for us the appropriate emotional elements. Or he may give us the merest

*I do not forget that at the death of Tennyson the writer in the *Daily Telegraph* averred that 'level beams of the setting moon streamed in upon the face of the dying bard'; but then, after all, in its way the *Daily Telegraph* is a work of art.

suggestion of natural forms, and rely almost entirely upon the force and intensity of the emotional elements involved in his presentment.

We may, then, dispense once for all with the idea of likeness to Nature, of correctness or incorrectness as a test, and consider only whether the emotional elements inherent in natural form are adequately discovered, unless, indeed, the emotional idea depends at any point upon likeness, or completeness of representation.

THE OTTOMAN AND THE WHATNOT

⁂

SUCH were the outlandish names of the two great clans that marched under the flag of the Antimacassar[1] to the resounding periods of Mr Podsnap's rhetoric.[2] For all the appearance of leisure, for all the absence of hustle, those were strenuous days. Respectability and 'the young person'[3] were perpetually menaced by inveterate human nature, and were always or nearly always just being saved as by a miracle. But in the end it was the boast of the Victorians that they had established a system of taboos almost as complicated and as all-pervading as that of the Ojibbeways or the Waramunga.[4] The Ottoman,[5] which seated two so conveniently, was liable to prove a traitor,[6] but what the Ottoman risked could be saved by the Whatnot,[7] with Tennyson and John Greenleaf Whittier to counsel and assuage.[8] One of the things they used to say in those days, quite loudly and distinctly, was: 'Distance lends enchantment to the view.'[9] It seemed so appropriate at the frequent and admirably organised picnics that at last it was repeated too often, and the time came when, under pain of social degradation, it was forbidden to utter the hated words. But now that we are busy bringing back the Ottoman and the Whatnot from the garret and the servants' hall to the drawing-room, we may once more repeat the phrase with impunity, and indeed this article has no other purpose than to repeat once more (and with how new a relish!): 'Distance lends enchantment to the view.'

Also, with our passion for science and exact measurement, we shall wish to discover the exact distance at which enchantment begins. And this is easier than might be supposed; for any one who has lived long enough will have noticed that a certain distance lends a violent disgust to the view – that as we recede there comes a period of oblivion and total unconsciousness, to be succeeded when consciousness returns by the ecstasy, the nature of which we are considering.

I, alas! can remember the time when the Ottoman and Whatnot still lingered in the drawing-rooms of the less fashionable and more conservative bourgeoisie; lingered despised, rejected, and merely awaiting their substitutes. I can remember the sham Chippendale and the sham old oak which replaced them. I can remember a still worse horror – a genuine modern style which as yet has no name, a period of black polished wood with spidery lines of conventional flowers incised in the wood and then gilt. These things must have belonged to the 'eighties – I think they went with the bustle; but as they are precisely at the distance where unconsciousness has set in, it is more difficult to me to write the history of this period than it would be to tell of the sequence of styles in the Tang dynasty. And now, having watched the Whatnot disappear, I have the privilege of watching its resurrection. I have passed from disgust, through total forgetfulness, into the joys of retrospection.

Now my belief is that none of these feelings have anything to do with our aesthetic reactions to the objects as works of art. The odd thing about either real or would-be works of art, that is to say, about any works made with something beyond a purely utilitarian aim – the odd thing is that they can either affect our aesthetic sensibilities or they can become symbols of a particular way of life. In this aspect they affect our historical imagination through our social emotions. That the historical images they conjure up in us are probably false has very little to do with it; the point is that they exist for us, and exist for most people, far more vividly and poignantly than any possible aesthetic feelings. And somehow the works of each period come to stand for us as symbols of some particular and special aspect of life. A Limoges casket[10] evokes the idea of a life of chivalrous adventure and romantic devotion; an Italian cassone[11] gives one a life of intellectual ferment and Boccaccian freedom[12]; before a Caffieri[13] bronze or a Riesener[14] bureau one imagines oneself an exquisite aristocrat proof against the deeper passions, and gifted with a sensuality so refined and a wit so ready that gallantry would be sufficient occupation for a lifetime. Who ever, handling a Louis XV tabatière,[15] reflected how few of the friends of its original owner ever washed, and how many of them were marked with small-pox? The fun of these historical evocations is precisely in what they leave out.

And in order that this process of selection and elimination may take place, precise and detailed knowledge must have faded from the collective memory, and the blurred but exquisite outlines of a generalisation must have been established.

We have just got to this point with the Victorian epoch. It has just got its vague and generalised *Stimmung*.[16] We think as we look at Leech's drawings,[17] or sit in a beadwork chair, of a life which was the perfect flower of bourgeoisie. The aristocracy with their odd irregular ways, the Meredith heroines and heroes, are away in the background; *the* Victorian life is of the upper bourgeoisie. It is immensely leisured, untroubled by social problems, unblushingly sentimental, impenitently unintellectual, and devoted to sport. The women are exquisitely trained to their social functions: they respond unfailingly to every sentimental appeal; they are beautifully ill-informed, and yet yearning for instruction; they have adorable tempers and are ever so mildly mischievous. The men can afford, without fear of impish criticism, to flaunt their whiskers in the sea breeze, and to expatiate on their contempt for everything that is not correct.

Here, I suppose, is something like the outline of that generalised historical fancy that by now emanates so fragrantly from the marble inlaid tables and the beadwork screens of the period. How charming and how false it is, one sees at once when one reflects that we imagine the Victorians for ever playing croquet without ever losing their tempers.

It is evident, then, that we have just arrived at the point where our ignorance of life in the Victorian period is such as to allow the incurable optimism of memory to build a quite peculiar little earthly paradise out of the boredoms, the snobberies, the cruel repressions, the mean calculations and rapacious speculations of the mid-nineteenth century. Go a little later, and the imagination is hopelessly hampered by familiarity with the facts of life which the roseate mist has not yet begun to transmute. But let those of us who are hard at work collecting Victorian paper-weights, stuffed humming-birds and wax flowers reflect that our successors will be able to create quite as amusing and wonderful interiors out of the black wood cabinets and 'aesthetic' crewel-work[18] of the eighties. They will not be able to do this until they have constructed the appropriate social picture, the outlines of which we cannot yet even dimly conceive. We have at this moment no inkling of the kind of lies they will invent about the 'eighties to amuse themselves; we only know that when the time comes the legend will have taken shape, and that, from that moment on, the objects of the time will have the property of emanation.

So far it has been unnecessary even to consider whether the objects of the Victorian period are works of art or not; all that is necessary is that they should have some margin of freedom from utility, some scope for the fancy of their creators. And the Victorian epoch is, I think, unusually rich in its capacity for emanation, for it was the great period of *fancy work*. As the age-long traditions of craftsmanship and structural design, which had lingered on from the Middle Ages, finally faded out under the impact of the new industrialism, the amateur stepped in, his brain teeming with fancies. Craftsmanship was dead, the craftsman replaced either by the machine or by a purely servile and mechanical human being, a man without tradition, without ideas of his own, who was ready to accomplish whatever caprices the amateur or the artist might set him to. It was an age of invention and experiment, an age of wildly irresponsible frivolity, curiosity and sentimentality. To gratify sentiment, nature was opposed to the hampering conventions of art; to gratify fatuous curiosity, the most improbable and ill-suited materials conceivable were used. What they call in France *le style coco*[19] is exactly expressive of this. A drawing of a pheasant is coloured by cutting up little pieces of real pheasant's feathers and sticking them on in the appropriate places. Realistic flowers are made out of shells glued together, or, with less of the pleasant shock of the unexpected, out of wax or spun glass. They experiment in colour, using the new results of chemistry boldly, greens from arsenic, magenta and maroons from coal-tar, with results sometimes happy, sometimes disastrous; but always we feel behind everything the capricious fancy of the amateur with his desire to contribute by some joke or conjuring trick to the social amenities. The general groundwork of design, so far as any tradition remains at all, is a kind of bastard baroque passing at times into a flimsy caricature of rococo, but almost always so overlaid and transfigured by the fancies of the amateur as to be hardly recognisable, and yet all, by now, so richly redolent of its social legend as to have become a genuine style.

There is reason enough, then, why we should amuse ourselves by collecting Victorian objects of art, or at least those of us who have the special social-historical sensibility highly developed. But so curiously intertwisted are our emotions that we are always apt to put a wrong label on them, and the label 'beauty' comes curiously handy for almost any of the more spiritual and disinterested feelings. So our collector is likely enough to ask us to admire his objects, not for their social emanations, but for their intrinsic aesthetic merit, which, to tell the truth, is far more problematical. Certain it is that the use of material at this period seems to be less discriminating, and the sense of quality feebler, than at any previous period of the world's history, at all events since Roman times – Pompeii, by-the-by, was a thoroughly Victorian city. The sense of design was also chaotically free from all the limitations of purpose and material, and I doubt if it attained to that perfect abstract sense of harmony which might justify any disregard of those conditions. No, on the whole it will be better to recognise fully how endearing, how fancy-free, how richly evocative are the objects of the Victorian period than to trouble our heads about their aesthetic value.

The discovery of Victorian art is due to a few enterprising and original artists. In a future article[20] I hope to show why it is to the artist rather than to the collector that we always owe such discoveries, and also why artists are of all people the most indifferent to the aesthetic value of the objects they recommend to our admiration.

THE ARTIST'S VISION

⁂

In the preceding article I stated that artists always lead the way in awakening a new admiration for forgotten and despised styles, and that in doing so they anticipate both the archaeologist and the collector. I also suggested that they were of all people the least fitted to report upon the aesthetic value of the objects they pressed upon us.

Biologically speaking, art is a blasphemy. We were given our eyes to see things, not to look at them. Life takes care that we all learn the lesson thoroughly, so that at a very early age we have acquired a very considerable ignorance of visual appearances. We have learned the meaning-for-life of appearances so well that we understand them, as it were, in shorthand. The subtlest differences of appearance that have a utility value still continue to be appreciated, while large and important visual characters, provided they are useless for life, will pass unnoticed. With all the ingenuity and resource which manufacturers put into their business, they can scarcely prevent the ordinary eye from seizing on the minute visual characteristics that distinguish margarine from butter. Some of us can tell Canadian cheddar at a glance, and no one was ever taken in by sham suede gloves.

The sense of sight supplies prophetic knowledge of what may affect the inner fortifications, the more intimate senses of taste and touch, where it may already be too late to avert disaster. So we learn to read the prophetic message, and, for the sake of economy, to neglect all else. Children have not learned it fully, and so they look at things with some passion. Even the grown man keeps something of his unbiological, disinterested vision with regard to a few things. He still looks at flowers, and does not merely see them. He also keeps objects which have some marked peculiarity of appearance that catches his eye. These may be natural, like precious stones, fossils, incrustations and such like; or they may be manufactured entirely with a view to pleasing by peculiarities of colour or shape, and these are called ornaments. Such articles, whether natural or artificial, are called by those who sell them 'curios', and the name is not an unhappy one to denote the kind of interest which they arouse. As I showed in a previous article, such objects get attached to them a secondary interest, arising from the kind of social milieu that they were made for, so that they become not merely curious for the eye, but stimulating to our social-historical imagination.

The vision with which we regard such objects is quite distinct from the practical vision of our instinctive life. In the practical vision we have no more concern after we have read the label on the object; vision ceases the moment it has served its biological function. But the curiosity vision does contemplate the object disinterestedly: the object *ex hypothesi* has no significance for actual life; it is a play or fancy object, and our vision dwells much more consciously and deliberately upon it. We notice to some extent its forms and colours, especially when it is new to us.

But human perversity goes further even than this in its misapplication of the gift of sight. We may look at objects not even for their curiosity or oddity, but for their harmony of form and colour. To arouse such a vision the object must be more than a 'curio': it has to be a work of art. I suspect that such an object must be made by some one in whom the impulse was not to please others, but to express a feeling of his own. It is probably this fundamental difference of origin between the 'curio' or ornament and the work of art that makes it impossible for any commercial system, with its eye necessarily on the customer, ever to produce works of art, whatever the ingenuity with which it is attempted.

But we are concerned here not with the origin, but with the vision. This is at once more intense and more detached from the passions of the instinctive life than either of the kinds of vision hitherto discussed. Those who indulge in this vision are entirely absorbed in apprehending the relation of forms and colour to one another, as they cohere within the object. Suppose, for example, that we are looking at a Sung bowl; we apprehend gradually the shape of the outside contour, the perfect sequence of the curves, and the subtle modifications of a certain type of curve which it shows; we also feel the relation of the concave curves of the inside to the outside contour; we realise that the precise thickness of the walls is consistent with the particular kind of matter of which it is made, its appearance of density and resistance; and finally we recognise, perhaps, how satisfactorily for the display of all these plastic qualities are the colour and the dull lustre of the glaze. Now while we are thus occupied there comes to us, I think, a feeling of purpose; we feel that all these sensually logical conformities are the outcome of a particular feeling, or of what, for want of a better word, we call an idea; and we may even say that the pot is the expression of an idea in the artist's mind. Whether we are right or not in making this deduction, I believe it nearly always occurs in such aesthetic apprehension of an object of art. But in all this no element of curiosity, no reference to actual life, comes in; our apprehension is unconditioned by considerations of space or time; it is irrelevant to us to know whether the bowl was made seven hundred years ago in China, or in New York yesterday. We may, of course, at any moment switch off from the aesthetic vision, and become interested in all sorts of quasi-biological feelings; we may inquire whether it is genuine or not, whether it is worth the sum given for it, and so forth; but in proportion as we do this we change the focus of our vision; we are more likely to examine the bottom of the bowl for traces of marks than to look at the bowl itself.

Such, then, is the nature of the aesthetic vision, the vision with which we contemplate works of art. It is to such a vision, if to anything outside himself, that the artist appeals, and the artist in his spare hours may himself indulge in the aesthetic vision; and if one can get him to do so, his verdict is likely to be as good as any one's.

The artist's main business in life, however, is carried on by means of yet a fourth kind of vision, which I will call the creative vision. This, I think, is the furthest perversion of the gifts of nature of which man is guilty. It demands the most complete detachment from any of the meanings and implications of appearances. Almost any turn of the kaleidoscope of nature may set up in the artist this detached and impassioned vision, and, as he contemplates the particular field of vision, the (aesthetically) chaotic and accidental conjunction of forms and colours begins to crystallise into a harmony; and as this becomes clear to the artist, his actual vision becomes distorted by the emphasis of the rhythm which has been set up within him. Certain relations of directions of line become for him full of meaning; he apprehends them no longer casually or merely curiously, but passionately, and these lines begin to be so stressed and stand out so clearly from the rest that he sees them far more distinctly than he did at first. Similarly colours, which in nature have almost always a certain vagueness and elusiveness, become so definite and clear to him, owing to their now necessary relation to other colours, that if he chooses to paint his vision he can state them positively and definitely. In such a creative vision the objects as such tend to disappear, to lose their separate unities, and to take their places as so many bits in the whole mosaic of vision. The texture of the whole field of vision becomes so close that the coherence of the separate patches of tone and colour within each object is no stronger than the coherence with every other tone and colour throughout the field.

In such circumstances the greatest object of art becomes of no more significance than any casual piece of matter; a man's head is no more and no less important than a pumpkin, or, rather, these things may be so or not according to the rhythm that obsesses the artist and crystallises his vision. Since it is the habitual practice of the artist to be on the look-out for these peculiar arrangements of objects that arouse the creative vision, and become material for creative contemplation, he is liable to look at all objects from this point of view. In so far as the artist looks at objects only as part of a whole field of vision which is his own potential picture, he can give no account of their aesthetic value. Every solid object is subject to the play of light and shade, and becomes a mosaic of visual patches, each of which for the artist is related to other visual patches in the surroundings. It is irrelevant to ask him, while he is looking with this generalised and all-embracing vision, about the nature of the objects which compose it. He is likely even to turn away from works of art in which he may be tempted to relapse into an aesthetic vision, and so see them as unities apart from their surroundings. By preference he turns to objects which make no strong aesthetic appeal in themselves. But he may like objects which attract by some oddity or peculiarity of form or colour, and thereby suggest to him new and intriguing rhythms. In his continual and restless preoccupation with appearance he is capable of looking at objects from which both the aesthetic and even the curious vision would turn away instinctively, or which they may never notice, so little prospect of satisfaction do they hold out. But the artist may always find his satisfaction, the material for his picture, in the most unexpected quarters. Objects of the most despised periods, or objects saturated for the ordinary man with the most vulgar and repulsive associations, may be grist to his mill. And so it happened that while the man of culture and the connoisseur firmly believed that art ended with the brothers Adam, Mr Walter Sickert was already busy getting hold of stuffed birds and wax flowers just for his own queer game of tones and colours. And now the collector and the art-dealer will be knocking at Mr Sickert's door to buy the treasures at twenty times the price the artist paid for them. Perhaps there are already younger artists who are getting excited about the tiles in the refreshment room at South Kensington, and, when the social legend has gathered round the names of Sir Arthur Sullivan and Connie Gilchrist, will inspire in the cultured a deep admiration for the 'aesthetic' period.

The artist is of all men the most constantly observant of his surroundings, and the least affected by their intrinsic aesthetic value. He is more likely on the whole to paint a slum in Soho than St Paul's, and more likely to do a lodging-house interior than a room at Hampton Court. He may, of course, do either, but his necessary detachment comes more easily in one case than the other. The artist is, I believe, a very good critic if you can make him drop his own job for a minute, and really attend to someone else's work of art; but do not go to him when he is on duty as an artist if you want a sound judgment about objects of art. The different visions I have discussed are like the different gears of a motor-car, only that we sometimes step from one gear into another without knowing it, and the artist may be on the wrong gear for answering us truly. Mr Walter Sickert is likely to have a Sickert in his eye when he gives us a panegyric on a bedroom candlestick.

ART AND SOCIALISM

✻

I AM not a Socialist, as I understand that word, nor can I pretend to have worked out those complex estimates of economic possibility which are needed before one can endorse the hopeful forecasts of Lady Warwick, Mr Money, and Mr Wells.[1] What I propose to do here is first to discuss what effect plutocracy, such as it is today, has had of late, and is likely to have in the near future, upon one of the things which I should like to imagine continuing upon our planet – namely, art. And then briefly to prognosticate its chances under such a regime as my colleagues have sketched.

As I understand it, art is one of the chief organs of what, for want of a better word, I must call the spiritual life. It both stimulates and controls those indefinable overtones of the material life of man which all of us at moments feel to have a quality of permanence and reality that does not belong to the rest of our experience. Nature demands with no uncertain voice that the physical needs of the body shall be satisfied first; but we feel that our real human life only begins at the point where that is accomplished, that the man who works at some uncreative and uncongenial toil merely to earn enough food to enable him to continue to work has not, properly speaking, a human life at all.

It is the argument of commercialism, as it once was of aristocracy, that the accumulation of surplus wealth in a few hands enables this spiritual life to maintain its existence, that no really valuable or useless work (for from this point of view only useless work has value) could exist in the community without such accumulations of wealth. The argument has been employed for the disinterested work of scientific research. A doctor of naturally liberal and generous impulses told me that he was becoming a reactionary simply because he feared that public bodies would never give the money necessary for research with anything like the same generosity as is now shown by the great plutocrats. But Sir Ray Lankester does not find that generosity sufficient, and is prepared at least to consider whether the State would not be more open-handed.[2]

The situation as regards art and as regards the disinterested love of truth is so similar that we might expect this argument in favour of a plutocratic social order to hold equally well for both art and science, and that the artist would be a fervent upholder of the present system. As a matter of fact, the more representative artists have rarely been such, and not a few, though working their life long for the plutocracy, have been vehement Socialists.

Despairing of the conditions due to modern commercialism, it is not unnatural that lovers of beauty should look back with nostalgia to the age when society was controlled by a landed aristocracy. I believe, however, that from the point of view of the encouragement of great creative art there is not much difference between an aristocracy and a plutocracy. The aristocrat usually had taste, the plutocrat frequently has not. Now taste is of two kinds, the first consisting in the negative avoidance of all that is ill-considered and discordant, the other positive and a by-product; it is that harmony which always results from the expression of intense and disinterested emotion. The aristocrat, by means of his good taste of the negative kind, was able to come to terms with the artist; the plutocrat has not. But both alike desire to buy something which is incommensurate with money. Both want art to be a background to their radiant self-consciousness. They want to buy beauty as they want to buy love; and the painter, picture-dealer, and the pander try perennially to persuade them that it is possible. But living beauty cannot be bought; it must be won. I have said that the aristocrat, by his taste, by his feeling for the accidentals of beauty, did manage to get on to some kind of terms with the artist. Hence the art of the eighteenth century, an art that is prone before the distinguished patron, subtly and deliciously flattering and yet always fine. In contrast to that the art of the nineteenth century is coarse, turbulent, clumsy. It marks the beginning of a revolt. The artist just managed to let himself be coaxed and cajoled by the aristocrat, but when the aristocratic was succeeded by the plutocratic patron with less conciliatory manners and no taste, the artist rebelled; and the history of art in the nineteenth century is the history of a band of heroic Ishmaelites, with no secure place in the social system, with nothing to support them in the unequal struggle but a dim sense of a new idea, the idea of the freedom of art from all trammels and tyrannies.

The place that the artists left vacant at the plutocrat's table had to be filled, and it was filled by a race new in the history of the world, a race for whom no name has yet been found, a race of pseudo-artists. As the prostitute professes to sell love, so these gentlemen professed to sell beauty, and they and their patrons rollicked good-humouredly through the Victorian era. They adopted the name and something of the manner of artists; they intercepted not only the money, but the titles and fame and glory which were intended for those whom they had supplanted. But, while they were yet feasting, there came an event which seemed at the time of no importance, but which was destined to change ultimately the face of things – the exhibition of ancient art at Manchester in 1857.[3] And with this came Ruskin's address on the Political Economy of Art,[4] a work which surprises by its prophetic foresight when we read it half a century later. These two things were the Mene Tekel[5] of the orgy of Victorian Philistinism. The plutocrat saw through the deception; it was not beauty the pseudo-artist sold him, any more than it was love which the prostitute gave. He turned from it in disgust and decided that the only beauty he could buy was the dead beauty of the past. Thereupon set in the worship of *patine* and the age of forgery and the detection of forgery. I once remarked to a rich man that a statue by Rodin might be worthy even of his collection. He replied, 'Show me a Rodin with the *patine* of the fifteenth century, and I will buy it.'

Patine, then, the adventitious material beauty which age alone can give, has come to be the object of a reverence greater than that devoted to the idea which is enshrined within the work of art. People are right to admire *patine*. Nothing is more beautiful than gilded bronze of which time has taken toll until it is nothing but a faded shimmering splendour over depths of inscrutable gloom; nothing finer than the dull glow which Pentelic marble[6] has gathered from past centuries of sunlight and warm Mediterranean breezes. *Patine* is good, but it is a surface charm added to the essential beauty of expression; its beauty is literally skin-deep. It can never come into being or exist in or for itself; no *patine* can make a bad work good, or the forgers would be justified. It is an adjectival and ancillary beauty scarcely worthy of our prolonged contemplation.

There is to the philosopher something pathetic in the Plutocrat's worship of *patine*. It is, as it were, a compensation for his own want of it. On himself all the rough thumb and chisel marks of his maker – and he is self-made – stand as yet unpolished and raw; but his furniture, at least, shall have the distinction of age-long acquaintance with good manners.

But the net result of all this is that the artist has nothing to hope from the plutocrat. To him we must be grateful indeed for that brusque disillusionment of the real artist, the real artist who might have rubbed along uneasily for yet another century with his predecessor, the aristocrat. Let us be grateful to him for this; but we need not look to him for further benefits, and if we decide to keep him the artist must be content to be paid after he is dead and vicariously in the person of an art-dealer. The artist must be content to look on while sums are given for dead beauty, the tenth part of which, properly directed, would irrigate whole nations and stimulate once more the production of vital artistic expression.

I would not wish to appear to blame the plutocrat. He has often honestly done his best for art; the trouble is not of his making more than of the artist's, and the misunderstanding between art and commerce is bound to be complete. The artist, however mean and avaricious he may appear, knows that he cannot really sell himself for money any more than the philosopher or the scientific investigator can sell himself for money. He takes money in the hope that he may secure the opportunity for the free functioning of his creative power. If the patron could give him that instead of money he would bless him; but he cannot, and so he tries to get him to work not quite freely for money; and in revenge the artist indulges in all manner of insolences, even perhaps in sharp practices, which make the patron feel, with some justification, that he is the victim of ingratitude and wanton caprice. It is impossible that the artist should work for the plutocrat; he must work for himself, because it is only by so doing that he can perform the function for which he exists; it is only by working for himself that he can work for mankind.

If, then, the particular kind of accumulation of surplus wealth which we call plutocracy has failed, as surely it has signally failed, to stimulate the creative power of the imagination, what disposition of wealth might be conceived that would succeed better? First of all, a greater distribution of wealth, with a lower standard of ostentation, would, I think, do a great deal to improve things without any great change in other conditions. It is not enough known that the patronage which really counts today is exercised by quite small and humble people. These people with a few hundreds a year exercise a genuine patronage by buying pictures at ten, twenty, or occasionally thirty pounds, with real insight and understanding, thereby enabling the young Ishmaelite to live and function from the age of twenty to thirty or so, when perhaps he becomes known to richer buyers, those experienced spenders of money who are always more cautious, more anxious to buy an investment than a picture. These poor, intelligent first patrons to whom I allude belong mainly to the professional classes; they have none of the pretensions of the plutocrat and none of his ambitions. The work of art is not for them, as for him a decorative backcloth to his stage, but an idol and an inspiration. Merely to increase the number and potency of these people would already accomplish much; and this is to be noticed, that if wealth were more evenly distributed, if no one had a great deal of wealth, those who really cared for art would become the sole patrons, since for all it would be an appreciable sacrifice, and for none an impossibility. The man who only buys pictures when he has as many motor-cars as he can conceivably want would drop out as a patron altogether.

But even this would only foster the minor and private arts; and what the history of art definitely elucidates is that the greatest art has always been communal, the expression – in highly individualised ways, no doubt – of common aspirations and ideals.

Let us suppose, then, that society were so arranged that considerable surplus wealth lay in the hands of public bodies, both national and local; can we have any reasonable hope that they would show more skill in carrying out the delicate task of stimulating and using the creative power of the artist?

The immediate prospect is certainly not encouraging. Nothing, for instance, is more deplorable than to watch the patronage of our provincial museums. The gentlemen who administer these public funds naturally have not realised so acutely as private buyers the lesson so admirably taught at Christie's, that pseudo or Royal-Academic art is a bad investment. Nor is it better if we turn to national patronage. In Great Britain, at least, we cannot get a postage stamp or a penny even respectably designed, much less a public monument. Indeed, the tradition that all public British art shall be crassly mediocre and inexpressive is so firmly rooted that it seems to have almost the prestige of constitutional precedent.* Nor will any one who has watched a committee commissioning a presentation portrait, or even buying an old master, be in danger of taking too optimistic a view. With rare and shining exceptions, committees seem to be at the mercy of the lowest common denominator of their individual natures, which is dominated by fear of criticism; and fear and its attendant, compromise, are bad masters of the arts.

Speaking recently at Liverpool, Mr Bernard Shaw placed the present situation as regards public art in its true light. He declared that the corruption of taste and the emotional insincerity of the mass of the people had gone so far that any picture which pleased more than ten per cent of the population should be immediately burned....[7]

This, then, is the fundamental fact we have to face. And it is this that gives us pause when we try to construct any conceivable system of public patronage.

For the modern artist puts the question of any socialistic – or, indeed, of any completely ordered – state, in its acutest form. He demands as an essential to the proper use of his powers a

* A precedent fully maintained by the war-monuments which have covered the English countryside since the above article was written.

freedom from restraint such as no other workman expects. He must work when he feels inclined; he cannot work to order. Hence his frequent quarrels with the burgher who knows he has to work when he is disinclined, and cannot conceive why the artist should not do likewise. The burgher watches the artist's wayward and apparently quite unmethodical activity, and envies his job. Now, in any Socialistic State, if certain men are licensed to pursue the artistic calling, they are likely to be regarded by the other workers with some envy. There may be a competition for such soft jobs among those who are naturally work-shy, since it will be evident that the artist is not called to account in the same way as other workers.

If we suppose, as seems not unlikely, in view of the immense numbers who become artists in our present social state, that there would be this competition for the artistic work of the community, what methods would be devised to select those required to fill the coveted posts? Frankly, the history of art in the nineteenth century makes us shudder at the results that would follow. One scarcely knows whether they would be worse if Bumble or the Academy were judge. We only know that under any such conditions *none* of the artists whose work has ultimately counted in the spiritual development of the race would have been allowed to practise the coveted profession.

There is in truth, as Ruskin pointed out in his 'Political Economy of Art',[8] a gross and wanton waste under the present system. We have thousands of artists who are only so by accident and by name, on the one hand, and certainly many – one cannot tell how many – who have the special gift but have never had the peculiar opportunities which are today necessary to allow it to expand and function. But there is, what in an odd way consoles us, a blind chance that the gift and the opportunity may coincide; that Shelley and Browning may have a competence, and Cézanne a farm-house he could retire to. Bureaucratic Socialism would, it seems, take away even this blind chance that mankind may benefit by its least appreciable, and most elusive treasures, and would carefully organise the complete suppression of original creative power; would organise into a universal and all-embracing tyranny the already overweening and disastrous power of endowed official art. For we must face the fact that the average man has two qualities which would make the proper selection of the artist almost impossible. He has, first of all, a touching proclivity to awe-struck admiration of whatever is presented to him as noble by a constituted authority; and, secondly, a complete absence of any immediate reaction to a work of art until his judgment has thus been hypnotised by the voice of authority. Then, and not till then, he sees, or swears he sees, those adorable Emperor's clothes that he is always agape for.

I am speaking, of course, of present conditions, of a populace whose emotional life has been drugged by the sugared poison of pseudo-art, a populace saturated with snobbishness, and regarding art chiefly for its value as a symbol of social distinctions. There have been times when such a system of public patronage as we are discussing might not have been altogether disastrous. Times when the guilds represented more or less adequately the genuine artistic intelligence of the time; but the creation, first of all, of aristocratic art, and finally of pseudo-art, have brought it about that almost any officially organised system would at the present moment stereotype all the worst features of modern art.

Now, in thus putting forward the extreme difficulties of any system of publicly controlled art, we are emphasising perhaps too much the idea of the artist as a creator of purely ideal and abstract works, as the medium of inspiration and the source of revelation. It is the artist as prophet and priest that we have been considering, the artist who is the articulate soul of mankind. Now, in the present commercial State, at a time when such handiwork as is not admirably fitted to some purely utilitarian purpose has become inanely fatuous and grotesque, the artist in this sense has undoubtedly become of supreme importance as a protestant, as one who proclaims that art is a reasonable function, and one that proceeds by a nice adjustment of means to ends. But if we suppose a state in which all the ordinary objects of daily life – our chairs and tables, our carpets and pottery – expressed something of this reasonableness instead of a crazy and vapid fantasy the artist as a pure creator might become, not indeed of less importance – rather more – but a less acute necessity to our general living than he is today. Something of the sanity and purposefulness of his attitude might conceivably become infused into the work of the ordinary craftsman, something, too, of his creative energy and delight in work.[9] We must, therefore, turn for a moment from the abstractly creative artist to the applied arts and those who practise them.

We are so far obliged to protect ourselves from the implications of modern life that without a special effort it is hard to conceive the enormous quantity of 'art' that is annually produced and consumed. For the special purpose of realising it I take the pains to write the succeeding paragraphs in a railway refreshment-room, where I am actually looking at those terribly familiar but fortunately fleeting images which such places afford. An one must remember that public places of this kind merely reflect the average citizen's soul, as expressed in his home.

The space my eye travels over is a small one, but I am appalled at the amount of 'art' that it harbours. The window towards which I look is filled in its lower part by stained glass; within a highly elaborate border, designed by some one who knew the conventions of thirteenth-century glass, is a pattern of yellow and purple vine leaves with bunches of grapes, and flitting about among these many small birds. In front is a lace curtain with patterns taken from at least four centuries and as many countries. On the walls, up to a height of four feet, is a covering of lincrusta walton[10] stamped with a complicated pattern in two colours, with sham silver medallions. Above that a moulding but an inch wide, and yet creeping throughout its whole with a degenerate descendant of a Graeco-Roman carved guilloche patten;[11] this has evidently been cut out of the wood by machine or stamped out of some composition – its nature is so perfectly concealed that it is hard to say which. Above this is a wallpaper in which an effect of eighteenth-century satin brocade is imitated by shaded staining of the paper. Each of the little refreshment-tables has two cloths, one arranged symmetrically with the table, the other a highly ornate printed cotton arranged 'artistically' in a diagonal position. In the centre of each table is a large pot in which every beautiful quality in the material and making of pots has been carefully obliterated by methods each of which implies profound scientific knowledge and great inventive talent. Within each pot is a plant with large dark green leaves, apparently made of india-rubber. This painful catalogue makes up only a small part of the inventory of the 'art' of the restaurant. If I were to go on to tell of the legs of the tables, of the electric-light fittings, of the chairs into the wooden seats of which some tremendous mechanical force has deeply impressed a large distorted anthemion[12] – if I were to tell of all these things, my reader and I might both begin to realise with painful acuteness something of the horrible toil involved in all this display. Display is indeed the end and explanation of it all. Not one of these things has been made because the maker enjoyed the making; not one has been bought because its contemplation would give any one any pleasure, but solely because each of these things is accepted as a symbol of a particular social status. I say their contemplation can give no one pleasure; they are there because their absence would be resented by the average man who regards a large amount of futile display as in some way inseparable from the conditions of that well-to-do life to which he belongs or aspires to belong. If everything were merely clean and serviceable he would proclaim the place bare and uncomfortable.

The doctor who lines his waiting-room with bad photogravures and worse etchings is acting on exactly the same principle; in short, nearly all our 'art' is made, bought, and sold merely for its value as an indication of social status.

Now consider the case of those men whose life-work it is to stimulate this eczematous eruption of pattern on the surface of modern manufactures. They are by far the most numerous 'artists' in the country. Each of them has not only learned to draw, but has learned by sheer application to put forms together with a similitude of that coherence which creative impulse gives. Probably each of them has somewhere within him something of that creative impulse which is the inspiration and delight of every savage and primitive craftsman; but in these manufacturer's designers the pressure of commercial life has crushed and atrophied that creative impulse completely. Their business is to produce, not expressive design, but dead patterns. They are compelled, therfore, to spend their lives behaving in an entirely idiotic and senseless manner, and that with the certainty that no one will ever get positive pleasure from the result; for one may hazard the statement that until I made the effort just now, no one of the thousands who use the refreshment-rooms ever really *looked* at the designs.

This question of the creation and consumption of art tends to become more and more pressing. I have shown just now what an immense mass of art is consumed, but this is not same art as that which the genuine artist produces. The work of the truly creative artist is not merely useless to the social man – it appears to be noxious and inassimilable. Before art can be 'consumed' the artistic idea must undergo a process of disinfection. It must have had extracted and removed from it all, or nearly all, that makes it aesthetically valuable. What occurs when a great artist creates a new idea is somewhat as follows: We know the process well enough, since an example of it has occurred within the last fifty years.[13] An artist attains to a new vision. He grasps this with such conviction that he is able to express it in his work. Those few people in his immediate surroundings who have the faculty of aesthetic perception become very much excited by the new vision. The average man, on the other hand, lacks this faculty and, moreover, instinctively protects the rounded perfection of his universe of thought and feeling from the intrusion of new experience; in consequence he becomes extremely irritated by the sight of works which appear to him completely unintelligible. The misunderstanding between this small minority and the public becomes violent. Then some of the more intelligent writers on art recognise that the new idea is really related to past aesthetic expressions which have become recognised. Then a clever artist, without any individual vision of his own, sees the possibility of using a modification of the new idea, and makes an ingenious compromise between it and the old, generally accepted notions of art. The public, which has been irritated by its incomprehension of the new idea, finding the compromise just intelligible, and delighted to find itself cleverer than it thought, acclaims the compromising intermediary as a genius. The process of disinfection thus begun goes on with increasing energy and rapidity, and before long the travesty of the new idea is completely assimilable by the social organism. The public, after swallowing innumerable imitations of the new idea, might even at last reluctantly accept the original creator as a great man, but generally not until he has been dead for some time and has become a vague and mythical figure.

It is literally true to say that the imitations of works of art are more assimilable by the public than originals, and therefore always tend to fetch a higher price in the market at the moment of their production.

The fact is that the average man uses art entirely for its symbolic value. Art is in fact the symbolic currency of the world. The possession of rare and much-coveted works of art is regarded as a sign of national greatness. The growth and development of the Kaiser-Friedrich-Museum was due to the active support of the Emperor William II, a man whose distaste for genuine art is notorious, but whose sense of the symbolic was highly developed.[14] Large and expensively ornamented buildings become symbols of municipal greatness. The amount of useless ornaments on the façades of their offices is a valuable symbol of the financial exuberance of big commercial undertakings; and, finally, the social status of the individual is expressed to the admiring or envious outer world by the streamlines of an aristocratic motor-car, or the superfluity of lace curtains in the front windows of a genteel suburban villa.

The social man, then, lives in a world of symbols, and though he presses other things into his service, such for instance, as kings, footmen, dogs, women, he finds in art his richest reservoir of symbolic currency. But in a world of symbolists the creative artist and the creative man of science appear in strange isolation as the only people who are not symbolists. They alone are up against certain relations which do not stand for something else, but appear to have ultimate value, to be real.

Art as a symbolic currency is an important means of the instinctive life of man, but art as created by the artist is in violent revolt against the instinctive life, since it is an expression of the reflective and fully conscious life. It is natural enough, then, that before it can be used by the instinctive life it must be deprived by travesty of its too violent assertion of its own reality. Travesty is necessary at first to make it assimilable, but in the end long familiarity may rob even original works of art of their insistence, so that, finally, even the great masterpieces may become the most cherished symbols of the lords of the instinctive life – may, as in fact they frequently do, become the property of millionaires.

A great deal of misunderstanding and ill-feeling between the artist and the public comes from a failure to realise the necessity of this process of assimilation of the work of art to the needs of the instinctive life.

I suspect that a very similar process takes place with regard to truth. In order that truth may not outrage too violently the passions and egoisms of the instinctive life, it too must undergo a process of deformation.

Society, for example, accepts as much of the ascertainable truth as it can stand at a given period in the form of the doctrine of its organised religion.

Now what effect would the development of the Great State which this book anticipates have upon all this? First, I suppose that the fact that every one had to work might produce a new reverence, especially in the governing body, for work, a new sense of disgust and horror at wasteful and purposeless work. Mr Money has written of waste of work;[15] here in unwanted pseudo-art is another colossal waste. Add to this ideal of economy in work the presumption that the workers in every craft would be more thoroughly organised and would have a more decisive voice in the nature and quality of their productions. Under the present system of commercialism the one object, and the complete justification, of producing any article is, that it can be made either by its intrinsic value, or by the fictitious value put upon it by advertisement, to sell with a sufficient profit to the manufacturer. In any socialistic state, I imagine – and to a large extent the Great State will be socialistic at least – there would not be this same automatic justification for manufacture; people would not be induced artificially to buy what they did not want, and in this way a more genuine scale of values would be developed. Moreover, the workman would be in a better position to say how things should be made. After years of a purely commercial standard, there is left even now, in the average workman, a certain bias in favour of sound and reasonable workmanship as opposed to the ingenious manufacture of fatuous and fraudulent objects; and, if we suppose the immediate pressure of sheer necessity to be removed, it is probable that the craftsman, acting through his guild organisations, would determine to some extent the methods of manufacture. Guilds might, indeed, regain something of the political influence that gave us the Gothic cathedrals of the Middle Ages. It is quite probable that this guild influence would act as a check on some innovations in manufacture which, though bringing in a profit, are really disastrous to the community at large. Of such a nature are all the so-called improvements whereby decoration, the whole value of which consists in its expressive power, is multiplied indefinitely by machinery. When once the question of the desirability of any and every production came to be discussed, as it would be in the Great State, it would inevitably follow that some reasonable and scientific classifications would be undertaken with regard to machinery. That is to say, it would be considered in what processes and to what degree machinery ought to replace handiwork, both from the point of view of the community as a whole and from that of the producer. So far as I know, this has never been undertaken even with regard to mere economy, no one having calculated with precision how far the longer life of certain hand-made articles does not more than compensate for increased cost of production. And I suppose that in the Great State other things besides mere economy would come into the calculation. The Great State will live, not hoard.

It is probable that in many directions we should extend mechanical operations immensely, that such things as the actual construction of buildings, the mere laying and placing of walls might become increasingly mechanical. Such methods, if confined to purely structural elements, are capable of beauty of a special kind, since they can express the ordered ideas of proportion, balance, and interval as conceived by the creative mind of the architect. But in process of time one might hope to see a sharp line of division between work of this kind and such purely expressive and non-utilitarian design as we call ornament; and it would be felt clearly that into this field no mechanical device should intrude, that, while ornament might be dispensed with, it could never be imitated, since its only reason for being is that it conveys the vital expressive power of a human mind acting constantly and directly upon matter.

Finally, I suppose that in the Great State we might hope to see such a considerable levelling of social conditions that the false values put upon art by its symbolising of social status would be largely destroyed, and, the pressure of mere opinion being relieved, people would develop some more immediate reaction to the work of art than they can at present achieve.

Supposing, then, that under the Great State it was found impossible, at all events at first, to stimulate and organise the abstract creative power of the pure artist, the balance might after all be in favour of the new order if the whole practice of applied art could once more become rational and purposeful. In a world where the objects of daily use and ornament were made with practical common sense, the aesthetic sense would need far less to seek consolation and repose in works of pure art.

Nevertheless, in the long run mankind will not allow this function, which is necessary to its spiritual life, to lapse entirely. I imagine, however, that it would be much safer to penalise rather than to stimulate such activity, and that simply in order to sift out those with a genuine passion from those who are merely attracted by the apparent ease of the pursuit. I imagine that the artist would naturally turn to one of the applied arts as his means of livelihood; and we should get the artist coming out of the *bottéga*,[16] as he did in fifteenth-century Florence. There are, moreover, innumerable crafts, even besides those that are definitely artistic, which, if pursued for short hours – Sir Leo Money has shown how short these hours might be[17] – would leave a man free to pursue other callings in his leisure.

The majority of poets today are artist in this position. It is comparatively rare for any one to make of poetry his actual means of livelihood. Our poets are, first of all, clerks, critics, civil servants, or postmen. I very much doubt if it would be a serious loss to the community if the pure graphic artist were in the same position. That is to say, that all our pictures would be made by amateurs. It is quite possible to suppose that this would be not a loss, but a great gain. The painter's means of livelihood would probably be some craft in which his artistic powers would be constantly occupied, though at a lower tension and in a humbler way. The Great State aims at human freedom; essentially, it is an organisation for leisure – out of which art grows; it is only a purely bureaucratic Socialism that would attempt to control the aesthetic lives of men.

So I conceive that those in whom the instinct for abstract creative art was strongest would find ample opportunities for its exercise, and that the temptation to stimulate this particular activity would be easily resisted by those who had no powerful inner compulsion.

In the Great State, moreover, and in any sane Socialism, there would be opportunity for a large amount of purely private buying and selling. Mr Wells's Modern Utopia, for example, hypothecates a vast superstructure of private trading.[18] A painter might sell his pictures to those who were engaged in more lucrative employment, though one supposes that with the much more equal distribution of wealth the sums available for this would be incomparably smaller than at present; a picture would not be a speculation, but a pleasure, and no one would become an artist in the hope of making a fortune.

Ultimately, of course, when art had been purified of its present unreality by a prolonged contact with the crafts, society would gain a new confidence in its collective artistic judgment, and might even boldly assume the responsibility which at present it knows it is unable to face. It might choose its poets and painters and philosophers and deep investigators, and make of such men and women a new kind of kings.

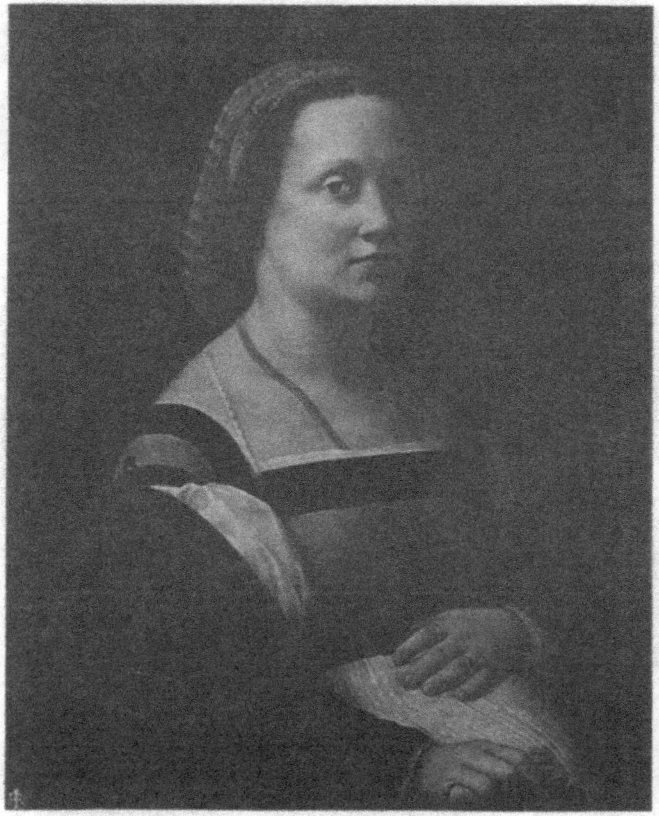

I.1 Raphael: La Donna gravida, *c.*1505. Oil on panel: 66 × 52 cm.

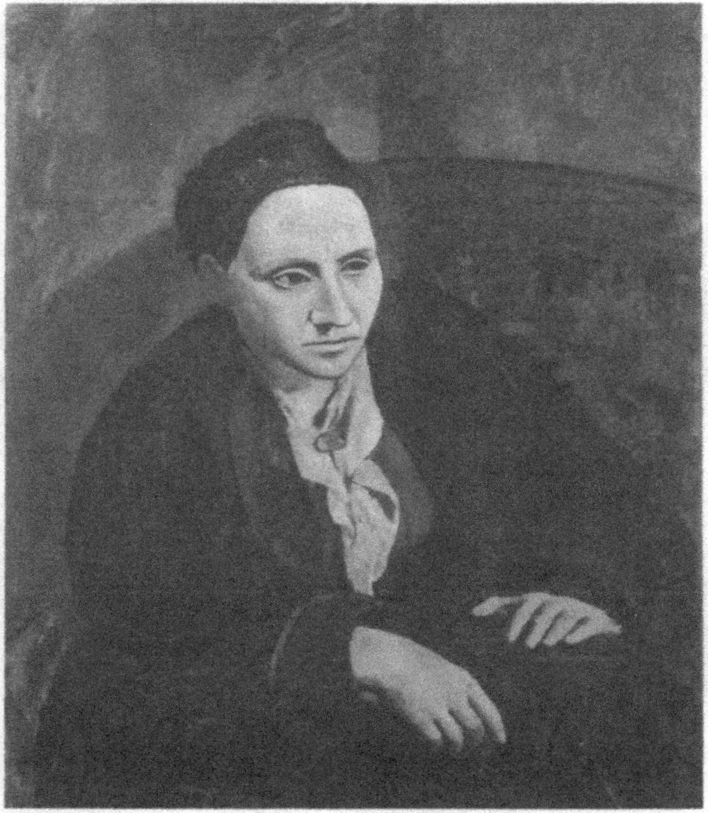

I.2 Pablo Picasso: Portrait of Gertrude Stein. 1906. Oil on canvas: 100 × 81,3 cm.

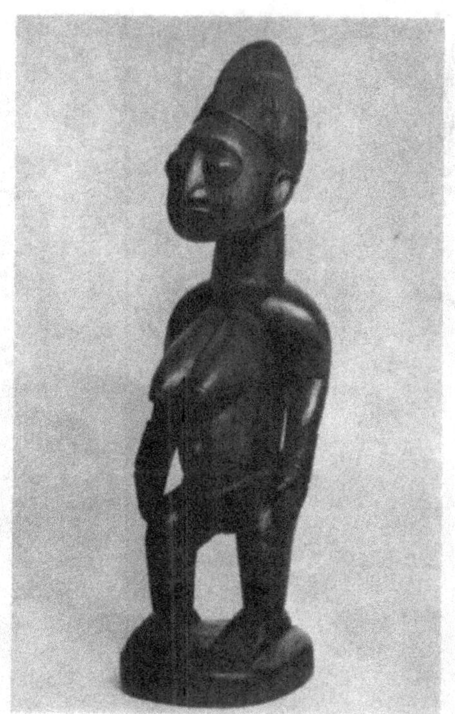

II.1 Yoruba sculpture. Wood.

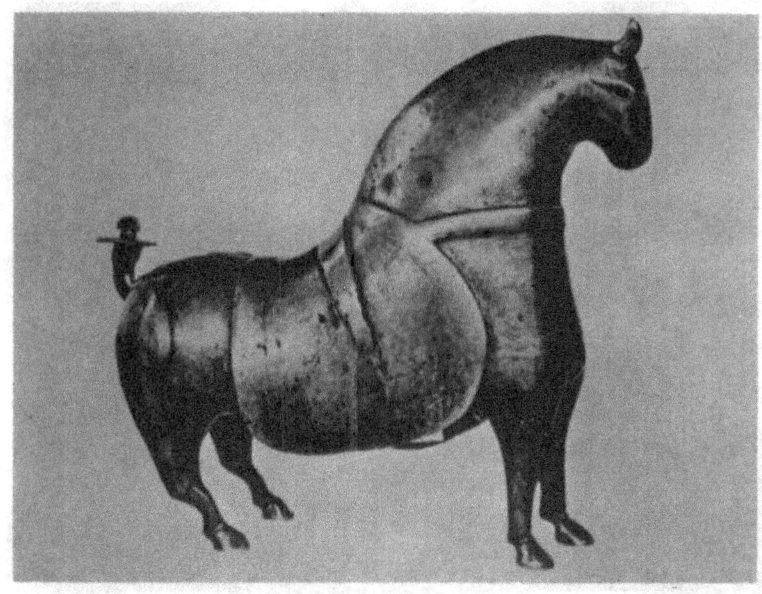

II.2 Fatimite bronze horse. 41 × 36 cm.

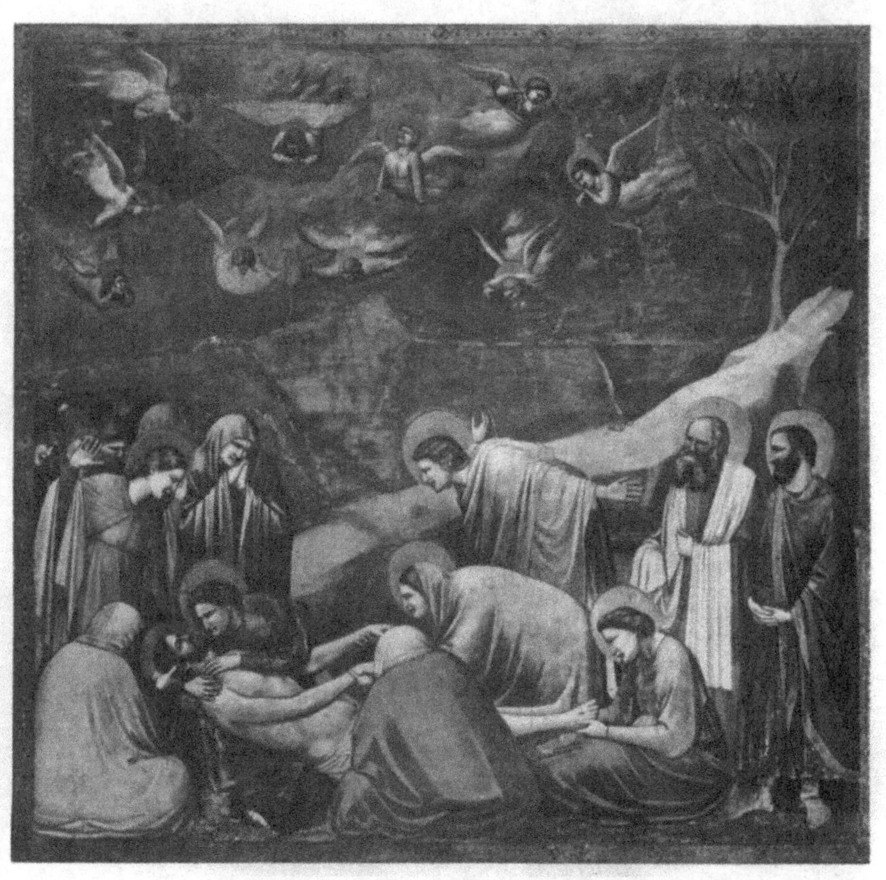

III Giotto: Descent from the Cross *or* Pietà. 1303–5. Fresco.

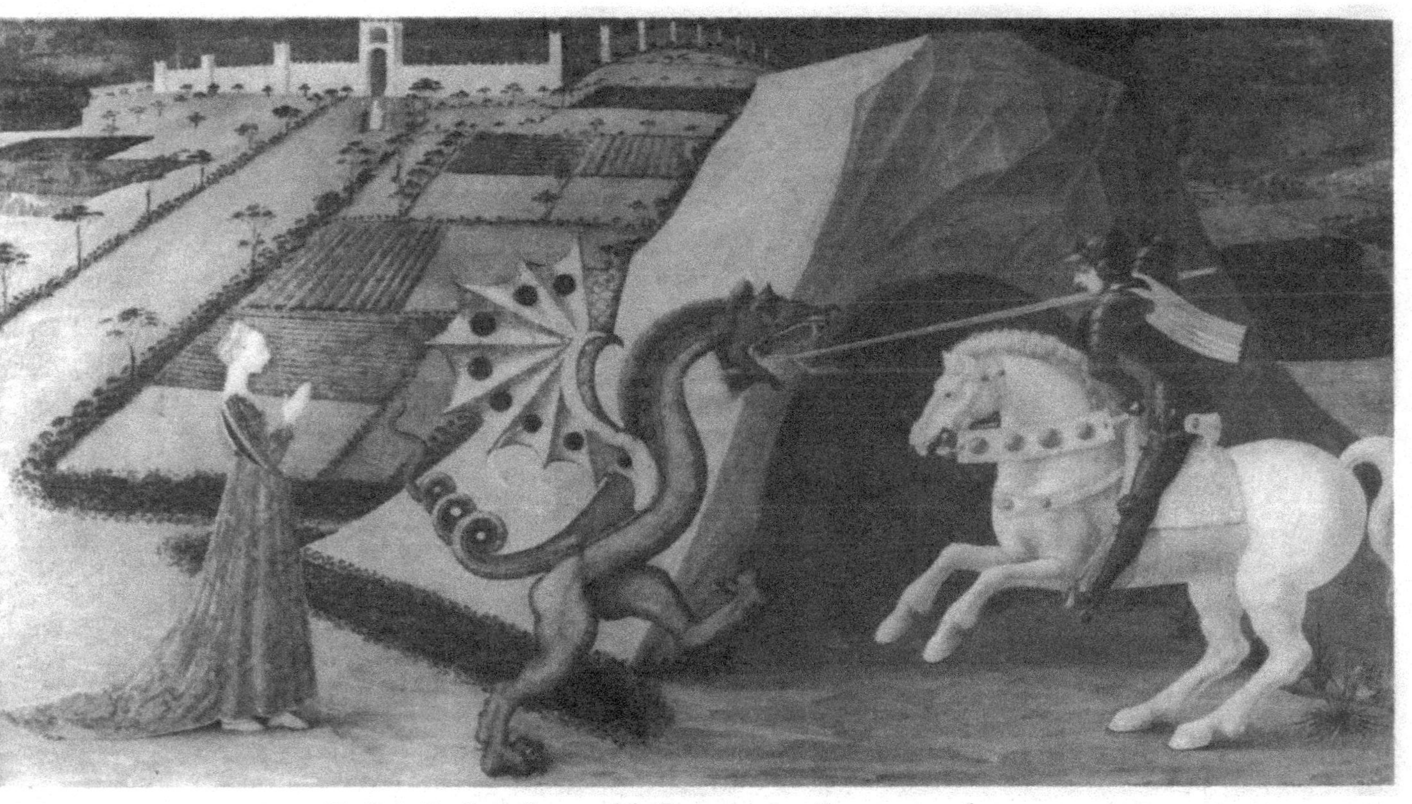

IV Paolo Uccello: St George and the Dragon. 1437–40. Tempera on panel: 52 × 90 cm.

ART AND SCIENCE

✱

THE author of an illuminating article, 'The Place of Science' in the *Athenaeum* for April 11th,[1] distinguishes between two aspects of intellectual activity in scientific work. Of these two aspects one derives its motive power from curiosity, and this deals with particular facts. It is only when, through curiosity, man has accumulated a mass of particular observations that the second intellectual activity manifests itself, and in this the motive is the satisfaction which the mind gets from the contemplation of inevitable relations. To secure this end the utmost possible generalisation is necessary.

In a later article S. says boldly that this satisfaction is an aesthetic satisfaction: 'It is in its aesthetic value that the justification of the scientific theory is to be found, and with it the justification of the scientific method.'[2] I should like to pose to S. at this point the question of whether a theory that disregarded facts would have equal value for science with one which agreed with facts. I suppose he would say No; and yet, so far as I can see, there would be no purely aesthetic reason why it should not. The aesthetic value of a theory would surely depend solely on the perfection and complexity of the unity attained, and I imagine that many systems of scholastic theology, and even some more recent systems of metaphysic, have only this aesthetic value. I suspect that the aesthetic value of a theory is not really sufficient to justify the intellectual effort entailed unless, as in a true scientific theory – by which I mean a theory which embraces all the known relevant facts – the aesthetic value is reinforced by the curiosity value which comes in when we believe it to be true. But now, returning to art, let me try to describe rather more clearly its analogies with science.

Both of these aspects – the particularising and the generalising – have their counterparts in art. Curiosity impels the artist to the consideration of every possible form in nature: under its stimulus he tends to accept each form in all its particularity as a given, unalterable fact. The other kind of intellectual activity impels the artist to attempt the reduction of all forms, as it were, to some common denominator which will make them comparable with one another. It impels him to discover some aesthetically intelligible principle in various forms, and even to envisage the possibility of some kind of abstract form in the aesthetic contemplation of which the mind would attain satisfaction – a satisfaction curiously parallel to that which the mind gets from the intellectual recognition of abstract truth.

If we consider the effects of these two kinds of intellectual activity, or rather their exact analogues, in art, we have to note that in so far as the artist's curiosity remains a purely intellectual curiosity it interferes with the perfection and purity of the work of art by introducing an alien and non-aesthetic element and appealing to non-aesthetic desires; in so far as it merely supplies the artist with new motives and a richer material out of which to build his designs, it is useful but subsidiary. Thus the objection to a 'subject picture', in so far as one remains conscious of the subject as something outside of, and apart from, the form, is a valid objection to the intrusion of intellect, of however rudimentary a kind, into an aesthetic whole. The ordinary historical pictures of our annual shows will furnish perfect examples of such an intrusion, since they exhibit innumerable appeals to intellectual recognitions without which the pictures would be meaningless. Without some previous knowledge of Caligula or Mary Queen of Scots we are likely to miss our way in a great deal of what passes for art today.

The case of the generalising intellect, or rather its analogue, in art is more difficult. Here the recognition of relations is immediate and sensational – perhaps we ought to consider it as curiously akin to those cases of mathematical geniuses who have immediate intuition of mathematical relations which it is beyond their powers to prove – so that it is by analogy that we may talk of it at all as intellectual. But the analogy is so close that I hope it may justify the use I here suggest. For in both cases the utmost possible generalisation is aimed at, and in both the mind is held in delighted equilibrium by the contemplation of the inevitable relations of all the parts in the whole, so that no need exists to make reference to what is outside the unity, and this becomes for the time being a universe.[3]

It will be seen how close the analogies are between the methods and aims of art and science, and yet there remains an obstinate doubt in the mind whether at any point they are identical. Probably in order to get much further we must wait for the psychologists to solve a number of problems; meanwhile this at least must be pointed out – that, allowing that the motives of science are emotional, many of its processes are purely intellectual, that is to say, mechanical. They could be performed by a perfectly non-sentient, emotionless brain, whereas at no point in the process of art can we drop feeling. There is something in the common phraseology by which we talk of *seeing* a point or an argument, whereas we *feel* the harmony of a work of art; and for some reason we attach a more constant emotional quality to feeling than to seeing, which is in more frequent request for coldly practical ends.

From the merest rudiments of pure sensation up to the highest efforts of design each point in the process of art is inevitably accompanied by pleasure; it cannot proceed without it. If we describe the process of art as a logic of sensation, we must remember that the premises are sensations, and that the conclusion can only be drawn from them by one who is in an emotional state with regard to them. Thus a harmony in music cannot be perceived by a person who merely hears accurately the notes which compose it – it can only be recognised when the relations of those notes to one another are accompanied by emotion. It is quite true that the recognition of inevitability in thought is normally accompanied by a pleasurable emotion, and that the desire for this mental pleasure is the motive force which impels to the making of scientific theory. But the inevitability of the relations remains equally definite and demonstrable whether the emotion accompanies it or not, whereas an aesthetic harmony simply does not exist without the emotional state. The harmony is not *true* – to use our analogy – unless it is felt with emotion.

None the less, perhaps, the highest pleasure in art is identical with the highest pleasure in scientific theory. The emotion which accompanies the clear recognition of unity in a complex seems to be so similar in art and in science that it is difficult not to suppose that they are psychologically the same. It is, as it were, the final stage of both processes. This unity-emotion in science supervenes upon a process of pure mechanical reasoning; in art it supervenes upon a process of which emotion has all along been an essential concomitant.

It may be that in the complete apprehension of a work of art there occurs more than one kind of feeling. There is generally a basis of purely physiological pleasure, as in seeing pure colours or hearing pure sounds; then there is the specifically aesthetic emotion by means of which the necessity of relations is apprehended, and which corresponds in science to the purely logical process; and finally there is the unity-emotion, which may not improbably be of an identical kind in both art and science.

In the art of painting we may distinguish between the unity of texture and the unity of design. I know quite well that these are not really completely separable, and that they are to some extent mutually dependent; but they may be regarded as separate for the purpose of focussing our attention. Certainly we can think of pictures in which the general architecture of the design is in no way striking or remarkable which yet please us by the perfection of the texture, that is to say, the ease with which we apprehend the necessary relationship of one shape, tone or colour with its immediately surrounding shapes, tones or colours; our aesthetic sense is continually aroused and satisfied by the succession of inevitable relationships. On the other hand, we know of works of art in which the unity and complexity of the texture strike us far less than the inevitable and significant relationship of the main divisions of the design – pictures in which we should say that the composition was the most striking beauty. It is when the composition of a picture, adequately supported as it must be by significance of texture, reveals to us the most surprising and yet inevitable relationships that we get most strongly the final unity-emotion of a work of art. It is these pictures that are, as S. would say of certain theories, the most significant for contemplation. Nor before such works can we help implicitly attributing to their authors the same kind of power which in science we should call 'great intellect', though perhaps in both the term 'great imaginative organisation' would be better.

THE ART OF THE BUSHMEN

✱

In the history of mankind drawing has at different times and among different races expressed so many different conceptions, and has used such various means, that it would seem to be not one art, but many. It would seem, indeed, that it has its origins in several quite distinct instincts of the human race, and it may not be altogether unimportant even for the modern draughtsman to investigate these instincts in their simpler manifestations in order to check and control his own methods. The primitive drawing of our own race is singularly like that of children. Its most striking peculiarity is the extent to which it is dominated by the concepts of language. In a child's drawing we find a number of forms which have scarcely any reference to actual appearances, but which directly symbolise the most significant concepts of the thing being represented. For a child, a man is the sum of the concept's head (which in turn consists of eyes, nose, mouth), of his arms, his hands (five fingers), his legs and his feet. Torso is not a concept which interests him, and it is, therefore, usually reduced to a single line which serves to link the concept-symbol head with those of the legs. The child does, of course, know that the figure thus drawn is not like a man, but it is a kind of hieroglyphic script for a man, and satisfies his desire for expression. Precisely the same phenomenon occurs in primitive art; the symbols for concepts gradually take on more and more of the likeness to appearances, but the mode of approach remains even in comparatively advanced periods the same. The artist does not seek to transfer a visual sensation to paper, but to express a mental image which is coloured by his conceptual habits.

Prof. Loewy[1] has investigated the laws which govern representation in early art, and has shown that the influence of the early artist's ideas of conceptual symbolism persist in Greek sculpture down to the time of Lysippus. He enumerates seven peculiarities of early drawing, of which the most important are that the figures are shown with each of their parts in its broadest aspect, and that the forms are stylised – i.e. present linear formations that are regular or tend to regularity.

Of the first of these peculiarities Egyptian and Assyrian sculpture, even of the latest and most developed periods, afford constant examples. We see there the head in profile, the eye full face, the shoulders and breast full face, and by a sudden twist in the body the legs and feet again in profile. In this way each part is presented in that aspect which most clearly expresses its corresponding visual concepts. Thus a foot is much more clearly denoted by its profile view than by the rendering of its frontal appearance – while no one who was asked to think of an eye would visualise it to himself in any other than a full-face view. In such art, then the body is twisted about so that each part may be represented by that aspect which the mental image aroused by the name of the part would have, and the figure becomes an ingenious compound of typical conceptual images. In the case of the head two aspects are accepted as symbolic of the concept 'head', the profile and the full-face; but it is very late in the development of art before men are willing to accept any intermediate position as intelligible or satisfactory. It is generally supposed that early art avoids foreshortening because of its difficulty. One may suppose rather that it is because the foreshortened view of a member corresponds so ill with the normal conceptual image, and is therefore not accepted as sufficiently expressive of the idea. Yet another of the peculiarities named by Prof. Loewy must be mentioned, namely, that the 'conformation and movement of the figures and their parts are limited to a few typical shapes.'[2] And these movements are always of the simplest kinds, since they are governed by the necessity of displaying each member in its broadest and most explicit aspect. In particular the crossing of one limb over another is avoided as confusing.

Such in brief outline, are some of the main principles of drawing both among primitive peoples and among our own children. It is not a little surprising then to find, when we turn to Miss Tongue's careful copies of the drawings executed by the

Bushmen of South Africa[3] that the principles are more often contradicted than exemplified. We find, it is true, a certain barbaric crudity and simplicity which give these drawings a superficial resemblance to children's drawings or those of primitive times, but a careful examination will show how different they are. The drawings are of different periods, though none of them probably are of any considerable antiquity, since the habit of painting over an artist's work when once he was forgotten obtained among the bushmen no less than with more civilised people. These drawings are also of very different degrees of skill. They represent for the most part scenes of the chase and war, dances and festivals, and in one case there is an illustration to a bushman story and one figure is supposed to represent a ghost. There is no evidence of deliberate decorative purpose in these paintings. The figures are cast upon the walls of the cave in such a way as to represent, roughly, the actual scenes.* Nothing could be more unlike primitive art than some of these scenes. For instance, the battle fought between two tribes over the possession of some cattle, is entirely unlike battle scenes such as we find in early Assyrian reliefs. There the battle is schematic, all the soldiers of one side are in profile to right, all the soldiers of the opposing side are in profile to left. The whole scene is perfectly clear to the intelligence, it follows the mental image of what a battle ought to be, but is entirely unlike what a battle ever is. Now, in the Bushman drawing there is nothing truly schematic; it is difficult to find out the soldiers of the two sides; they are all mixed up in a confused hurly-burly, some charging, others flying, and here and there single combats going on at a distance from the main battle. But more than this, the men are in every conceivable attitude, running, standing, kneeling, crouching, or turning sharply round in the middle of flight to face the enemy once more.

* This absence of decorative feeling may be due to the irregular and vague outlines of the picture space. It is when the picture must be fitted within determined limits that decoration begins. I have noticed that children's drawings are never decorative when they have the whole surface of a sheet of paper to draw on, but they will design a frieze with well-marked rhythm when they have only a narrow strip.

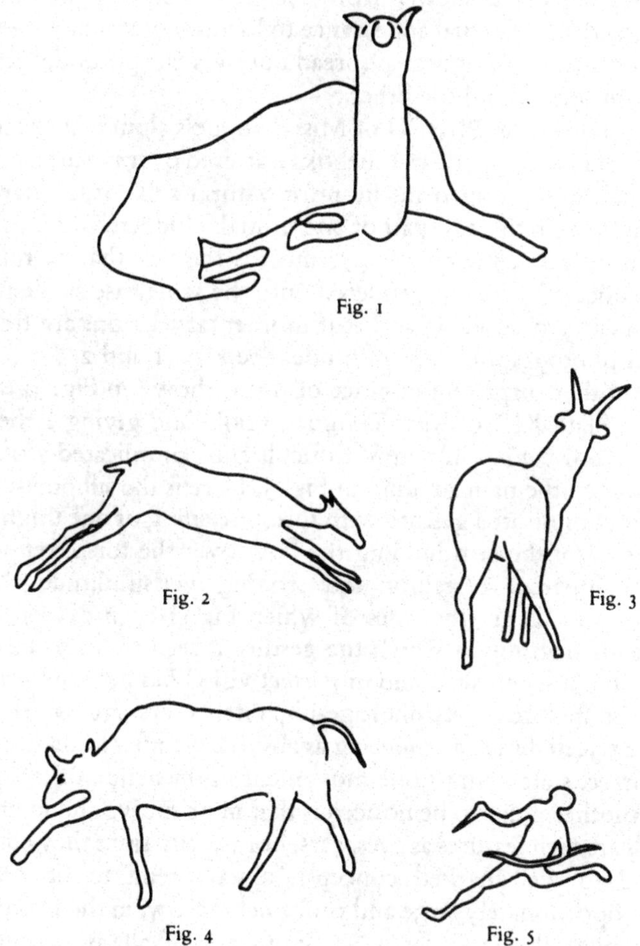

Fig. 1

Fig. 2

Fig. 3

Fig. 4

Fig. 5

In fact we have, in all its confusion, all its indeterminate variety and accident, a rough silhouette of the actual appearance of such a scene as viewed from above, for the Bushman makes this sacrifice of actual appearance to lucidity of statement – that he represents the figures as spread out over the ground, and not as seen one behind the other.

Or take again Plate XI of Miss Tongue's album; the scene is the Veldt with elands and rheboks scattered over its surface. The animals are arranged in the most natural and casual manner; sometimes in this case part of one animal is hidden by the animal in front; but what strikes one most is the fact that extremely complicated poses are rendered with the same ease as the more frequent profile view, and that momentary actions are treated with photographic verisimilitude. See Figs. 1 and 2.

Another surprising instance of this is shown in Fig. 3, taken from Plate XIX of Miss Tongue's book, and giving a rhebok seen from behind in a most difficult and complicated attitude. Or again, the man running in Fig. 5. Here is the silhouette of a most complicated gesture with foreshortening of one thigh and crossing of the arm holding the bow over the torso, rendered with apparent certainty and striking verisimilitude. Most curious of all are the cases of which Fig. 4 is an example, of animals trotting, in which the gesture is seen by us to be true only because our slow and imperfect vision has been helped out by the instantaneous photograph. Fifty years ago we should have rejected such a rendering as absurd; we now know it to be a correct statement of one movement in the action of trotting.

Another point to be noticed is that in primitive and in children's art such features as eyes, ears, horns, tails, since they correspond to well-marked concepts, always tend to be drawn disproportionately large and prominent. Now, in the Bushman drawings, the eye, the most significant of all, is frequently omitted, and when represented bears its true proportion to the head. Similarly, horns, ears, and tails are never exaggerated. Indeed, however faulty these drawings may be, they have one great quality, namely that each figure is seen as a single entity, and the general character of the silhouette is aimed at rather than a sum of the parts. Those who have taught drawing to children will know with what infinite pains civilised man arrives at this power.

By way of contrast to these extraordinary performances of the Bushman draughtsman, I give in outline, Fig. 6, the two horses of a chariot on an early – Dipylon – Greek vase. The man

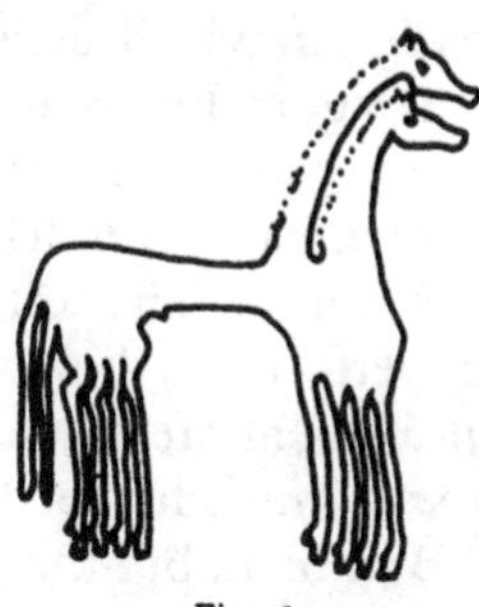

Fig. 6

who drew it was incomparably more of an artist; but how entirely his intellectual and conceptual way of handling phenomena has obscured his vision! His two horses are a sum of the concept-symbols, arranged with great orderliness and with a decorative feeling, but without any sort of likeness to appearance. Mr Balfour,[4] in his preface to Miss Tongue's book, notices briefly some of these striking characteristics of the Bushman drawings. He says:

> The paintings are remarkable not only for the realism exhibited by so many, but also for a freedom from the limitation to delineation in profile which characterises for the most part the drawings of primitive peoples, especially where animals are concerned. Attitudes of a kind difficult to render were ventured upon without hesitation, and an appreciation even of the rudiments of perspective is occasionally to be noted, though only in a crude and uncertain form. The practice of endeavouring to represent more than could be seen at one time, a habit so characteristic of the art of primitive peoples as also of civilised children, is far less noticeable in Bushman art than might have been expected from the rudimentary general culture of these people, and one does not see instances of *both* eyes being indicated upon a profile face, or a mouth in profile on a full face, such as are so familiar in the undeveloped art of children and of most backward races.[5]

Since, then, Bushman drawing has little analogy to the primitive art of our own races, to what can we relate it? The Bushmen of Australia have apparently something of the same power of transcribing pure visual images, but the most striking case is that of Palaeolithic man. In the caves of the Dordogne and of Altamira in Spain, Palaeolithic man has left paintings which date from about 10,000 B. C., in which, as far as mere naturalism of representation of animals goes, he has surpassed anything that not only our own primitive peoples, but even the most accomplished animal draughtsmen have ever achieved. Fig. 7 shows in outline a bison from Altamira. The certainty and completeness of the pose, the perfect rhythm and the astonishing verisimilitude of the movement are evident even in this. The Altamira drawings show a much higher level of accomplishment than those of the Bushmen, but the general likeness is so great as to have suggested the idea that the Bushmen are descendants of Palaeolithic man who have remained at the same rudimentary stage as regards the other arts of life, and have retained something of their own unique power of visual transcription.

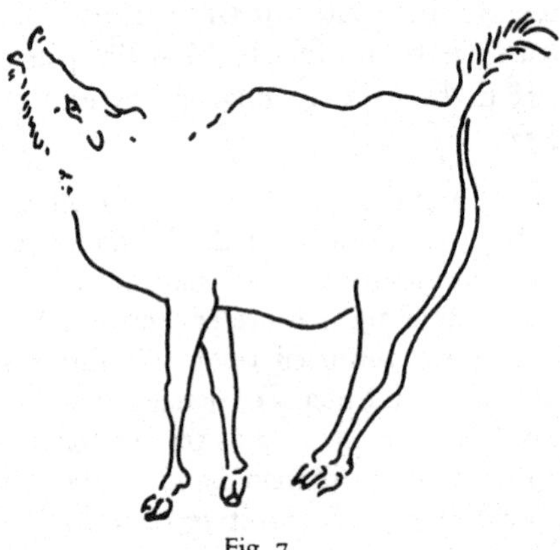

Fig. 7

Whether this be so or not, it is to be noted that all the peoples whose drawing shows this peculiar power of visualisation belong to what we call the lowest of savages; they are certainly the least civilisable, and the South African Bushmen are regarded by other native races in much the same way that we look upon negroes. It would seem not impossible that the very perfection of vision, and presumably of the other senses* with which the Bushmen and Palaeolithic man were endowed, fitted them so perfectly to their surroundings that there was no necessity to develop the mechanical arts beyond the elementary instruments of the chase. We must suppose that Neolithic man, on the other hand, was less perfectly adapted to his surroundings, but that his sensual defects were more than compensated for by increased intellectual power. This greater intellectual power manifested itself in his desire to classify phenomena, and the conceptual view of nature began to predominate. And it was this habit of thinking of things in terms of concepts which deprived him for ages of the power to see what they looked like. With Neolithic man drawing came to express man's thought about things rather than his sensations of them, or rather, when he tried to reproduce his sensations, his habits of thought intervened, and dictated to his hand orderly, lucid, but entirely non-naturalistic forms.

How deeply these visual-conceptual habits of Neolithic man have sunk into our natures may be seen by their effects upon hysterical patients, a statement which I owe to the kindness of Dr Henry Head, F.R.S.[6] If the word 'chest' is mentioned most people see a vague image of a flat surface on which are marked the sternum and the pectoral muscles; when the word 'back' is given, they see another flat or almost flat surface with markings of the spine and the shoulder-blades; but scarcely any one, having these two mental images called up, thinks of them as parts of a continuous cylindrical body. Now, in the case of some hysterical patients anaesthesia is found just over some part of the body which has been isolated from the rest in thought by means of the conceptual image. It will occur, for instance, in the chest, but will not go beyond the limits which the conceptualised visual image of a chest defines. Or it will be associated with the concept hand, and will stop short at the wrists. It is not surprising, then,

* This is certainly the case with the Australian Bushmen.

that a mode of handling the continuum of natural appearance, which dictates even the behaviour of disease, should have profoundly modified all artistic representations of nature since the conceptual habit first became strongly marked in Neolithic man. An actual definition of drawing given by a child may be quoted in this connection, 'First I think, and then I draw a line round my think.'

It would be an exaggeration to suppose that Palaeolithic and Bushman drawings are entirely uninfluenced by the concepts which even the most primitive people must form. Indeed, the preference for the profile view of animals – though as we have seen other aspects are frequent – would alone indicate this, but they appear to have been at a stage of intellectual development where the concepts were not so clearly grasped as to have begun to interfere with perception, and where therefore the retinal image passed into a clear memory picture with scarcely any intervening mental process. In the art of even civilised man we may, I think, find great variations in the extent to which the conceptualising of visual images has proceeded. Egyptian and Assyrian art remained intensely conceptual throughout, no serious attempt was made to give greater verisimilitude to the symbols employed. The Mycenaean artists, on the other hand, seem to have been appreciably more perceptual, but the Greeks returned to an intensely conceptualised symbolism in which some of their greatest works of art were expressed, and only very gradually did they modify their formulae so as to admit of some approach to verisimilitude, and even so the appeal to vision was rather by way of correcting and revising accepted conceptual images than as the foundation of a work of art. The art of China, and still more of Japan, has been distinctly more perceptual. Indeed, the Japanese drawings of birds and animals approach more nearly than those of any other civilised people to the immediacy and rapidity of transcription of Bushman and Palaeolithic art. The Bushman silhouettes of cranes (Fig. 8) might almost have come from a Japanese screen. Like Japanese drawings, they show an alertness to accept the silhouette as a single whole instead of reconstructing it from separately apprehended parts. It is partly due to Japanese influence that our

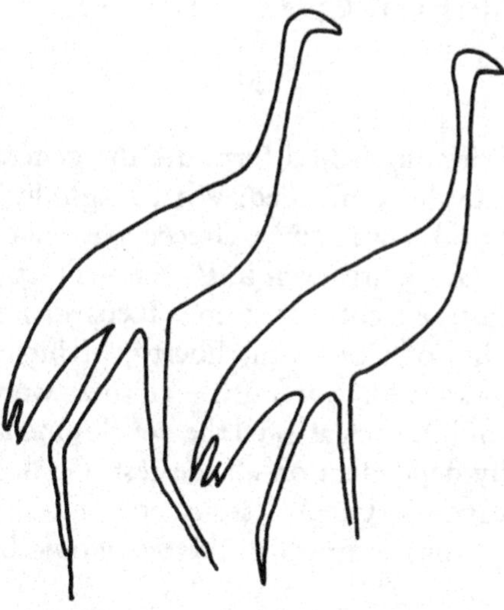

Fig. 8

own Impressionists have made an attempt to get back to that ultra-primitive directness of vision. Indeed they deliberately sought to deconceptualise art. The artist of today has therefore to some extent a choice before him of whether he will *think* form like the early artists of European races or merely *see* it like the Bushmen. Whichever his choice, the study of these drawings can hardly fail to be of profound interest. The Bushmen paintings on the walls of caves and sheltered rocks are fast disappearing; the race itself, of which Miss Bleek[7] gives a fascinating account, is now nothing but a remnant. The treatment that they have received at the hands of the white settlers does not seem to have been conspicuously more sympathetic or intelligent than that meted out to them by negro conquerors, and thus the opportunity of solving some of the most interesting problems of human development has been for ever lost. The gratitude of all students of art is due to Miss Tongue and Miss Bleek, by whose zeal and industry these remains of a most curious phase of primitive art have been adequately recorded.

NEGRO SCULPTURE

✻

WHAT a comfortable mental furniture the generalisations of a century ago must have afforded! What a right little, tight little, round little world it was when Greece was the only source of culture, when Greek art, even in Roman copies, was the only indisputable art, except for some Renaissance repetitions! Philosophy, the love of truth, liberty, architecture, poetry, drama, and for all we know music – all these were the fruits of a special kind of life, each assisted the development of the other, each was really dependent on all the rest. Consequently if we could only learn the Greek lessons of political freedom and intellectual self-consciousness all the rest would be added unto us.

And now, in the last sixty years, knowledge and perception have poured upon us so fast that the whole well-ordered system has been blown away, and we stand bare to the blast, scarcely able to snatch a hasty generalisaton or two to cover our nakedness for a moment.

Our desperate plight comes home to one at the Chelsea Book Club, where are some thirty chosen specimens of negro sculpture. If to our ancestors the poor Indian had 'an untutored mind', the Congolese's ignorance and savagery must have seemed too abject for discussion. One would like to know what Dr Johnson would have said to any one who had offered him a negro idol for several hundred pounds. It would have seemed then sheer lunacy to listen to what a negro savage had to tell us of his emotions about the human form. And now one has to go all the way to Chelsea in a chastened spirit and prostrate oneself before his 'stocks and stones'.

We have the habit of thinking that the power to create expressive plastic form is one of the greatest of human achievements, and the names of great sculptors are handed down from generation to generation, so that it seems unfair to be forced to admit that certain nameless savages have possessed this power not only in a higher degree than we at this moment, but than we as a nation have ever possessed it. And yet that is where I find myself. I have to admit that some of these things are great sculpture – greater, I think, than anything we produced even in the Middle Ages. Certainly they have the special qualities of sculpture in a higher degree. They have indeed complete plastic freedom; that is to say, these African artists really conceive form in three dimensions. Now this is rare in sculpture. All archaic European sculpture – Greek and Romanesque, for instance – approaches plasticity from the point of view of bas-relief. The statue bears traces of having been conceived as the combination of front, back, and side bas-reliefs. And this continues to make itself felt almost until the final development of the tradition. Complete plastic freedom with us seems only to come at the end of a long period, when the art has attained a high degree of representational skill and when it is generally already decadent from the point of view of imaginative significance.

Now, the strange thing about these African sculptures (Plate II. 1) is that they bear, as far as I can see, no trace of this process. Without ever attaining anything like representational accuracy they have complete freedom. The sculptors seem to have no difficulty in getting away from the two-dimensional plane. The neck and the torso are conceived as cylinders, not as masses with a square section. The head is conceived as a pear-shaped mass. It is conceived as a single whole, not arrived at by approach from the mask, as with almost all primitive European art. The mask itself is conceived as a concave plane cut out of this otherwise perfectly unified mass.

And here we come upon another curious difference between negro sculpture and our own, namely, that the emphasis is utterly different. Our emphasis has always been affected by our preferences for certain forms which appeared to us to mark the nobility of man. Thus we shrink from giving the head its full development; we like to lengthen the legs and generally to force the form into a particular type. These preferences seem to be dictated not by a plastic bias, but by our reading of the physical symbols of certain inner qualities which we admire in our kind, such, for instance, as agility, a commanding presence, or a pensive brow. The negro, it seems, either has no such preferences, or his preferences happen to coincide more nearly with what his feeling for pure plastic design would dictate. For instance, the length, thinness, and isolation of our limbs render them extremely refractory to fine plastic treatment, and the negro scores heavily by his willingness to reduce the limbs to a succession of ovoid masses sometimes scarcely longer than they are broad. Generally speaking, one may say that his plastic sense leads him to give its utmost amplitude and relief to all the protuberant parts of the body, and to get thereby an extraordinarily emphatic and impressive sequence of planes. So far from clinging to two dimensions, as we tend to do, he actually underlines, as it were, the three-dimensionalness of his forms. It is in some such way, I suspect, that he manages to give to his forms their disconcerting vitality, the suggestion that they make of being not mere echoes of actual figures, but of possessing an inner life of their own. If the negro artist wanted to make people believe in the potency of his idols he certainly set about it in the right way.

Besides the logical comprehension of plastic form which the negro shows, he has also an exquisite taste in his handling of material. No doubt in this matter his endless leisure has something to do with the marvellous finish of these works. An instance of this is seen in the treatment of the tattoo cicatrices. These are always rendered in relief, which means that the artist has cut away the whole surface around them. I fancy most sculptors would have found some less laborious method of interpreting these markings. But this patient elaboration of the surface is characteristic of most of these works. It is seen to perfection in a wooden cup covered all over with a design of faces and objects that look like clubs in very low relief. The *galbe*[1] of this cup shows a subtlety and refinement of taste comparable to that of the finest Oriental craftsmen.

It is curious that a people who produced such great artists did not produce also a culture in our sense of the word. This shows that two factors are necessary to produce the cultures which distinguish civilised peoples. There must be, of course, the creative artist, but there must also be the power of conscious critical appreciation and comparison. If we imagined such an apparatus of critical appreciation as the Chinese have possessed from the earliest times applied to this negro art, we should have no difficulty in recognising its singular beauty. We should never have been tempted to regard it as savage or unrefined. It is for want of a conscious critical sense and the intellectual powers of comparison and classification that the negro has failed to create one of the great cultures of the world, and not from any lack of the creative aesthetic impulse, nor from lack of the most exquisite sensibility and the finest taste. No doubt, also, the lack of such a critical standard to support him leaves the artist much more at the mercy of any outside influence. It is likely enough that the negro artist, although capable of such profound imaginative understanding of form, would accept our cheapest illusionist art with humble enthusiasm.

ANCIENT AMERICAN ART

✱

NOTHING in the history of our Western civilisation is more romantic nor for us more tantalising than the story of the discovery and the wanton destruction of the ancient civilisations of America. Here were two complex civilisations which had developed in complete independence of the rest of the world; even so completely independent of each other that, for all their general racial likeness, they took on almost opposite characters. If only we could know these alternative efforts of the human animal to come to terms with nature and himself with something like the same fullness with which we know the civilisations of Greece and Rome, what might we not learn about the fundamental necessities of mankind? They would have been for us the opposite point of our orbit; they would have given us a parallax from which we might have estimated the movements of that dimmest and most distant phenomenon, the social nature of man. And as it is, what scraps of ill-digested and ill-arranged information and what fragments of ruined towns have to suffice us! Still, so fascinating is the subject that we owe Mr Joyce[1] a debt of gratitude for the careful and thorough accumulation of all the material which the archaeological remains afford. These by themselves would be only curious or beautiful as the case may be; their full value and significance can only come out when they are illustrated by whatever is known of their place in the historical sequence of the civilisations. Mr Joyce gives us what is known of the outlines of Mexican and Peruvian history as far as it can be deciphered from the early accounts of Spanish invaders and from the original documents, and he brings the facts thus established to bear on the antiquities. Unfortunately for the reader of these books, the story is terribly involved and complicated even when it is not dubious. Thus in Mexico we have to deal with an almost inextricable confusion of tribes and languages having much in common, but each interpreting their common mythology and religion in a special manner. Even Greek mythology, which we once seemed to know fairly well, takes on under the pressure of modern research an unfamiliar formlessness – becomes indistinct and shifting in its outlines; and the various civilisations of Mexico, each with its innumerable gods and goddesses with varying names and varying attributes, produce on the mind a sense of bewildering and helpless wonder, and still more a sense of pervading horror at the underlying nature of the human imagination. For one quality emerges in all the different aspects of their religions, its hideous inhumanity and cruelty, its direct inspiration of all the most ingenious tortures both in peace and war – above all, the close alliance between religion and war and going with both of these the worship of suffering as an end in itself. Only at one point in this nightmare of inhumanity do we get a momentary sense of pleasure – itself a savage one – that is in the knowledge that at certain sacred periods the priests, whose main business was the torturing of others, were themselves subjected to the purificatory treatment. A bas-relief in the British Museum shows with grim realism the figure of a kneeling priest with pierced tongue, pulling a rope through the hole. Under such circumstances one would at least hesitate to accuse the priesthood of hypocrisy.

When we turn to Peru the picture is less grim. The Incas do not seem to have been so abjectly religious as the Aztecs; they had at least abolished human sacrifice, which the Aztecs practised on a colossal scale, and though the tyranny of the governing classes was more highly organised, it was inspired by a fairly humane conception.

But we must leave the speculations on such general questions, which are as regards these books incidental to the main object, and turn to the consideration of the archaeological remains and the investigation of their probable sequence and dating.

Our attitude to the artistic remains of these civilisations has a curious history. The wonder of the Spanish invaders at the sight of vast and highly organised civilisations where only savagery was expected has never indeed ceased, but the interest in their remains has changed from time to time. The first emotion they excited besides wonder was the greed of the conquerors for the accumulated treasure. Then among the more cultivated Spaniards supervened a purely scientific curiosity to which we owe most of our knowledge of the indigenous legend and history. Then came the question of origins, which is still as fascinating and unsettled as ever, and to the belief that the Mexicans were the lost ten tribes of Israel we owe Lord Kingsborough's monumental work in nine volumes on Mexican antiquities.[2] To such odd impulses perhaps, rather than to any serious appreciation of their artistic merits, we owe the magnificent collection of Mexican antiquities in the British Museum. Indeed, it is only in this century that, after contemplating them from every point of view, we have begun to look at them seriously as works of art. Probably the first works to be admitted to this kind of consideration were the Peruvian pots in the form of highly realistic human heads and figures.[3]

Still more recently we have come to recognise the beauty of Aztec and Maya sculpture, and some of our modern artists have even gone to them for inspiration.[4] This is, of course, one result of the general aesthetic awakening which has followed on the revolt against the tyranny of the Graeco-Roman tradition.

Both in Mexico and Peru we have to deal with at least two, possibly four, great cultures, each overthrown in turn by the invasion of less civilised, more warlike tribes, who gradually adopt the general scheme of the older civilisation. In Mexico there is no doubt about the superiority, from an artistic point of view, of the earlier culture – the Aztecs had everything to learn from the Maya, and they never rose to the level of their predecessors. The relation is, in fact, curiously like that of Rome to Greece. Unfortunately we have to learn almost all we know of Maya culture through their Aztec conquerors, but the ruins of Yucatan and Guatemala are by far the finest and most complete vestiges left to us.

In Peru also we find in the Tiahuanaco gateway[5] a monument of some pre-Inca civilisation, and one that in regard to the art of sculpture far surpasses anything that the later culture reveals. It is of special interest, moreover, for its strong stylistic likeness to the Maya sculpture of Yucatan. This similarity prompts the interesting speculation whether the earlier civilisations of the two continents had either a common origin or points of contact, whereas the Inca and Aztec cultures seem to drift entirely apart. The Aztecs carry on at a lower level the Maya art of sculpture, whereas the Incas seem to drop sculpture almost entirely, a curious fact in view of the ambitious nature of their architectural and engineering works. One seems to guess that the comparatively humane socialistic tyranny of the Incas developed more and more along purely practical lines, whilst the hideous religiosity of the Aztecs left a certain freedom to the imaginative artist.

In looking at the artistic remains of so remote and strange a civilisation one sometimes wonders how far one can trust one's aesthetic appreciation to interpret truly the feelings which inspired it. In certain works one cannot doubt that the artist felt just as we feel in appreciating his work. This must, I think, hold on the one hand of the rich ornamental arabesques of Maya buildings or the marvellous inlaid feather and jewel work of either culture; and on the other hand, when we look at the caricatural realistic figures of Truxillo[6] pottery we need scarcely doubt that the artist's intention agrees with our appreciation, for such a use of the figure is more or less common to all civilisations. But when we look at the stylistic sculpture of Maya and Aztec art, are we, one wonders, reading in an intention which was not really present? One wonders, for instance, how far external and accidental factors may not have entered in to help produce what seems to us the perfect and delicate balance between representational and purely formal consideration. Whether the artist was not held back both by ritualistic tradition and the difficulty of his medium from pushing further the actuality of his presentation – whether, in fact, the artist deplored or himself approved just that reticence which causes our admiration. At times Maya sculpture has a certain similarity to Indian religious sculptural reliefs, particularly in the use of flat surfaces entirely incrusted with ornaments in low relief; but on the whole the comparison is all in favour of the higher aesthetic sensibility of the Maya artists, whose co-ordination of even the most complicated forms compares favourably with the incoherent luxuriance of most Indian work.

In this, as in so many of its characteristics, Maya art comes much nearer to early Chinese sculpture; and again one wonders that such a civilisation should have produced such sensitive and reasoned designs – designs which seem to imply a highly developed self-conscious aesthetic sensibility. Nor do the Maya, for all their hieratic ritualism, seem to fall into the dead, mechanical repetition which the endless multiplication of religious symbols usually entails, as, for instance, most markedly in Egyptian art. But this strange difference between what we know of Mexican civilisation and what we might have interpreted from the art alone is only one more instance of the isolation of the aesthetic from all other human activities.

The sculptures of Pedras Negras, of which casts may be seen in the British Museum, are among the finest remains of Maya sculpture. They show at once the extreme richness of the decorative effect and the admirable taste with which this is coordinated in a plastic whole in which the figure has its due predominance. Though the relief of the ornamental part is kept flat and generally square in section, it has nothing of the dryness and tightness that such a treatment often implies.

Mr Joyce's books are compiled with amazing industry, and contain a vast accumulation of information. If we have a complaint, it is that for those who are not specialists this information is poured out in almost too uniform a flood, with too little by way of general ideas to enable the mind to grasp or relate them properly. If some of the minor details of obscure proper names had been relegated to the notes, it would have been possible to seize the general outlines more readily. The books are rather for reference than adapted to consecutive reading. In his judgments on the various speculations to which these civilisations have given rise Mr Joyce is, as one would expect from so careful a scholar, cautious and negative. He does not, as far as I remember, even allude to the theory of the Lost Ten Tribes, but he does condescend to discuss the theory of cultural influence from Eastern Asia which has more than once been put forward by respectable ethnologists. He decides against this fascinating hypothesis more definitely than one would expect – more definitely, I should say, than the facts before us allow. He declares, for instance, that the calendrical system of Mexico shows no similarity with those of Eastern Asia, whereas Dr Lehmann[7] gives a circumstantial account of a very curious likeness, the almost exact correspondence of two quite peculiar systems of reckoning. My own bias in favour of the theory of Eastern Asiatic influence is, I confess, based on what may seem very insufficient grounds, namely, the curious likeness of the general treatment of naturalistic forms and the peculiar character of the stylisation of natural forms in early Chinese and American art. It is of course impossible to define a likeness of general character which depends so largely on feeling, but it consists to some extent in the predilection for straight lines and rectangles – a spiral in nature becoming in both early Chinese and American art a sequence of rectangular forms with rounded corners. What is more remarkable is that the further back we go in Chinese art the greater the resemblance becomes, so that a Chou bronze, or still more the carved horns which have survived from Shang dynasty,[8] are extraordinarily like Maya or Tiahuanaco sculpture. Again, it is curious to note how near to early Chinese bronzes are the tripod vases of the Guetar Indians. All these may of course be of quite independent origin, but their similarity cannot be dismissed lightly in view of the long persistence in any civilisation of such general habits of design. Thus the general habits of design of the Cretan civilisation persisted into Greek and even Roman and Christian art; the habits of design of Chinese artists have persisted, though through great modifications, for more than three thousand years. One other fact which may seem almost too isolated and insignificant may perhaps be put forward here. In a history of the Mormons, published in 1851,[9] there is given a figure of an inscribed bronze (see Figure 9) which was dug up by the Mormons in Utah in 1843. Since Brigham Young[10] pretended to have dug up the original book of Mormon his followers had a superstitious reverence for all such treasure trove, and probably the bronze still exists and might be worth investigation. Now this drawing, here reproduced, looks to me like an extremely bad and unintelligent reproduction of an early Chinese object, in general appearance not unlike certain pieces of jade. It is fairly certain that at the time the Mormons discovered this, no such objects had found their way out of China, since the interest in and knowledge of this period of Chinese art is of much later growth. So it appears conceivable that the object, whatever its nature, is a relic of some early cultural invasion from Eastern Asia. The physical possibilities of such invasions from the Far East certainly seem to be underestimated by Mr Joyce.

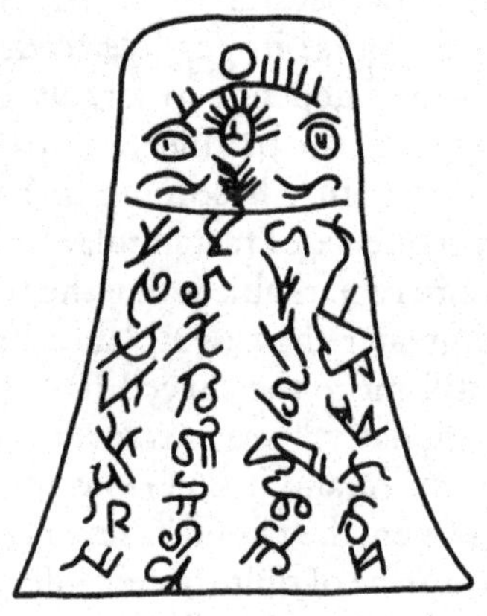

Fig. 9

THE MUNICH EXHIBITION OF MOHAMMEDAN ART

⁎

It would be hard to exaggerate the importance of this exhibition for those who are interested in the history not alone of Oriental but of European art. One of the most fascinating of the problems that present themselves to the art historian is that of the origins of mediaeval art. Until we understand more or less completely how in the dim centuries of the later Empire and early middle ages the great transformation of Graeco-Roman into mediaeval art was accomplished, we cannot quite understand the Renaissance itself, nor even the form which the whole modern art of Europe has come in the course of centuries to assume. And on this problem the Munich exhibition throws many illuminating side-lights. Early Mohammedan art is seen here to be a meeting-point of many influences. There are still traces of the once widespread Hellenistic tradition, though this is seen to be retreating before the refluent wave of aboriginal ideas. Sassanid art[1] had already been the outcome of these contending forces, and the pre-eminence of Sassanid art in forming early Mohammedan styles is clearly brought out in this exhibition. Then there is a constant exchange with Byzantium, and finally continual waves of influence, sometimes fertilising, sometimes destructive, from that great reservoir of Central Asian civilisation, the importance of which is now at last being gradually revealed to us by the discoveries of Dr Stein, Drs Lecoq and Grunwedel, and M. Pelliot.[2]

And through this great clearing-house of early Mohammedan art there are signs of influences passing from West to East. The most striking example is that of the plate in cloisonnée enamel[3] from the Landes Museum at Innsbruck. Here we have the one certain example of Mohammedan cloisonnée enamel established by its dedication to a prince of the Orthokid dynasty of the twelfth century.[4] It is extraordinary that this solitary example should alone have survived from what must, judging from the technical excellence of this specimen, have once been a flourishing craft. The general effect of the intricate pattern of animal forms upon a whitish ground suggests, on the one hand, the earliest examples of Limoges enamels,[5] and on the other the early Chinese, and there can be little doubt that the Chinese did in fact derive their knowledge of cloisonnée, which they themselves called 'Western ware', from these early Mohammedan craftsmen, who had themselves learned the technique from Byzantium.

But on the whole the stream of influence is in the opposite direction, from East to West, and one realises at Munich that in the great period of artistic discovery and formation of styles the near East and the West were developing in closest contact and harmony. Indeed the most fertile, if not actually the most resplendent, period of both arts was attained whilst they were still almost indistinguishable. If it were not for the habit of these early Mohammedan craftsmen of interweaving inscriptions into their designs, a habit which endears them quite especially to art-historians, how many works of Oriental manufacture would have been ascribed to Europe? In spite of these inscriptions, indeed, such an authority as M. Babelon has sought to place to the account of Western artists the superb cut crystal vessels,[6] of which the noblest example is the inscribed ewer of the tenth century in the treasury of S. Mark's. Or take again the textiles. In the exhibition there are a number of fragments of textiles of the tenth to the twelfth centuries, in which the general principle of design is the same; for the most part the surface is covered by circular reserves in which severely conventionalised figures of hunters, lions, or monsters are placed in pairs symmetrically confronted. Only minute study has enabled specialists to say that some were made in Sassanid Persia, some in Byzantium, some in Sicily, and some in Western Europe. The dominant style in all these is again derived from Sassanid art. And here once more one must note the strange recrudescence after so long of Assyrian types and motives, and its invasion of Western Europe, through Byzantium, Sicily, and Spain.

What strikes us most in comparing Graeco-Roman art with

the new art which gradually emerges in the middle ages is that, on the one hand, we have a series of decorative designs never so remarkable for vitality as for their elegance, and become by the time of the Roman Empire only a little less perfunctory and mechanical than the patterns of modern times; and on the other hand an art in which the smallest piece of pattern-making shows a tense vitality even in its most purely geometrical manifestations, and the figure is used with a new dramatic expressiveness unhindered by the artist's ignorance of actual form. Now in the splendid photographs of the Sassanid rock carvings which Dr Sarre[7] has taken and which are exposed at Munich, we can see something of this process of the creation of the new vital system of design. In the earlier reliefs, those of the time of Sapor,[8] we have, it is true, a certain theatrical splendour of pose and setting, but in the actual forms some flaccidity and inflation. The artists who wrought them show still the predominance of the worn-out Hellenistic tradition which spread in Alexander's wake over Asia. In the stupendous relief of Chosroes at Taq-i-Bostan,[9] on the other hand, we have all the dramatic energy, the heraldic splendour of the finest mediaeval art, and the source of this new inspiration is seen to be the welling up once more of the old indigenous Mesopotamian art. We have once more that singular feeling for stress, for muscular tension, and for dramatic oppositions which distinguish the bas-reliefs of Babylon and Nineveh from all other artistic expressions of the antique world. It would be possible by the help of exhibits at Munich to trace certain Assyrian forms right through to mediaeval European art. Take, for instance, the lion heads on the pre-Babylonian mace from Goudea in the Louvre; one finds a precisely similar convention for the lion head on the Sassanid repoussé[10] metalwork found in Russia. Once again it occurs in the superb carved rock crystal waterspout lent by the Karlsruhe Museum, and one finds it again on the font of Lincoln Cathedral and in the lions that support the doorway columns of Italian cathedrals. In all these there is a certain community of style, a certain way of symbolising the leonine nature which one may look for in vain in Greek and Graeco-Roman art.

Even if this seems too forced an interpretation of facts, it is none the less clear that everywhere in early Mohammedan art this recrudescence of Assyrian forms may be traced, and that their influence was scarcely less upon Europe than upon the near East. Dr Sarre has taken a tracing of the pattern which is represented in low relief upon the robes of Chosroes in the Taq-i-Bostan relief. In South Kensington Museum there is an almost identical piece of silk brocade which actually comes from the ruins of Khorsabad,[11] and in the same museum one may find more than one Byzantine imitation of this design and closely similar ones made in Sicily; and the conventional winged monster which forms the basis of these designs has a purely Assyrian air.

In Egypt, too, it would seem that there was before the Arab invasion a marked recrudescence of indigenous native design which enabled the Coptic[12] craftsmen gradually to transform the motives given to them by Roman conquerors into something entirely non-Hellenistic. And the incredible beauty of the Fatimite textiles of the tenth, eleventh, and twelfth centuries, of which a few precious relics are shown in another room, preserve something, especially in the bird forms, of this antique derivation.

But to return once more to Sassanid art. The specimens from the Hermitage and Prince Bobrinsky's[13] collections form an object lesson of extraordinary interest in the development of early Mohammedan art. They have inherited and still retain that extreme realisation of massive splendour, that fierce assertion of form and positive statement of relief which belongs to the art of the great primitive Empires, and most of all to the art of Mesopotamia, and yet they already adumbrate the forms of Mohammedan art into which they pass by insensible degrees. Here, too, we find vestiges of the dying Hellenistic tradition. One of Prince Bobrinsky's bronzes, a great plate, has, for instance, a design composed of classic vases, from which spring stems which bend round into a series of circles, a design which might almost be matched as regards form, though not as regards spirit, in the wall decorations of Pompeii. Or take again the superb repoussé silver plate representing a Sassanid king spearing a lion. Here the floating drapery of the king and the edge of his tunic show a deliberately schematised rendering of the traditional folds of the Greek peplos. But how much more Assyrian than Greek is the whole effect – the dramatic tension of the figures expressed by an emphasis on all the lines of muscular effort, as in the legs of the horse and the lions! How Assyrian, too, is the feeling for relief, and the predilection for imbricated or closely set parallel lines as in the lions' manes! In the conventional rock under one of the lions one seems to see also a hint of Chinese forms.

Still more Assyrian is another plate, the arrangement of which recalls the reliefs of Assurbanipal or Sennacherib,[14] and yet already there are forms which anticipate Mohammedan art; the gate of the city, its crenelations, and the forms of the helmets of the soldiers, all have an air of similarity with far later Mohammedan types. Another plate shows a Sassanid king regaling himself with wine and music, and gives already more than a hint of the favourite designs of the Rhages[15] potters or the bronze workers of Mossoul.[16]

Among Prince Bobrinsky's bronzes which were found in the Caucasus is a late Sassanid aquamanile[17] in the form of a bird. It is already almost Mohammedan, though retaining something of the extreme solidity and weight of earlier art. Once more, in the aggressive schematisation of the form of the tail and the suggestion of feathers by a series of deeply marked parallel lines, we get a reminiscence of Assyrian art, while in the treatment of the crest there is the more florid interweaving of curves which adumbrate not only Mohammedan but Indian forms.

In the aquamanile in the form of a horse, the Sassanid influence is still predominant, but there can be no doubt that this is already Mohammedan, probably of the eighth or ninth century. We have already here the characteristics of Fatimite bronzes, of which a few specimens are shown at Munich. The great griffin of Pisa could not, of course, be moved from the Campo Santo,[18] nor are the two specimens in the Louvre shown,[19] but the stag from the Bavarian National Museum is there and affords a most interesting comparison with Prince Bobrinsky's horse (Plate II. 2). Both have the same large generalisation of form, and in both we have the curious effect of solidity and mass produced by the shortened hind legs, with the half-squatting movement to which that gives rise.

The Bobrinsky horse is obviously more primitive, and probably indicates the beginnings of a school of bronze plastic in Mesopotamia nearly parallel to that of Egypt. This school, however, never developed as fully along sculptural lines, and at a comparatively early date abandoned sculpture for the art of bronze inlay, of which Mossoul was the great centre in the twelfth and thirteenth centuries. In the incised designs on the horse we have an example of the early forms of the palmette ornament[20] and of the interlacing curves which form the basis of most subsequent Mohammedan patterns. Within the reserves formed by the *intreccie*[21] are small figures, of which one – that of a man seated and playing the lute – can just be made out in the reproduction. It is already typical of the figure design which the Mohammedan artists developed in the twelfth and thirteenth centuries.

It shows the peculiar characteristics of all the art produced for the Fatimite court, its exquisite perfection and refinement of taste, its minuteness of detail and finish together with a large co-ordination of parts, a rhythmic feeling for contour and the sequence of planes, which have scarcely ever been equalled. And all these qualities of refinement, almost of sophistication, which Fatimite art possesses do not, as we see here, destroy the elementary imaginative feeling for the vitality of animal forms. With this Mesopotamian example we may compare the lion from the Kassel Museum. This is a splendid example of Fatimite sculpture. It causes one to regret that Mohammedan artists so soon abandoned an art for which they show such extraordinary aptitude. The lion which comes from the Kassel Museum has been published by M. Migeon,[22] and is of rare beauty and interest in relation to the Sassanid works here described. In the case in which this masterpiece of Mohammedan sculpture is shown there is also seen the celebrated lion which once belonged to the painter Fortuny.[23] Noble though this is in general conception, the coarseness of its workmanship and the want of subtlety in its proportions, in comparison with the Kassel lion, makes it evident that it is not from the same school of Egyptian craftsmen, but probably of Spanish origin.

Yet another of the Bobrinsky bronzes of about the same date as the horse is already typically Mohammedan as may be seen by the leaf forms and the *intreccie* of the crest, but how much of the antique Sassanid proportions and sense of relief is still retained! It is believed to be from Western Turkestan and of the eighth or ninth century. One must suppose that Sassanid forms travelled North and East as well as South and West, and helped in the formation of that Central Asian art which becomes the dominant factor in the later centuries of Mohammedan, more especially of Persian, art.

Before leaving the question of Sassanid influences I must mention the series of bronze jugs in the Bobrinsky and Sarre collections. The general form is obviously derived from classic originals, but they have a peculiar spout of a rectangular shape placed at right angles on the top of the main opening. The effect of this is to give two openings, one for pouring the water in, the other for pouring it out at right angles. Now in the early Mossoul water-jugs we see numerous examples of what are clearly derivations of this form passing by gradual degrees into the familiar neck with spout attached but not separated, which is typical of later Mohammedan water-jugs. This evolution can be traced step by step in the Munich Exhibition, and leaves no doubt of the perfect continuity of Sassanid and Mohammedan forms.*

One of the features of early Mohammedan art is the vitality of its floral and geometrical ornament, the system of which is uniformly spread throughout the Mohammedan world. The question of where and how this system of ornament arose is not easily solved, but there are indications that Egypt was the place of its earliest development. Its characteristic forms seem certainly derived from the universal palmette of Graeco-Roman decoration. The palmette, so rigid, unvarying and frequently so lifeless in the hands of Graeco-Roman artists,

* I cannot help calling attention, though without any attempt at explaining it, to the striking similarity to these Sassanid and early Mohammedan water-jugs shown by an example of Sung pottery lent by Mr Eumorfopoulos to the recent exhibition at the Burlington Fine Arts Club,[24] Case A, No. 43. Here a very similar form of spout is modelled into a phoenix's head.

became the source of the flexible and infinitely varied systems of Mohammedan design, so skilfully interwoven, so subtly adapted to their purpose, that the supremacy of Mohammedan art in this particular has been recognised and perpetuated in the word Arabesque. It is curious to note that the history of this development is almost a repetition of what occurred many centuries before in the formation of the system of Celtic ornament. There, too, the Greek palmette was the point of departure. The Celtic bronze-workers adopted a cursive abbreviation of it which allowed of an almost too unrestrained flexibility in their patterns, but one peculiarly adapted to their bronze technique. In the case of Mohammedan art it would seem that the change from the palmette was effected by Coptic wood-carvers and by the artists who decorated in plaster the earliest Egyptian mosques. Indeed, one may suspect that the transformation of Graeco-Roman ornament had already been initiated by Coptic workers in pre-Mohammedan times. One or two exhibits of Coptic reliefs in woodwork show how far this process had already gone. The Coptic wood-carvers arrived at an extremely simple and economical method of decoration by incisions with a gouge, each ending in a spiral curve, and so set as to leave in relief a sequence of forms resembling a half-palmette, and at times approaching very closely to the characteristic interlacing 'trumpet' forms of Celtic ornament. A similar method was employed with even greater freedom and with a surprising richness and variety of effect in the plaster decorations of the earliest mosques, such as that of Ibn Tulun.[25] In this way there was developed a singularly easy and rhythmic manner of filling any given space with interlaced and confluent forms suited to the calligraphic character of Mohammedan design. It cannot be denied that in course of time it pandered to the besetting sin of the oriental craftsman, his intolerable patience and thoughtless industry, and became in consequence as dead in its mere intricacy and complexity as the Graeco-Roman original in its frigid correctness. The periods of creation in ornamental design seem indeed to be even rarer than those of creation in the figurative arts, and if the greater part of Mohammedan art shows, along with increasing technical facility, a constant degradation in ornamental design it is no exception to a universal rule. At any rate, up to the end of the thirteenth century its vitality was as strong and its adaptability even greater than the ornamental design of Christian Europe.

The design based on the half-palmette adapted itself easily to other materials than wood and plaster. In an even more cursive form it was used alike by miniaturists and the closely allied painters on pottery. Of the former a good instance is that of a manuscript of Dioscorides, written and painted by Abdullah ben el-Fadhl in the year 1223 AD.[26] It is of Mesopotamian origin and shows in the decorative treatment of the figures a close affinity with the painting on contemporary pottery from Rakka.[27] It is surprising how much character and even humour the artist gives to figures which are conceived in a purely calligraphic and abstract manner, and what richness and nobility of style there is in the singularly economical and rapid indications of brocaded patterns in the robes. Here we see how, in the hands of the miniaturists, the half-palmette ornament becomes even more cursive and flexible, more readily adapted to any required space than in the hands of the wood-carver and plasterer.

The whole of the figure-design of this period, as seen in the pottery of Rakka, Rhages, and Sultanabad, shows the same characteristics. It is all calligraphic rather than naturalistic, but it is notable how much expression is attained within the flexible formula which these Mohammedan artists had evolved. The requirements of the potter's craft stimulated the best elements of such a school of draughtsmanship, and for their power of creating an illusion of real existence by the sheer swiftness and assurance of their rhythm, few draughtsmen have surpassed the unknown masters who threw their indications of scenes from contemporary life upon the fragile bowls and lustred cups of early Syrian and Persian pottery.

It is generally believed now that not only in ceramics and metal-work, but even in glass, Fatimite culture was preeminent. Probably no such collection of enamelled oriental glass has ever been brought together as that at Munich.

An example of glass of Egyptian origin bearing the date

737 A.D., belonging to Dr Fouquet,[28] shows how early the manufacture of glass was already established in Egypt. To Egypt, too, must be ascribed the splendid crystals and carved glass-work in which the Munich Exhibition is particularly rich. One of these is the so-called Hedwig glass from the Rijksmuseum at Amsterdam. It has two finely conventionalised lions and eagles which resemble the types of Fatimite sculpture. It is described by Migeon (*Manuel*, p.378) as being of moulded glass, but the design is probably cut on the wheel in the manner employed for rock-crystal. Among the examples of carved crystal one of the finest is the less well-known example of a water-spout in the shape of a lion's head, lent by the Karlsruhe Museum. In all these figures the distinctive quality of Fatimite art, its combination of massive grandeur of design with extreme refinement, are apparent.

None the less, the evidence in favour of Syrian and Mesopotamian centres of glass-industry is very strong, and if many of the pieces, especially the earliest ones, are still relegated to Egypt, some of the finest are still ascribed, though on no very conclusive grounds, to the Syrian workshops. The finest of these belong to the late twelfth and early thirteenth centuries, and, generally speaking, the work of the fourteenth century shows a decline. Perhaps the most splendid specimen known is the large bottle from the treasury of S. Stephen's, Vienna. The glass in this and the kindred piece from the same place shows a peculiar brownish-yellow tone almost of the colour of honey, which gives the most perfect background to the enamelled figure-decoration. In the choice of subjects with a predominance of scenes from the chase there is undoubtedly a considerable resemblance to the scenes on the encrusted bronze work of Mossoul, and this, so far as it goes, makes in favour of a Syrian origin. But whatever their origin, the finest of these pieces show a decorative splendour and a perfection of taste which have assured their appreciation from the days of the Crusaders. Already in the inventory of Charles V of France[29] such pieces, frequently mounted on silver stands, figure among the King's choicest treasures. Nor was the appreciation of this beautiful craft confined to Europe. One of the many proofs of a continual interchange between the Mohammedan and Chinese civilisations is seen in the number of examples of this glass which have come from China. In Munich there is a magnificent bowl lent by Dr Sarre which is of Chinese provenance, and numerous other pieces have been recorded.

The collection of incrusted bronzes at Munich is extremely rich, ranging from the twelfth-century work, in which plastic relief is still used, accompanied by sparse incrustations of red copper upon the almost strawy yellow bronze, to the fourteenth- and fifteenth-century work, in which plastic relief has altogether disappeared, and elaborate incrustations of silver and even gold give to the surface an extreme profusion of delicate interwoven traceries. Here, too, the earliest work shows the finest sense of design. The specimen from the Piet Latauderie collection still retains in its relief of stylistic animals a feeling for mass and grandeur inherited from Sassanid metal-workers, and the incrustations, though exquisitely wrought, are kept in due subordination to the general design. Some of the thirteenth-century pieces, though already tending to too great intricacy, still attain to a finely co-ordinated effect by the use of reserves filled with boldly designed figures. Some of the best of these contain scenes borrowed from Christian mythology, among which I may mention, as a superb example, the great bowl belonging to the Duc d'Arenberg.

I have alluded at various points to the influence of Chinese art upon Mohammedan. Among the most decisive and curious instances of this is a bronze mirror with the signs of the Zodiac in relief. Round the edge is an inscription of dedication to one of the Orthokid princes. It is of Mesopotamian workmanship. Here the derivation from Chinese mirrors, which date back to Han times, is unmistakable, and is seen in every detail, even to the griffin head in the centre, pierced to allow of the string by which it was carried.

GIOTTO

✱

THE CHURCH OF S. FRANCESCO AT ASSISI*

WE find abundant evidences in studying early Christian art that Christianity at its origin exercised no new stimulating influence upon its development, but if it were claimed for the Franciscan movement that it brought about the great outburst of Italian art the position would be harder to refute: and indeed what S. Francis accomplished, the literal acceptance by official Christendom of Christ's teaching, was tantamount to the foundation of a new religion, and the heresy of some of his followers, who regarded his as a final dispensation superseding that of the New Testament, can scarcely have seemed unreasonable to those who witnessed the change in the temper of society which his example brought about. S. Francis was the great orthodox heretic. What he effected within the bounds of the Church, for a time at all events, was only accomplished for later times by a rupture with the Papal power. He established the idea of the equality of all men before God and the immediate relationship of the individual soul to the Deity. He enabled every man to be his own priest. To the fervour with which these ideas were grasped by his countrymen we may ascribe to some extent the extreme individualism of the Italian Renaissance, the

* The following, from the *Monthly Review*, 1901, is, perhaps more than any other article here reprinted, at variance with the more recent expressions of my aesthetic ideas. It will be seen that great emphasis is laid on Giotto's expression of the dramatic idea in his pictures. I still think this is perfectly true so far as it goes, nor do I doubt that an artist like Giotto did envisage such an expression. I should be inclined to disagree wherever in this article there appears the assumption not only that the dramatic idea may have inspired the artist to the creation of his form, but that the value of the form for us is bound up with recognition of the dramatic idea. It now seems to me possible by a more searching analysis of our experience in front of a work of art to disentangle our reaction to pure form from our reaction to its implied associated ideas.

absence of the barriers of social caste to the aspirations of the individual and the passionate assertion on his part of the right to the free use of all his activities. No doubt the individualism of, say, a Sigismondo Malatesta[1] in the fifteenth century was very different from anything which S. Francis would have approved; none the less such a view of life was rendered possible by the solvent action of his teaching on the fixed forms of society.

But of more immediate importance to our purpose is the aesthetic element in S. Francis' teaching. To say that in his actions S. Francis aimed at artistic effect would perhaps give a wrong impression of his character, but it is true that his conception of holiness was almost as much an aesthetic as a moral one. To those who know S. Bonaventura's life[2] a number of stories will suggest themselves, which indicate a perfectly harmonious attitude to life rather than a purely moral one: stories such as that of the sheep which was given to him, and which he received joyfully because of its simplicity and innocence, 'and holding it in his hands he admonished it to be intent to praise God and to keep itself from offending the brethren; and the sheep observed fully the commandment of the Blessed Francis, and when it heard the brethren singing in the choir ran thither quickly, and without any teaching bent before the altar of the Blessed Virgin and bleated, as though it had human reason.'[3]

S. Francis, the 'Jongleur de Dieu', was actually a poet before his conversion, and his whole life had the pervading unity and rhythm of a perfect work of art. Not that he was a conscious artist. The whole keynote of the Franciscan teaching was its spontaneity, but his feelings for moral and aesthetic beauty were intimately united. Indeed, his life, like the Italian art which in a sense arose from it, like the Gothic French art which was a simultaneous expression of the same spirit, implies an attitude, as rare in life as in art, in which spiritual and sensuous beauty are so inextricably interwoven that instead of conflicting they mutually intensify their effects.

Not only was the legend of S. Francis' life full of suggestions of poetical and artistic material, but his followers rewrote the New Testament from the Franciscan point of view, emphasising the poetical and dramatic elements of the story. In particular they shifted the focus of interest by making the relationship of the Virgin to her son the central motive of the whole. It will be seen that Italian artists down to Raphael turned rather to the Franciscan than the Vulgate version.[4] In fact, S. Bonaventura and the great poet of the movement, the cultivated and ecstatic Jacopone da Todi,[5] did for the Christian legend very much what Pindar[6] did for classical mythology; without altering the doctrine they brought into full relief its human and poetical significance.

It is not surprising, then, to find that the great church at Assisi, built with all the magnificence that the whole of Italy could contribute to honouring the spouse of Divine Poverty, should be the cradle of the new art of Italy – the neo-Christian or Franciscan art, as we might almost call it.

The lower church of S. Francesco was probably decorated almost immediately after the building was finished, between 1240 and 1250, but these early works are almost obliterated by a second decoration undertaken after 1300. We must therefore turn to the upper church, the paintings of which were probably completed before 1300, as the chief source of our knowledge of the emergence of the new Italian style. It was there that the Italian genius first attained to self-expression in the language of monumental painting – a language which no other nation of modern Europe has ever been able to command except in rare and isolated instances.

And here we plunge at once into a very difficult, perhaps an insoluble problem: who were the painters who carried out this immense scheme of decoration? The archives of the church have been searched in vain, and we are left with a sentence of Ghiberti's commentary, and Vasari,[7] who here proves an uncertain guide, so that we are thrown chiefly on the resources of internal evidence.

The paintings of the upper church may be briefly enumerated thus: In the choir are faint remains of frescoes of the life of the Virgin: in the right transept a Crucifixion and other subjects almost obliterated; in the left transept another Crucifixion, better preserved, and archangels in the triforium. The nave is divided into an upper and lower series; the upper series contains scenes of the Old and New Testaments, the lower is devoted to the legend of S. Francis, and in alternate vaults of the roof are paintings of single figures.

It would be out of place to discuss all these frescoes in detail, but it may be worth while to select certain typical ones, around which the rest may be grouped, and see how far they bear out what little documentary and traditional authority we have.

We will begin with the Crucifixion of the left transept, which is clearly by an artist of decided and marked personality. It is certainly less pleasing and less accomplished than the works of the later Byzantine school, and in spite of certain motives, such as the floating drapery of the Christ, which show Byzantine reminiscences, it is derived in the main from the native Italian tradition. This is shown in the stumpy proportions of the figures and the crude, not to say hideous, realism of the faces of the crowd. The classical origin of the tradition is still traceable in the sandalled feet and the reminiscence of the toga in some of the draperies. But the chief interest lies in the serious attempt made by the artist to give dramatic reality to the scene in a way never attempted by the less human Byzantines. The action of the Magdalen throwing up both arms in despair is really impressive, and this is a more vivacious rendering of a gesture traditional in Western early Christian art; an instance occurs in the fifth-century MS of Genesis at Vienna.[8] But the artist shows his originality more in the expressive and sometimes beautiful poses of the weeping angels and the natural movements of the Virgin and S. John.

Very nearly allied to this are the archangels of the triforium,[9] and some of the frescoes of the upper scenes in the nave, such as the Nativity and the Betrayal. These belong to the same group, though they are not necessarily by the master of the Crucifixion himself.

As we proceed along the nave, still keeping to the upper series, we come upon another distinct personality, whose work is typified in the Deception of Isaac.[10] In certain qualities this master is not altogether unlike the master of the Crucifixion. Like him, he replaces the purely schematic linear rendering of drapery by long streaks of light and dark paint, so arranged as to give the idea of actual modelling in relief. But he does this not only with greater naturalism, but with a greatly increased sense of pure beauty. The painting is not hieratic and formal as the Byzantine would have made it, nor has it that overstrained attempt at dramatic vehemence which we saw in the Crucifixion. The faces have remarkable beauty, and throughout there is a sense of placid and dignified repose which is rare in mediaeval work. It is, in fact, decidedly classical, and classical, too, in a sense different from the vague reminiscences of classic origin which permeate early Christian art, and were faintly echoed in the Crucifixion. Rachel especially, with her full, well-rounded eyes, wide apart and set deep in their sockets, her straight nose and small mouth, might almost have come straight from a Pompeian picture.

The hair, too, instead of being in tangled masses, as in the Crucifixion, or rendered by parallel lines, as in the Sacrifice of Isaac, is drawn into elegantly disposed curls, which yet have something of the quality of hair, and which remind us of the treatment in classic bronzes.

The last vault of the nave, with the Doctors of the Church, is by an artist who is extremely similar to the last, and clearly belongs to the same group. The level brows nearly meeting over the bridge of the nose, the straight profile and the curled hair show the similarity, as does also the drapery. The classic tendencies of this artist may be seen in the amorini caryatides[11] in the extreme corners of the spandrill,[12] while the decoration of one of the arches of the church by the same hand has, arising from an urn of pure classic design, a foliated scroll-work, in which centaurs disport themselves.

In the lower series representing the Life of S. Francis we are at once struck by the resemblances to the last two paintings. The Pope, who is approving the rule of S. Francis, is almost a repetition of one of the Doctors of the Church. We have the same peculiar drapery with shiny, slippery, highlights, broadly washed on in well-disposed folds. The faces too, though they are more individual and far more expressive, are, nevertheless, built on the same lines. They have similar straight profiles, the same deeply cut level brows, which tend to meet in a line across the nose. The general impression it makes is that it is by a younger artist than the master of the Esau fresco,[13] but one who has a keener feeling for reality and a far deeper sense of the dramatic situation.

We will now turn to the historical evidence. The earliest and best is that of Ghiberti (early fifteenth century),[14] who tells us simply that Giotto painted the S. Francis legend. Vasari says that Cimabue worked first in the lower church with Greek artists, and then did the whole of the upper church, except the S. Francis legend, which he ascribes to Giotto. In addition to these we have a sixteenth-century MS and an account of the church by Petrus Rudolphus of the same period, which agree that both Giotto and Cimabue painted in the upper church.[15]

We may take it, then, that we have fairly good evidence for ascribing the S. Francis series in the main to Giotto, and a consensus of traditional opinion that somewhere in the other frescoes we ought to discover Cimabue.

The name of Cimabue is fraught with tender associations. To the last generation, happy in its innocence, it was familiar as a household word. Browning could sing without a qualm: 'My painter – who, but Cimabue?'[16] The cult of Cimabue became fashionable; it offended Philistine nostrils and received its due castigation from Mr Punch.[17] And now, alas, he would be a bold man who dared to say that he admired Cimabue, who dared to do more than profess a pious belief in his existence. Only recently a distinguished critic[18] has endeavoured to hand over to Duccio di Buoninsegna the very stronghold of the Cimabue faith, the altar-piece of the Rucellai Chapel in Sta Maria Novella. But the myth dies hard, and Florentine guides will still point out the portraits of all Cimabue's relations in the little figures round the frame. Ever since the time of Rumohr,[19] however, who considered him to be little more than an emanation of Vasari's brain heated by patriotic fervour, it has been established that we have no documentary evidence for any single picture by him. We do know, however, that at the very end of his life he executed the mosaic of the apse in the cathedral at Pisa. But this is a much-restored work, and originally can have been little but an adaptation of a Byzantine design, and it throws no light on his work as a painter. In any case, all criticisms of his reputation in his own day, whether deserved or not, must fall to the ground before Dante's celebrated lines, 'Credette Cimabue nella pittura Tener lo campo, ed ora ha Giotto il grido',[20] for on this point Dante is first-rate evidence. And that being the case, there is a probability, almost amounting to certainty, that the man who 'held the field' in painting would be requisitioned for the greatest national undertaking of his day, the decoration of S. Francesco at Assisi, even though, as we have seen, it would be impossible to accept Vasari's statement that he did the whole.

In looking for Cimabue among the groups of the upper church which we have selected, it will be worth while to take as an experimental guide other works ascribed traditionally to our artist. If these should agree in their artistic qualities with one another and with any one group at Assisi, we shall have some probability in favour of our view. And the result of such a process is to find in the master of the Crucifixion our elusive and celebrated painter.

It would be wearisome to go in detail through all these works; it will suffice to say that in certain marked peculiarities they all agree with one another and with the Crucifixion. The most striking likeness will be found between the heads which appear under the Virgin's throne in the picture in the Academy at Florence,[21] which Vasari attributes to Cimabue, and the grotesque heads to the right of the Crucifixion. There is the same crude attempt at realism, the same peculiar matted hair, the same curious drawing of the eye-socket which gives the appearance of spectacles. The characteristics of this picture will again be found in the Cimabue of the Louvre[22] which comes from Pisa, where he is known to have worked. Very similar, too, in innumerable details of architectural setting, of movement of hands and heads, and of drapery is the fresco of the Madonna Enthroned and S. Francis, in the lower church at Assisi. Finally, the Rucellai Madonna, in spite of its very superior qualities, which must be due to its being a later work, answers in many detailed tests to the characteristics of this group of paintings.*

And now, having found our Cimabue in the master of the

Crucifixion, what must our verdict be on his character as an artist? Frankly we must admit that he is not to be thought of in the same category with the master of the Esau fresco, much less with Duccio or Giotto.† There is, however, in his work that spark of vitality which the Italians rightly prized above Byzantine accomplishment. He gave to his historical compositions a rude dramatic vigour, and to his Madonnas and Angels a suggestion of sentimental charm which borders on affection; he was, in fact, a sentimental realist whose relation to the Byzantine

* One picture, however, ascribed by Vasari to Cimabue, namely, the Madonna of the National Gallery, does not bear the characteristics of this group. Dr Richter's argument for giving the Rucellai painting to Duccio depends largely on the likeness of this to the Maesta,[23] but there is no reason to cling so closely to Vasari's attributions. If we except the National Gallery Madonna, which shows the characteristics of the Sienese school, these pictures, including the Rucellai Madonna, will be found to cohere by many common peculiarities not shared by Duccio. Among these we may notice the following: The eye has the upper eyelid strongly marked; it has a peculiar languishing expression, due in part to the large elliptical iris (Duccio's eyes have a small, bright, round iris with a keen expression); the nose is distinctly articulated into three segments; the mouth is generally slewed round from the perpendicular; the hands are curiously curved, and in all the Madonnas clutch the supports of the throne; the hair bows seen upon the halos have a constant and quite peculiar shape; the drapery is designed in rectilinear triangular folds, very different from Duccio's more sinuous and flowing line. The folds of the drapery where they come to the contour of the figure have no effect upon the form of the outline, an error which Duccio never makes. Finally, the thrones in all these pictures have a constant form; they are made of turned wood with a high foot-stool, and are seen from the side; Duccio's is of stone and seen from the front. That the Rucellai Madonna has a morbidezza[24] which is wanting in the earlier works can hardly be considered a sufficient distinction to set against the formal characteristics. It is clearly a later work, painted probably about the year 1300, and Cimabue, like all the other artists of the time, was striving constantly in the direction of greater fusion of tones.

† I should speak now both with greater confidence and much greater enthusiasm of Cimabue. The attempt of certain scholars to dispose of him as a myth has broken down. The late Mr H.P. Horne found that the documents cited by Dr Richter to prove that Duccio executed the Rucellai Madonna referred to another picture.[25] I had also failed in my estimate to consider fully the superb crucifix by Cimabue in the Museum of Sta Croce, a work of supreme artistic merit. In general my defence of Cimabue, though right enough as far as it goes, appears to me too timid and my estimate of his artistic quality far too low (1920).

masters must have been something like that of Caravaggio to the academic school of the Carracci.[26]

We come next to the master of the Deception of Isaac, and the closely allied, if not identical, painter who did the Four Doctors of the vault. We have already noticed the likeness of these works to the legend of S. Francis, which we may take provisionally to be Giotto's; but, in spite of the similarity of technique, they are inspired by a very diverse sentiment. They are not dramatic and intense as Giotto's; they show a more conscious aspiration after style; the artist will not allow the requirements of formal beauty to be disturbed by the desire for expressive and life-like gestures. Where, then, could an artist of this period acquire such a sense of pure classic beauty in painting? In sculpture it might be possible to find classic models throughout Italy as Nicòla[27] did at Pisa, but Rome was the only place which could fulfil the requirements for a painter. There must at this time have been many more remains of classical painting among the ruins of the Palatine than are now to be seen, and it is a natural conclusion that the artist who painted the figure of Rachel was directly inspired by them. Nor is there anything difficult in the assumption that this unknown precursor of Giotto was a Roman artist, for the Roman school of painting was by far the most precocious of any in Italy. At Subiaco there are frescoes,[28] some of which must date from the lifetime of S. Francis, which already, as in the portrait of S. Francis himself, show a certain freedom from Byzantine formalism. But it is in the works of the Cosmati, Jacopo Torriti, Rusutti, and Cavallini[29] in the latter half of the thirteenth century that we see how vigorous and progressive an art was springing up in Rome.* Had not the removal of the Popes to Avignon in the fourteenth century left the city a prey to internal discord, we can hardly doubt that the Roman would have been one of the greatest and earliest developed schools of Italian painting. As it is, we find in the mosaics under the apse of Sta Maria in Trastevere, executed about the year 1290, compo-

*The important position here assigned to the Roman school has been confirmed by the subsequent discovery[30] of Cavallini's frescoes in Sta Cecilia at Rome (1920).

sitions in every way comparable to Giotto's frescoes. These mosaics, too, have architectural accessories which are very similar to the architecture of the 'Doctors of the Church'[31] at Assisi. The architecture based on a study of classic forms is of the kind always associated with the Cosmati family. It will be seen that it is quite distinct from the architecture of Cimabue's and Duccio's Madonnas, but that it becomes the normal treatment in Giotto's frescoes.

There is, then, a curiously close analogy between the origins of neo-Christian painting and neo-Christian sculpture in Italy; just as Giovanni Pisano's[32] work was preceded by the purely classic revival which culminated in Nicòla's Baptistery pulpit,[33] so in painting Giotto's work emerges from a similar classic revival based on the study of Roman wall-paintings. The perfect similarity between Nicòla Pisano's sentiment and that of the master of the Esau fresco may be realised by comparing the action of Rachel's hand in the fresco with that of the Virgin in the Annunciation of the Baptistery pulpit. In both we have the same autarchic conception of character conveyed by the same measured ease of gesture, which contrasts vividly with the more expansive ideals of neo-Christian art, of which Giotto appears from the first as the most perfect representative.

In examining the series of frescoes describing the life of S. Francis we find varieties in the proportions of the figures and in the types of features which suggest the co-operation of more than one artist, but the spirit that inspires the compositions throughout is one. And this afflatus which suddenly quickens so much that was either tentative or narrowly accomplished into a new fulness of life, a new richness of expression, is, we may feel certain, due to the genius of Giotto.

If we look at one of these frescoes, such, for example, as the Presepio at Greccio,[34] and at the same time endeavour to transport ourselves into the position of a contemporary spectator, what will strike us most immediately and make the most startling general impression is its actuality. Here at last after so many centuries of copying the traditional forms handed down from a moribund Pagan art – centuries during which these abstractions had become entirely divorced from the life of the time –

here at last was an artist who gave a scene as it must have happened, with every circumstance evidently and literally rendered. The scene of the institution of the Presepio takes place in a little chapel divided from the body of the church by a marble wall. The pulpit and crucifix are therefore seen from behind, the latter leaning forward into the church and showing from the chapel only the wooden battens and fastenings of the back. The singing-desk in the centre is drawn with every detail of screws and adjustments, while the costume of the bystanders is merely the ordinary fashionable dress of the day. The research for actuality could not be carried farther than this. When some years ago a French painter painted the scene of Christ at the house of the Pharisee with the figures in evening dress[35] it aroused the most vehement protests, and produced for a time a shock of bewilderment and surprise. This is not to suggest any real analogy between the works of the two artists, but merely that the innovation made by Giotto must have been in every way as surprising to his contemporaries. Nor was Giotto's, like M. Beraud's, a *succès de scandale*; on the contrary, it was immediately recognised as satisfying a want which had been felt ever since the legend of S. Francis, the setting of which belonged to their own time and country, had been incorporated by the Italians in their mythology. The earliest artists had tried to treat the subject according to the formulae of Byzantine biblical scenes, but with such unsatisfactory results as may be seen in the altar-piece of the Bardi Chapel of Sta Croce at Florence. In Giotto's frescoes at Assisi it acquired for the first time a treatment in which the desire for actuality was fully recognised. But actuality alone would not have satisfied Giotto's patrons; it was necessary that the events should be presented as scenes of everyday life, but it was also necessary that they should possess that quality of universal and eternal significance which distinguishes a myth from a mere historical event. It was even more necessary that they should be heroic than that they should be actual. And it was in his power to satisfy such apparently self-contradictory conditions that Giotto's unique genius manifested itself. It was this that made him the greatest story-teller in line, the supreme epic-painter of the world. The reconciliation of these two aims, actuality and universality, is indeed the severest strain on the power of expression. To what a temperature must the imagination be raised before it can fuse in its crucible those refractory squalid trivialities unconsecrated by time and untinged by romance with which the artist must deal if he is to be at once 'topical' and heroic, to be at one and the same time in 'Ercles' vein' and Mrs Gamp's.[36] Even in literature it is a rare feat. Homer could accomplish it, and Dante, but most poets must find a way round. In Dante the power is constantly felt. He could not only introduce the politics and personalities of his own time, but he could use such similes as that of old tailors peering for their needles' eyes, a half-burnt piece of paper, dogs nozzling for fleas, and still more unsavoury trivialities, without for a moment lowering the high key in which his comedy was pitched. The poet deals, however, with the vague and blurred mental images which words call up, but the painter must actually present the semblance of the thing in all its drab familiarity. And yet Giotto succeeded. He could make the local and particular stand for a universal idea.

But, without detracting in any way from what was due to Giotto's superlative genius, it may be admitted that something was given by the propitious moment of his advent. For the optics of the imagination are variable: in an age like the present, men and events grow larger as they recede into the mist of the past; it is rarely that we think of a man as truly great till he has for long received the consecration of death. But there must be periods when men have a surer confidence in their own judgments – periods of such creative activity that men can dare to measure the reputations of their contemporaries, which are of their own creation, against the reputations of antiquity – and in such periods the magnifying, mythopoetical effect, which for us comes only with time, takes place at once, and swells their contemporaries to heroic proportions. It was thus that Dante saw those of his own time – could even see himself – in the proportions they must always bear. The fact that S. Francis was canonised two years after death, and within twenty years was commemorated by the grandest monument in Italy, is a striking proof of that superb self-confidence.

We will return to the frescoes: the evidence for their being in the main by Giotto himself rests not only on the general consensus of tradition, but upon the technical characteristics and, most of all, upon the imaginative conception of the subjects. None the less, in so big a work it is probable that assistants were employed to carry out Giotto's designs, and this will account for many slight discrepancies of style. Certain frescoes, however – notably the last three of the series – show such marked differences that we must suppose that one of these assistants rose to the level of an original creative artist.

In the fresco of S. Francis kneeling before the Pope, we have already noticed Giotto's close connection with the artists of the Roman school. Their influence is not confined to the figures and drapery; the architecture – in which it may be noted, by the way, that Giotto has already arrived instinctively at the main ideas of linear perspective – with its minute geometrical inlays, its brackets and mouldings, derived from classic forms, is entirely in the manner of the Cosmati.[37] But the composition illustrates, none the less, the differences which separate him from the master of the Esau fresco. Giotto is at this stage of his career not only less accomplished, but he has nothing of that painter's elegant classical grace. He has, instead, the greatest and rarest gift of dramatic expressiveness. For though the poses, especially of the bishop seated on the Pope's left, lack grace, and the faces show but little research for positive beauty or regularity of feature, the actual scene, the dramatic situation, is given in an entirely new and surprising way. Of what overwhelming importance for the history of the world this situation was, perhaps Giotto himself could scarcely realise. For this probably represents, not the approbation of the order of minor brethren by Honorius III, which was a foregone conclusion, but the permission to preach given by Innocent III, a far more critical moment in the history of the movement. For Innocent III, in whom the Papacy reached the zenith of its power, had already begun the iniquitous Albigensian crusade,[38] and was likely to be suspicious of any unofficial religious teaching. It cannot have been with unmixed pleasure that he saw before him this poverty-stricken group of Francis and his eleven followers, whose appearance declared in the plainest terms their belief in that primitive communistic Christianity which, in the case of Petrus Waldus, had been branded by excommunication.[39] In fact, the man who now asked for the Papal blessing on his mission was in most respects a Waldensian. Francis – the name Francesco is itself significant – was probably by birth, certainly by predilection* and temperament, half a Frenchman; his mother came from Provence, and his father had business connections at Lyons; so that it is not impossible that Francis was influenced by what he knew, through them, of the Waldensian movement. In any case, his teaching was nearly identical with that of Petrus Waldus; both taught religious individualism and, by precept at all events, communism. It was, therefore, not unnatural that Innocent should not respond at once to S. Francis' application. According to one legend, the Pope's first advice to him was to consort with swine, as befitted one of his miserable appearance. But, whatever his spontaneous impulses may have been, he had the good sense to accept the one man through whom the Church could again become popular and democratic.

Of all that this acceptance involved, no one who lived before the Reformation could understand the full significance, but Giotto has here expressed something of the dramatic contrasts involved in this meeting of the greatest of saints and the most dominating of popes – something of the importance of the moment when the great heretic was recognised by the Church.

In the fresco of S. Francis before the Sultan we have a means of comparing Giotto at this period with the later Giotto of the Bardi Chapel, in Florence, where the same scene is treated with more intimate psychological imagination; but here already the story is told with a vividness and simplicity which none but

* 'Drunken with the love of compassion of Christ, the blessed Francis would at times do such-like things as this; for the passing sweet melody of the spirit within him, seething over outwardly, did often find utterance in the French tongue, and the strain of the divine whisper that his ear had caught would break forth into a French song of joyous exulting.' Then pretending with two sticks to play a viol, 'and making befitting gestures, (he) would sing in French of our Lord Jesus Christ' (*The Mirror of Perfection*, ed. P. Sabatier, trans. S. Evans (1898), p.150).

Giotto could command. The weak and sinuous curves of the discomfited sages, the ponderous and massive contour of the indignant Sultan, show that Giotto's command of the direct symbolism of line is at least as great as Duccio's in the *Three Maries*,[40] while his sense of the roundness and solid relief of the form is, as Mr Berenson[41] has ably pointed out, far greater. We find in the Sultan, indeed, the type for which Giotto showed a constant predilection – a well-formed, massive body, with high rounded shoulders and short neck, but with small and shapely hands. As is natural in the work of an artist who set himself so definitely to externalise the tension of a critical moment, his hands are always eloquent; it is impossible to find in his work a case where the gestures of the hands are not explicit indications of a particular emotion. The architecture in this fresco is a remarkable evidence of the classical tendencies which he inherited from the Cosmati school. The Sultan's throne has, it is true, a quasi-Gothic gable, but the coffered soffit,[42] and the whole of the canopy opposite to it, with its winged genii, pilasters, and garlands are derived from classic sources.

We have already considered the Presepio as an example of Giotto's power of giving the actual setting of a scene without losing its heroic quality. It is also an example of his power of visualising the psychological situation; here, the sudden thrill which permeates an assembly at a moment of unwonted exaltation. It depicts the first representation of the Nativity instituted at Greccio by S. Francis; it is the moment at which he takes the image of the Infant Christ in his arms, when, to the ecstatic imaginations of the bystanders, it appeared for an instant transformed into a living child of transcendent beauty. The monks at the back are still singing the Lauds (one can almost tell what note each is singing, so perfect is Giotto's command of facial expression), but the immediate bystanders and the priest are lost in rapt contemplation of S. Francis and the Child.*

* This was the first 'representation' of the kind in Italy, and is of interest as being the beginning of the Italian Drama, and also of that infinite series of allegorical pageants, sometimes sacred, sometimes secular, which for three centuries played such a prominent part in city life and affected Italian art very intimately.

One of the most beautiful of the whole series is the fresco which represents the nuns of S. Clare meeting the Saint's body as it is borne to burial. Throughout the series Giotto took Bonaventura's Life as his text, and it is interesting to see how near akin the two renderings are, both alike inspired by that new humanity of feeling which S. Francis' life had aroused. Having described the beauty of the Saint's dead body,

> of which the limbs were so soft and delicate to the touch that they seemed to have returned to the tenderness of a child's, and appeared by manifest signs to be innocent as never having done wrong, so like a child's were they,

he adds,

> Therefore it is not to be marvelled at if seeing a body so white and seeing therein those black nails and that wound in the side which seemed to be a fresh red rose of spring, if those that saw it felt therefor great wonder and joy. And in the morning when it was day the companies and people of the city and all the country round came together, and being instructed to translate that most holy body from that place to the city of Assisi, moved with great solemnity of hymns and songs and divine offices, and with a multitude of torches and of candles lighted and with branches of trees in their hands; and with such solemnity going towards the city of Assisi and passing by the church of S. Damiano, in which stayed Clara the noble virgin who is today a saint on earth and in heaven, they rested there a little. She and her holy virgins were comforted to see and kiss that most holy body of their father the blessed Francis adorned with those holy stigmata and white and shining as has been said.[43]

Bonaventura, we see, had already conceived the scene with such consummate artistic skill that it was, as it were, ready made for Giotto. He had only to translate that description into line and colour; and in doing so he has lost nothing of its beauty. Giotto, like Bonaventura, is apparently perfectly simple, perfectly direct and literal, and yet the result is in both cases a work of the rarest imaginative power. Nor is it easy to analyse its mysterious charm. Giotto was a great painter in the strictest and most technical sense of the word, but his technical perfection is not easily appreciated in these damaged works and one cannot explain the effect this produces by any actual beauty of the surface quality of the painting; it depends rather on our perception, through the general disposition and action of the figures, of Giotto's attitude to life, of the instinctive rightness of feeling through which he was enabled to visualise the scene in its simplest and most inevitable form.

We come now to the last three frescoes of the series which show such marked differences from the rest, though some of the peculiarities, the minute hands and elegant features, appear in parts of some of the preceding frescoes, notably in our last: we may imagine that an assistant working under Giotto was, as the work progressed, given a larger and larger share in the execution, and finally carried out the last three frescoes alone. But this is pure hypothesis; all we can do at present is to note the difference not only of types, but even to some extent in the manner of conception, that they evince. One of them recounts the story of a woman of Benevento devoted to S. Francis, who died after forgetting one of her sins in her last confession. At the intercession of the dead Saint she was allowed to come to life again, finish her confession, and so defeat of his prey the black devil who had already come for her soul. Here the whole spacing out of the composition indicates a peculiar feeling, very different from Giotto's. The artist crowds his figures into narrow, closely-packed groups, and leaves vast spaces of bare wall between. In this particular instance the result is very impressive; it intensifies the supreme importance of the confession and emphasises the loneliness and isolation of the soul that has already once passed away. When we look at the individual figures the differences are even more striking; the long thin figures, the repetition of perpendicular lines, the want of variety in the poses of the heads, a certain timidity in the movements, the long masks, too big in proportion for the heads, the tiny elegant features, elongated necks, and minute hands – all these characteristics contrast with Giotto's tendency to massive proportions and easy expansive movements. Not that these figures have not great beauty; only it is of a recondite and exquisite kind. The artist that created these types must have loved what was sought out and precious; though living so long before Raphael, he must have been something of a 'pre-Raphaelite'.

We have no clue to the identity of this pseudo-Giotto; he is quite distinct from Giotto's known pupils, and indeed may rather have been a contemporary artist who came under Giotto's influence than one trained by him. Besides the frescoes at Assisi, we are fortunate enough to possess one other picture by this interesting artist. It is a small altar-piece dedicated to S. Cecilia, which hangs in the corridor of the Uffizi, and has been attributed both to Cimabue and to Giotto. The long Rossetti-like necks and heads, the poses, in which elegance is preferred to expressiveness, and the concentration of the figures so as to leave large empty spaces even in these small compositions, are sufficient grounds for attributing it to Giotto's fellow-worker at Assisi.*

In the year 1298 Giotto entered into a contract with Cardinal Stefaneschi to execute for him the mosaic of the 'Navicella', now in the porch of S. Peter's. We have in this the first ascertainable date of Giotto's life. It is one which, however, fits very well with the internal evidences of his style, as it would give the greater part of the last decade of the thirteenth century as the period of Giotto's activity in the Upper Church at Assisi. One other work on the evidence of style we may attribute to the master's pre-Roman period, and that is the Madonna of the Academy at Florence. Here Giotto followed the lines of Cimabue's enthroned Madonnas, though with his own greatly increased sense of solidity in the modelling and vivacity in the poses. It cannot, however, be considered as a prepossessing work. It may be due to restoration that the picture shows no signs of Giotto's peculiar feeling for tonality; but even the design is scarcely satisfactory, the relation of the Madonna to the throne is such that her massive proportions leave an impression of ungainliness rather than of grandeur. In the throne itself he has made an experiment in the new Gothic architecture, but he

* The Master of the Cecilia altar-piece has been the object of much research since this article was written, and a considerable number of important works are now ascribed to him with some confidence. He has been tentatively identified with Buffalmacco by Dr Sirén (Osvald Sirén, 'A Great Contemporary of Giotto', part I, *Burlington Magazine* 35 (Dec. 1919), 229–40; part II, *Burlington Magazine* 36 (Jan. 1920), 4–11).

has hardly managed to harmonise it with the earlier classic forms of the Cosmati, which still govern the main design. We shall see that in his work at Rome he overcame all these difficulties.

In Rome Giotto worked chiefly for Cardinal Stefaneschi.[44] This is significant of Giotto's close relations with the Roman school, for it was Bartolo, another member of the same family, who commissioned the remarkable mosaics of Sta Maria in Trastevere, executed in 1290, mosaics which show how far the Roman school had already advanced towards the new art, of which Giotto's work was the consummation.

The mosaic of the *Navicella* which was the greatest undertaking of Giotto's activity in Rome, is unfortunately terribly restored.[45] We can, however, still recognise the astonishing dramatic force of the conception and the unique power which Giotto possessed of giving a vivid presentation of a particular event, accompanied by the most circumstantial details, and at the same time suggesting to the imagination a symbolical interpretation of universal and abstract significance. Even the surprising intrusion of a *genre* motive in the fisherman peacefully angling on the shore does not disturb our recognition of this universal interpretation, which puts so clearly the relation of the ship of the Church, drifting helplessly with its distraught crew, to the despairing Peter, who has here the character of an emissary and intermediary, and the impassive and unapproachable figure of Christ himself.

The daring originality which Giotto shows in placing the predominant figure at the extreme edge of the composition, the feeling for perspective which enabled him to give verisimilitude to the scene by throwing back the ship into the middle distance, the new freedom and variety in the movements of the Apostles in the boat, by which the monotony of the eleven figures crowded into so limited a space is avoided, are proofs of Giotto's rare power of invention, a power which enabled him to treat even the most difficult abstractions with the same vivid sense of reality as the dramatic incidents of contemporary life. It is not to be wondered at that this should be the work most frequently mentioned by the Italian writers of the Renaissance. The storm-gods blowing their

Triton's horns are a striking instance of how much Giotto assimilated at this time from Pagan art.

But of far greater beauty are the panels for the high altar of S. Peter's, also painted for Cardinal Stefaneschi, and now to be seen in the sacristy,[46] where the more obvious beauties of Melozzo da Forli's[47] music-making angels too often lead to their being overlooked. And yet, unnoticed in the dark corners of the room, they have escaped the attentions of restorers and glow with all the rare translucency of Giotto's tempera.

These are the first pictures we have examined by Giotto in which we are able to appreciate at all the beauty and subtlety of his tone contrasts, for not only have the frescoes of the upper church at Assisi and the *Madonna* of the Academy suffered severely from restoration, but it is probable that in his youthful works he had not freed himself altogether from the harsher tonality of earlier art. Here, however, Giotto shows that power which is distinctive of the greatest masters of paint, of developing a form within a strictly limited scale of tone, drawing out of the slightest contrasts their fullest expressiveness for the rendering of form; a method which, though adopted from an intuitive feeling for pure beauty, gives a result which can only be described as that of an enveloping atmosphere surrounding the forms.*

The kneeling figure, presumably Cardinal Stefaneschi himself, in the *Christ enthroned* is an admirable instance of this quality. With what tender, scarcely perceptible gradations, with what a limited range from dark to light is the figure expressed! and yet it is not flat, the form is perfectly realised between the two sweeping curves whose simplicity would seem, but for the masterly modelling, to prevent the possibility of their containing a human figure. The portrait is as remarkable in sentiment as in execution. The very conception of introducing a donor into such a composition was new.† It was a sign of the new individualism which

* This quality is to be distinguished from that conscious naturalistic study of atmospheric envelopment which engrossed the attention of some artists of the cinquecento; it is a decorative quality which may occur at any period in the development of painting if only an artist arises gifted with a sufficiently delicate sensitiveness to the surface-quality of his work.

† I cannot recall any example in pre-Giottesque art.

marked the whole of the great period of Italian art, and finally developed into extravagance. The donor having once found his way into pictures of sacred ceremonial remained, but he not infrequently found it difficult to comport himself becomingly amid celestial surroundings; as he became more important, and heaven itself became less so, he asserted himself with unseemly self-assurance, until at last his matter-of-fact countenance, rendered with prosaic fidelity, stares out at the spectator in contemptuous indifference to the main action of the composition, the illusion of which it effectually destroys.

But here, where the idea is new, it has no such jarring effect; it is not yet a stereotyped formula, an excuse for self-advertisement or social display, but the direct outcome of a poetical and pious thought; and Giotto, with his unique rightness of feeling, has expressed, by the hand clinging to the throne and the slightly bent head, just the appropriate attitude of humble adoration, which he contrasts with the almost nonchalant ease and confidence of the angels. Even in so purely ceremonial a composition as this Giotto contrives to create a human situation.

In the planning of this picture Giotto has surpassed not only Duccio's and Cimabue's versions of the Enthronement motive but his own earlier work at Florence. The throne, similar in construction to that in the Academy picture, no longer shows the inconsistencies of two conflicting styles, but is of pure and exquisitely proportioned Gothic; the difficult perspective of the arches at the side is rendered with extraordinary skill though without mathematical accuracy. The relation of the figure of Christ to the throne is here entirely satisfactory, with the result that the great size of the figure no longer appears unnatural, but as an easily accepted symbol of divinity. In the drawing of the face of the Christ he has retained the hieratic solemnity given by the rigid delineation of Byzantine art.

But if the *Christ enthroned* is a triumph of well-calculated proportions, the *Crucifixion of S. Peter* which formed one side of the triptych is even more remarkable for the beauty of its spacing and the ingenuity of its arrangement.

In designing such a panel with its narrow cusped arch and gold background, the artist's first consideration must be its effect as mere pattern when seen on the altar at the end of a church. In his frescoes, Giotto's first preoccupation was with the drama to be presented; here it was with the effect of sumptuous pattern.

And the given data out of which the pattern was to be made were by no means tractable. The subject of the Crucifixion of S. Peter was naturally not a favourite one with artists, and scarcely any succeeded in it entirely, even in the small dimensions of a predella piece, to which it was generally relegated. For it is almost impossible to do away with the unpleasant effect of a figure seen thus upside down. The outstretched arms, which in the crucifixion of Christ give a counterbalancing line to the long horizontal of the spectators, here only increase the difficulty of the single upright. But Giotto, by a brilliant inspiration,* found his solution in the other fact given by his subject – namely, that the martyrdom took place between the goals of the Circus of Nero. By making these huge pyramids adapted from two well-known Roman monuments – the Septizonium and the pyramid of Cestius – he has obtained from the gold background just that dignified effect of spreading out above and contracting below which is so effective in renderings of the crucifixion of Christ, an effect which he still further emphasises by the two angels, whose spreading wings and floating draperies increase the brocade-like richness of the symmetrical pattern.

Nor, the pattern once assured, has Giotto failed of vivid dramatic presentation. It is surprising to find crowded into so small a space so may new poses all beautifully expressive of the individual shades of a common feeling; the woman to the left of the cross leaning her head on her hand as though sorrow had become a physical pain: the beautiful figure of the youth, with long waving hair, who throws back both arms with a despairing gesture; the woman lifting her robe to wipe her tears; and, most exquisite of all, and most surprising, in its novelty and truth to life, the figure of the girl to the left, drawn towards the terrible scene by a motion of sympathy and yet shrinking back with instinctive shyness and terror. In the child alone Giotto has, as

*Derived, no doubt, but greatly modified, from Cimabue's treatment of the subject at Assisi.

was usually the case, failed of a rhythmical and expressive pose. And what an entirely new study of life is seen here in the variety of the types! In one – the man whose profile cuts the sky to the left – he seems to have been indebted to some Roman portrait-bust; another, on horseback to the left, is clearly a Mongolian type, with slant eyes and pigtail, a curious proof of the intercourse with the extreme East which the Franciscan missionaries had already established. In the drawing of the nude figure of S. Peter, in spite of the unfortunate proportion of the head, the same direct study of nature has enabled Giotto to realise the structure of the figure more adequately than any artist since Roman times. One can well understand the astonishment and delight of Giotto's contemporaries at this unfolding of the new possibilities of art, which could now interpret all the variety and richness of human life and could so intensify its appeal to the emotions. One other peculiarity of this picture is interesting and characteristic of Giotto's attitude. In painting the frame of his panel he did not merely add figures as decorative and symbolic accessories, he brought them into relation with the central action, for each of them gazes at S. Peter with a different expression of pity and grief. Giotto had to be dramatic even in his frames.*

That Giotto remained in Rome till after the great Jubilee of 1300 is shown by the fragment of his fresco of the Papal Benediction which still remains on a pillar of S. John Lateran. There is every probability that at this time he met Dante, who was collecting the materials for the terrible portrait of Boniface VIII which he drew in the *Inferno*.

The next ascertainable date in Giotto's life is that of the decoration of the Arena chapel at Padua, begun in 1305. Here at last we are on indisputable ground. The decoration of this chapel was conceived by Giotto as a single whole, and was entirely carried out by him, though doubtless with the help of assistants, and although it has suffered from restoration it remains the completest monument to his genius. The general

* The attribution of the Stefaneschi altar-piece to Giotto is much disputed and some authorities give it to Bernardo Daddi. I still incline to the idea that it is the work of Giotto and the starting point of Bernardo Daddi's style (1920).

effect of these ample silhouettes of golden yellow and red on a ground of clear ultramarine is extraordinarily harmonious, and almost gay. But essentially the design is made up of the sum of a number of separate compositions. The time had not come for co-ordinating these into a single scheme, as Michelangelo did in the ceiling of the Sistine. In the composition of the separate scenes Giotto here shows for the first time his full powers. Nearly every one of these is an entirely original discovery of new possibilities in the relation of forms to one another. The contours of the figures evoke to the utmost the ideal comprehension of volume and mass. The space in which the figures move is treated almost as in a bas-relief, of which they occupy a preponderant part. As compared with the designs at Assisi the space is restricted, and the figures amplified so that the plastic unity of the whole design is more immediately apprehended. I doubt whether in any single building one can see so many astonishing discoveries of formal relations as Giotto has here made. Almost every composition gives one the shock of a discovery at once simple, inevitable, and instantly apprehended, and yet utterly unforeseeable. In most compositions one can guess at some of the steps by which the formal relations were established. Here one is at a loss to conceive by what flight of imagination the synthesis has been attained. We will consider a few in greater detail.

Giotto was, I believe, the first artist to represent the Resurrection by the *Noli me tangere*. The Byzantines almost invariably introduced the Descent into Hades or the Three Maries at the Tomb. In any case it is characteristic of Giotto to choose a subject where the human situation is so intimate and the emotions expressed are so poignant. Here, as in the *Navicella*, where he was free to invent a new composition, he discards the bilateral arrangement, which was almost invariable in Byzantine art, and concentrates all the interest in one corner of the composition. The angels on the tomb are damaged and distorted, but in the head and hands of the Magdalene we can realise Giotto's greatly increased power and delicacy of modelling as compared with the frescoes at Assisi. It is impossible for art to convey more intensely than this the beauty of such a movement of impetuous yearning. The action of the Christ is as vividly realised; almost too obviously, indeed, does he seem to be edging out of the composition in order to escape the Magdalene's outstretched hands. This is a striking instance of that power which Giotto possessed more than any other Italian, more indeed than any other artist except Rembrandt, the power of making perceptible the flash of mutual recognition which passes between two souls at a moment of sudden illumination.

In the *Pietà* (Plate III) a more epic conception is realised, for the impression conveyed is of a universal and cosmic disaster: the air is rent with the shrieks of desperate angels whose bodies are contorted in a raging frenzy of compassion. And the effect is due in part to the increased command, which the Paduan frescoes show, of simplicity and logical directness of design. These massive boulderlike forms, these draperies cut by only a few large sweeping folds, which suffice to give the general movement of the figure with unerring precision, all show this new tendency in Giotto's art as compared with the more varied detail, the more individual characterisation, of his early works. It is by this consciously acquired and masterly simplicity that Giotto keeps here, in spite of the unrestrained extravagance of passion, the consoling dignity of style. If one compares it, for example, with the works of Flemish painters, who explored the depths of human emotion with a similar penetrating and sympathetic curiosity, one realises the importance of what all the great Italians inherited from Graeco-Roman civilisation – the urbanity of a great style. And nowhere is it felt more than here, where Giotto is dealing with emotions which classical art scarcely touched.

It is interesting that Giotto should first have attained to this perfect understanding of style at Padua, where he was, as we know, in constant intercourse with Dante. Dante must have often watched him, perhaps helped him by suggestions, in decorating the chapel built with the ill-gotten wealth of that Scrovegni whom he afterwards seated amid the usurers on the burning sands of Hell.[48]

It is mainly by means of the composition and the general conception of pose and movement that Giotto expresses the dramatic idea. And regarded from that point of view, these frescoes are an astounding proof of Giotto's infallible intuitions. The characters he has created here are as convincing, as ineffaceable, as any that have been created by poets. The sad figure of Joachim is one never to be forgotten. In every incident of his sojourn in the wilderness, after the rejection of his offering in the temple, his appearance indicates exactly his mental condition. When he first comes to the sheepfold, he gazes with such set melancholy on the ground that the greeting of his dog and his shepherds cannot arouse his attention; when he makes a sacrifice he crawls on hands and knees in the suspense of expectation, watching for a sign from heaven; even in his sleep we guess at his melancholy dreams; and in the scene where he meets his wife at the Golden Gate on his return, Giotto has touched a chord of feeling at least as profound as can be reached by the most consummate master of the art of words.

It is true that in speaking of these one is led inevitably to talk of elements in the work which modern criticism is apt to regard as lying outside the domain of pictorial art. It is customary to dismiss all that concerns the dramatic presentation of the subject as literature or illustration, which is to be sharply distinguished from the qualities of design. But can this clear distinction be drawn in fact? The imaginings of a playwright, a dramatic poet, and a dramatic painter have much in common, but they are never at any point identical. Let us suppose a story to be treated by all three: to each, as he dwells on the legend, the imagination will present a succession of images, but those images, even at their first formation, will be quite different in each case, they will be conditioned and coloured by the art which the creator practises, by his past observation of nature with a view to presentment in that particular art. The painter, like Giotto, therefore, actually imagines in terms of figures capable of pictorial presentment, he does not merely translate a poetically dramatic vision into pictorial terms. And to be able to do this implies a constant observation of natural forms with a bias towards the discovery of pictorial beauty. To be able, then, to conceive just the appropriate pose of a hand to express the right idea of character and emotion in a picture, is surely as much a matter of a painter's vision as to appreciate the relative 'values' of a tree and cloud so as to convey the mood proper to a particular landscape.

Before leaving the Paduan frescoes, I must allude to those allegorical figures of the virtues and vices in which Giotto has, as it were, distilled the essence of his understanding of human nature. These personified virtues and vices were the rhetorical commonplaces of the day, but Giotto's intuitive understanding of the expression of emotion enabled him to give them a profound significance. He has in some succeeded in giving not merely a person under the influence of a given passion, but the abstract passion itself, not merely an angry woman, but anger. To conceive thus a figure possessed absolutely by a single passion implied an excursion beyond the regions of experience; no merely scientific observation of the effects of emotion would have enabled him to conceive the figure of Anger. It required an imagination that could range the remotest spaces thus to condense in visible form the bestial madness of the passion, to depict what Blake would have called the 'diabolical abstract' of anger.

We come now to the last great series of frescoes by Giotto which we possess, those of the Bardi and Peruzzi chapels of Sta Croce, his maturest and most consummate works. From the very first Giotto had to the full the power of seizing upon whatever in the forms of nature expressed life and emotion, but the perfect understanding of the conditions of a suave and gracious style was only slowly acquired. In the Florentine frescoes it is the geniality, the persuasiveness of the style which first strikes us. They have, indeed, an almost academic perfection of design.

The comparison of the *Death of S. Francis* here with the early fresco of the subject at Assisi shows how far Giotto has moved from the literal realism of his first works. At Assisi crowds of people push round the bier, soldiers and citizens come in to see, there is all the shifting variety of the actual event. Here the composition is sublimated and refined, reduced to its purest elements. The scene is still vividly, intensely real, but it is apprehended in a more pensive and meditative vein. There is in the composition a feeling for space which imposes a new mood of placidity and repose. This composition became the typical formula for such subjects throughout the Renaissance, but it was never again equalled. In spite of its apparent ease and simplicity, it is really by the subtlest art that all these figures are grouped in such readily apprehended masses without any sense of crowding and with such variety of gesture in the figures. The fresco, which had remained for more than a century under a coat of whitewash, was discovered in 1841 and immediately disfigured by utter restoration. The artist,[49] with a vague idea that Giotto was a decorative artist, and that decoration meant something ugly and unnatural, surrounded the figures with hard inexpressive lines. We can, therefore, only guess, by our knowledge of Giotto elsewhere, and by the general idea of pose, how perfect was the characterisation of the actors in the scene, how each responded according to his temperament to the general sorrow, some in humble prostration, one with a more intimate and personal affection, and one, to whom the vision of the ascending soul is apparent, wrapt in mystic ecstasy.

An interesting characteristic of these late frescoes is the revival which they declare of Giotto's early love for classical architecture. He may well have recognised the pictorial value of the large untroubled rectangular spaces which it allowed. In the *Salome* he has approached even more nearly to purely classic forms than in his earliest frescoes at Assisi. The building has an almost Palladian effect with its square parapets surmounted by statues, some of which are clearly derived from the antique. In the soldier who brings in the Baptist's head he has reverted to the costume of the Roman soldier, whereas, in the allegory of Chastity, the soldiers wear mediaeval winged helmets.

The fact that there is a free copy of this fresco by the Lorenzetti[50] at Siena made in 1331 gives us the period before which this must have been finished. Here again the mood is singularly placid, but the intensity with which Giotto realised a particularly dramatic moment is shown by a curious detail in which this differs from the usual rendering of the scene. Most artists, wishing to express the essentials of the story, make Salome continue her dance while the head is brought in. But

Giotto was too deep a psychologist to make such an error. At the tragic moment she stops dancing and makes sad music on her lyre, to show that she, too, is not wanting in proper sensibility.

There is evidence in these frescoes of an artistic quality which we could scarcely have believed possible, and yet, as it is most evident in those parts which are least damaged, it is impossible not to believe that Giotto possessed it; and that is the real feeling for chiaroscuro which these paintings show. It is not merely that the light falls in one direction, though even that was a conception which was scarcely grasped before Masaccio, but that Giotto actually composes by light and shade, subordinates figures or groups of figures by letting them recede into gloom and brings others into prominent light. This is particularly well seen in the *Ascension of S. John*, where the shadow of the building is made use of to unify the composition and give depth and relief to the imagined space. It is also an example of that beautiful atmospheric tonality of which I have already spoken. In the figure of S. John himself, Giotto seems to have the freedom and ease which we associate with art of a much later date. There is scarcely a hint of archaism in this figure. The head, with its perfect fusion of tones, its atmospheric envelopment, seems already nearly as modern as a head by Titian. Even the colour scheme, the rich earthy reds, the intense sweet blues of the figures relieved against a broken green-grey, is a strange anticipation of Cinquecento art. It seems as though Giotto in these works had himself explored the whole of the promised land to which he led Italian painting.

It is true that we are conscious of a certain archaism here in the relations of the figures and the architecture. A certain violence is done to that demand for verisimilitude which, perhaps wrongly, we now invariably make. But in the *Raising of Drusiana* even this demand is met. Here the figures all have their just proportions to one another, and to the buildings, and to the town wall which stretches behind them. The scene is imagined, not merely according to the conditions of the dramatic idea, but according to the possibilities and limitations of actual figures moving in a three-dimensional space; even the perspective of the ground is understood. Such an imaginative construction of three-dimensional space had its disadvantages as well as its advantages for art, but in any case it is an astonishing indication of Giotto's genius that he thus foresaw the conditions which in the end would be accepted universally in European art. There is scarcely anything here that Raphael would have had to alter to adapt the composition to one of his tapestry cartoons.

Of the dramatic power of this I need add nothing to what has already been said, but as this is the last of his works which we shall examine it may afford an example of some of the characteristics of Giotto's draughtsmanship. For Giotto was one of the greatest masters of line that the world has seen, and the fact that his knowledge of the forms of the figure was comparatively elementary in no way interferes with his greatness. It is not how many facts about an object an artist can record, but how incisive and how harmonious with itself the record is, that constitutes the essence of draughtsmanship.

In considering the qualities of line, three main elements are to be regarded: First, the decorative rhythm, our sense of sight being constructed like our sense of sound, so that certain relations, probably those which are capable of mathematical analysis, are pleasing, and others discordant. Secondly, the significance of line as enabling us imaginatively to reconstruct a real, not necessarily an actual, object from it. The greatest excellence of this quality will be the condensation of the greatest possible suggestion of real form into the simplest, most easily apprehended line; the absence of confusing superfluity on the one hand, and mechanical, and therefore meaningless simplicity, on the other. Finally, we may regard line as a gesture, which impresses us as a direct revelation of the artist's personality in the same way that handwriting does.

Now, with Giotto, beautiful as his line undoubtedly is, it is not the first quality, the decorative rhythm, that most immediately impresses us. That is not the object of such deliberate and conscious research as with some artists. It is in its significance for the expression of form with the utmost lucidity, the most logical interrelation of parts that his line is so impressive. Here, for instance, in the figure of the kneeling woman, the form is expressed with perfect clearness; we feel at once the relation of the shoulders to one another, the relation of the torso to the pelvis, the main position of the thighs, and all this is conveyed by a curve of incredible simplicity capable of instant apprehension. To record so much with such economy requires not only a rare imaginative grasp of structure, but a manual dexterity which makes the story of Giotto's O perfectly credible should one care to believe it.[51]

Giotto's line, regarded as an habitual gesture, is chiefly striking for its breadth and dignity. It has the directness, the absence of preciosity, which belongs to a generous and manly nature. The large sweeping curves of his loose and full draperies are in part the direct outcome of this attitude.

It is difficult to avoid the temptation to say of Giotto that he was the greatest artist that ever lived, a phrase which has been used of too many masters to retain its full emphasis. But at least he was the most prodigious phenomenon in the known history of art. Starting with little but the crude realism of Cimabue, tempered by the effete accomplishment of the Byzantines,* to have created an art capable of expressing the whole range of human emotions; to have found, almost without a guide, how to treat the raw material of life itself in a style so direct, so pliant to the idea, and yet so essentially grandiose and heroic; to have guessed intuitively almost all the principles of representation which it required nearly two centuries of enthusiastic research to establish scientifically – to have accomplished all this is surely a more astounding performance than any other one artist has ever achieved.

But the fascination Giotto's art exercises is due in part to his position in the development of modern culture. Coming at the same time as Dante, he shares with him the privilege of seeing life as a single, self-consistent, and systematic whole. It was a moment of equilibrium between the conflicting tendencies of human activity, a moment when such men as Dante and Giotto could exercise to the full their critical and analytical powers without destroying the unity of a cosmic theory based on theo-

* This passage now seems to me to underestimate the work of Giotto's predecessors with which we are now much better acquainted (1920).

logy. Such a moment was in its nature transitory: the free use of all the faculties which the awakening to a new self-consciousness had aroused, was bound to bring about antitheses which became more and more irreconcilable as time went on. Only one other artist in later times was able again to rise, by means of the conception of natural law, to a point whence life could be viewed as a whole. Even so, it was by a more purely intellectual effort, and Leonardo da Vinci could not keep the same genial but shrewd sympathy for common humanity which makes Giotto's work so eternally refreshing.

THE ART OF FLORENCE

✱

THE 'artistic temperament' – as used in the press and the police court, these words betray a general misunderstanding of the nature of art, and of the artist whenever he becomes fully conscious of its purpose. The idea of the artist as the plaything of whim and caprice, a hypersensitive and incoherent emotionalist, is, no doubt, true of a certain class of men, many of whom practise the arts; nothing could be further from a true account of those artists whose work has had the deepest influence on the tradition of art; nothing could be less true of the great artists of the Florentine School.

From the rise of modern art in the thirteenth century till now Florence and France have been the decisive factors in the art of Europe. Without them our art might have reflected innumerable pathetic or dramatic moods, it might have illustrated various curious or moving situations, it would not have attained to the conception of generalised truth of form.

To Florence of the fourteenth and fifteenth centuries and to France of the seventeenth and succeeding centuries we owe the creation of generalised or what, for want of a better word, we may call 'intellectual' art.

In speaking of intellect it is necessary to discriminate between two distinct modes of its operation. The intellect may seek to satisfy curiosity by observation of the distinctions between one object and another by means of analysis; but it may concern itself with the discovery of fundamental relations between these objects, by the construction of a synthetic system which satisfies the mind, both for its truth to facts and its logical coherence. The artist may employ both these modes. His curiosity about the phenomena of nature may lead him to accurate observation and recognition of the variety and distinctness of characters, but he also seeks to construe these distinct forms into such a coherent whole as will satisfy the aesthetic desire for unity. Perhaps the process employed by the artist may not be identical with the intellectual processes of science, but it is evident that they present a very close analogy to them.

It is a curious fact that at the beginning of the fifteenth century in Italy, art was deeply affected by both kinds of intellectual activity. Curiosity about natural forms in all their variety and complexity – *naturalism* in the modern sense – first manifested itself in European art in Flanders, France, and North Italy about the second decade of the fifteenth century. It appears that Italy actually led the way in this movement, and that Lombardy was the point of origin. Pisanello and Jacopo Bellini[1] are the great exemplars in Italy of this idea of exploring indefatigably and somewhat recklessly all those detailed aspects of nature which their predecessors, occupied in the grand Giottesque style, had scorned to notice.

In Florence, too, this impulse was undoubtedly felt, but it is the great distinction of the Florentine artists that, however much their curiosity about particular forms may have been excited, their high intellectual passion for abstract ideas impelled them more to the study of some general principles underlying all appearance. They refused to admit the given facts of nature except in so far as they could become amenable to the generalising power of their art. Facts had to be digested into form before they were allowed into the system.

We can get an idea of what Florence of the fifteenth century meant for the subsequent tradition of European art if we consider that if it had not been for Florence the art of Italy might have been not altogether unlike the art of Flanders and the Rhine – a little more rhythmical, a little more gracious, perhaps, but fundamentally hardly more significant.

Although this typically Florentine attitude defined itself most clearly under the stress of naturalism it was, of course, already characteristic of earlier Florentine art. Giotto, indeed, had left the tradition of formal completeness so firmly fixed in Florence that whatever new material had to be introduced it could only be introduced into a clearly recognized system of design.

Of Giotto's own work we rarely get a sight in England, the National Gallery having missed the one great chance of getting him represented some twenty years ago.[2] But though Lady Jekyll's single figure of Christ[3] can by its nature give no idea of his amazing and almost unequalled power of discovering unexpected inevitabilities of formal relations, it gives none the less something of Giotto's peculiar beauty of drawing, wherein the completest reality is attained without any attempted verisimilitude. In Mr Harris's Bernardo Daddi[4] we get nearer perhaps to Giotto as a composer, and even in his Giovanni da Milano[5] in spite of some Lombard grossness and sentimentality, the great traditon still lives.

Masaccio, represented here by Mr Rickett's single figure,[6] is one of the most mysterious personalities in art, and typically Florentine. His mystery lies partly in our ignorance about him, partly in the difficulty of grasping the rapidity of action, the precocity, of genius such as his. Coming at the very beginning of the naturalistic movement he seized with a strange complacency and ease upon the new material it offered, but – and this is what astounds one – he instantly discovered how to assimilate it perfectly to the formal requirements of design. So that not only the discovery of the new material, but its digestion was with him a simultaneous and almost instantaneous process. He was helped perhaps by the fact that the new naturalism was as yet only a general perception of new aspects of natural form. It was left for his younger contemporaries to map out the new country methodically – to the group of adventurous spirits – Brunelleschi, Donatello, Castagno, and Uccello[7] – who founded modern science, and gave to the understanding of classic art a methodical basis. It is in this group that the fierce intellectual passion of the Florentine genius manifests itself most clearly. Perspective and anatomy were the two studies which promised to reveal to them the secrets of natural form. The study of anatomy exemplifies mainly the aspect of curiosity, though even in this the desire to find the underlying principles of appearance is evident – on the other hand perspective, to its first discoverers, appeared to promise far more than an aid to verisimilitude, it may have seemed a visual revelation of the structure of space, and through that a key to the construction of pictorial space.

To our more penetrating study of aesthetic (for of all sciences, aesthetic has been the greatest laggard) it is evident that neither perspective nor anatomy has any very immediate bearing upon art – both of them are means of ascertaining facts, and the question of art begins where the question of fact ends. But artists have always had to excite themselves with some kind of subsidiary intoxicant, and perspective and anatomy, while they were still in their infancy, acted admirably as stimulants. That they have by now become, for most artists, the dreariest of sedatives may make it difficult to conceive this. But at all events in that first generation they excited their devotees to an ardent search for abstract unity of design. And this excitement went on to the next generation as exemplified by the works of the Umbro-Florentines – Piero della Francesca and Signorelli – and in Florence itself of Pollaiuolo.[8]

But the scientific spirit once aroused was destined not to remain for long so stimulating and helpful an assistant to the creation of design. It was bound in the end to start trains of thought too complex and too absorbing to occupy a subordinate place. Already in the rank and file of Florentine artists, the Ghirlandaios, Filippino Lippis, and their kindred, mere curiosity – naïve literalism – had undermined the tradition, so that towards the last quarter of the century hardly any artist knew how to design intelligibly on the scale of a fresco, whereas the merest duffer of the fourteenth century could be certain of the volumes and quantities of his divisions.

But it is with Leonardo da Vinci[9] that the higher aspects of the scientific spirit first came into conflict with art. Doubtless this conflict is not fundamental nor final, but only an apparent result of human limitations; but to one who, like Leonardo, first had a Pisgah prospect of that immense territory, to the exploration of which four centuries of the intensest human effort have been devoted without yet getting in sight of its boundaries – to such a man it was almost inevitable that the scientific content of art should assume an undue significance. Up till Leonardo one can say that the process of digesting the new-found material into aesthetic form had kept pace with observation, though already in Verrocchio[10] there is a sign of yielding to the crude phenomenon. But with Leonardo himself the organising faculty begins to break down under the stress of new matter. Leonardo himself shared to the full the Florentine passion for abstraction, but it was inevitable that he should be dazzled and fascinated by the vast prospects that opened before his intellectual gaze. It was inevitable that where such vast masses of new particulars revealed themselves to his curiosity their claim for investigation should be the most insistent. Not but what Leonardo did recognise the necessity for his art of some restriction and choice. His keen observation had revealed to him the whole gamut of atmospheric colour which first became a material for design under Monet and his followers. But having described a picture which would exactly correspond to a French painting of 1870, he rejects the whole of this new material as unsuitable for art. But even his rejection was not really a recognition of the claims of form, but only, alas! of another scientific trend with which his mind had become possessed. It was his almost prophetic vision of the possibilities of psychology which determined more than anything else the lines of his work. In the end almost everything was subordinated to the idea of a kind of psychological illustration of dramatic themes – an illustration which was not to be arrived at by an instinctive reconstruction from within, but by deliberate analytic observation. Now in so far as the movements of the soul could be interpreted by movements of the body as a whole, the new material might lend itself readily to plastic construction, but the minuter and even more psychologically significant movements of facial expression demanded a treatment which hardly worked for aesthetic unity. It involved a new use of light and shade, which in itself tended to break down the fundamental divisions of design, though later on Caravaggio and Rembrandt[11] managed, not very successfully, to pull it round so as to become the material for the basic rhythm. And in any case the analytic trend of Leonardo's mind became too much accentuated to allow of a successful synthesis. Michelangelo, to some extent, and Raphael still more, did, of course, do much to re-establish a system of design on an enlarged basis which would admit of some of Leonardo's new content, but one might hazard the speculation that European art has hardly yet recovered from the shock which Leonardo's passion for psychological illustration delivered. Certainly literalism and illustration have through all these centuries been pressing dangers to art – dangers which it has been the harder to resist in that they allow of an appeal to that vast public to whom the language of form is meaningless.

In Florentine art, then, one may see at happy moments of equilibrium the supreme advantages of intellectual art and at other and less fortunate moments the dangers which beset so difficult an endeavour. It was after all a Florentine who made the best prophecy of the results of modern aesthetic when he said: 'Finally, good painting is a music and a melody which intellect only can appreciate and that with difficulty.'[12]

THE JACQUEMART-ANDRÉ COLLECTION

⁕

THE Jacquemart-André collection[1] is not merely one of those accumulations of the art of the past by which it has become the fashion for rich people to impose themselves on the wonder of an ignorant public. It shows that the lady who created it did so partly, at all events, because of a quite personal and intimate love of beautiful things, a love which did not have to seek for its justification and support in the opinion of the world.

The three pictures discussed here are proof of the sincerity and courage of Mme André's artistic convictions. They offer scarcely any foothold for the sentimental and associative understanding of pictures. The *St George*[2] of Paolo Uccello (Plate IV) might, it is true, be taken as a 'naïve', 'quaint', or 'primitive' rendering of an 'old world' legend – indeed, whilst I was admiring it I gathered from the comments of those who lingered before it for a few seconds that this was the general attitude – but to do so would be to misunderstand the picture completely. Uccello, in fact, lends himself to misunderstanding, and Vasari, with his eye to literary picturesqueness, has done his best to put us off the scent. He made him an 'original', a harmless, ingenious, slightly ridiculous crank – gifted, no doubt, – but one whose gifts were wasted by reason of his crankiness.[3] And the legend created by Vasari has stuck. Uccello has always seemed to be a little aside from the main road of art, an agreeable, amusing diversion, one that we can enjoy with a certain humorous and patronising detachment, as we enjoy the innocence of some mediaeval chronicler. Uccello, I admit, has lent himself to this misunderstanding because from every other point of view but that of pure design he comes up to the character Vasari has made current. No artist was ever so helpless as he at the dramatic presentment of his theme. Nothing can well be imagined less like a battle than his battle-pieces, not if we think of the Deluge would our wildest fancies have ever conceived anything remotely resembling the scene which he painted with such literal precision, with such a mass of inconclusive and improbable invention, in the Chiostro Verde of Sta Maria Novella.

The idea of verisimilitude is entirely foreign to him. And here comes in the oddity and irony of his situation. He was the first or almost the first great master of linear perspective. The study of perspective became so engrossing to him that according to Vasari it wasted his talent as an artist.

Now perspective is the scientific statement of the nature of visual appearance. To the modern artist it becomes an occasional assistance in giving to his images an air of verisimilitude. Wherever a strict adherence to the laws of perspective would give to his objects a strange or unlikely look he frankly neglects it. But to Uccello perspective seemed, perhaps wrongly, to have an altogether different value. To him it appears to have been a method of recreating a visual world. That is to say, he took certain data of appearance from observation, and by handling them according to the laws of perspective he created a world, which, owing to the simplicity of his data and the rigid application of his laws, has far less resemblance to what we see than his contemporaries and predecessors had contrived by rule of thumb. Had he taken the whole of the data of observed form the application of the laws of perspective would have become impossible, and he would have been thrown back upon imitative realism and the literal acceptance of appearance. Such was indeed what happened to the painters of Flanders and the north, and such has become the usual method of modern realistic art. But nothing was more abhorrent to the spirit of fifteenth-century Florence than such an acceptance of the merely casual, and nothing is more fundamentally opposed to the empirical realism of a Van Eyck or a Frith[4] than the scientific and abstract realism of Paolo Uccello.

This passion, then, for an abstract and theoretical completeness of rendering led Uccello to simplify the data of observed form to an extraordinary extent, and his simplification anticipates in a curious way that of the modern cubists, as one may see from the treatment of his horses in the National Gallery battle-piece.[5]

It is one of the curiosities of the psychology of the artist that he is generally trying very hard to do something which has nothing to do with what he actually accomplishes; that the fundamental quality of his work seems to come out unconsciously as a by-product of his concious activity. And so it was in Uccello's case. If one had asked him what his perspective was for, he would probably have said that when once it was completely mastered it would enable the artist to create at will any kind of visual whole, and that this would have the same completeness, the same authenticity as an actual scene. As a matter of fact such a conception is unrealisable; the problem is too complex for solution in this way, and what happened to Uccello was that the simplifications and abstractions imposed upon observations of nature by the desire to construct his whole scene perspectively, really set free in him his power of creating a purely aesthetic organisation of form. And it is this, in fact, that makes his pictures so remarkable. In the Jacquemart-André picture, for instance, we see how the complex whole which such a scene as the legend of St. George suggests is reduced to terms of astounding simplicity; saint, horse, dragon, princess are all seen in profile because the problems of representation had to be approached from their simplest aspect. The landscape is reduced to a system of rectilinear forms seen at right angles to the picture plane for the same reason.

And out of the play of these almost abstract forms mainly rectangular, with a few elementary curves repeated again and again, Uccello has constructed the most perfect, the most amazingly subtle harmony. In Uccello's hands painting becomes almost as abstract, almost as pure an art as architecture. And as his feeling for the interplay of forms, the rhythmic disposition of planes, was of the rarest and finest, the most removed from anything trivial or merely decorative (in the vulgar sense), he passes by means of this power of formal organisation into a region of feeling entirely remote from that which is suggested if we regard his work as mere illustration. Judged as illustration the *S. George* is quaint, innocent and slightly childish; as design it must rank among the great masterpieces.

Two other pictures in the Jacquemart-André collection illustrate the same spirit of uncompromising aesthetic adventure which distinguishes one branch of the Florentine school of the fifteenth century, and lifts it above almost all that was being attempted elsewhere in Italy even at this period of creative exuberance.

Baldovinetti[6] was at one time in close contact with Uccello, and of all his works the *Madonna and Child* in the Jacquemart-André collection is the most heroically uncompromising. No doubt he accepted more material directly from nature than Uccello did. He was beginning to explore the principles of atmospheric perspective which were destined ultimately to break up the unity of pictorial design, but everything that he takes is used with the same spirit of obedience to the laws of architectonic harmony. The spacing of this design, the relations of volume of the upright mass of the Virgin's figure to the spaces of sky and landscape have the unmistakable interdependence of great design.[7] Only a great creative artist could have discovered so definite a relationship. The great mass of the rocky hill in the landscape and the horizontal lines of the Child's figure play into the central idea with splendid effect. Only in the somewhat rounded and insensitive modelling of the Virgin's face does the weakness of Baldovinetti's genius betray itself. The contours are everywhere magnificently plastic; only when he tries to create the illusion of plastic relief by modelling, Baldovinetti becomes literal and uninspired. In his profile portrait in the National Gallery[8] he relies fortunately almost entirely on the plasticity of the contour – in his late *Trinità* at the Accademia in Florence[9] the increasing desire for imitative realism has already gone far to destroy this quality.

The third picture which I have taken as illustrating my theme is not, it is true, Florentine, but its author, Signorelli,[10] kept so constantly in touch with the scientific realists of Florence that he may be counted almost as one of them, nor indeed did any of them surpass him in uncompromising fidelity to the necessities of pure design. Certainly there is nothing of the flattering or seductive qualities of the common run of Umbrian art in this robust and audacious composition, in which everything is arranged as it were concentrically around the imposing mass of the Virgin's figure. The gestures interpreted psychologically are not on the same imaginative plane as the design itself. Signorelli was ill at ease in interpreting any states but those of great tension, and here the gestures are meant to be playful and intimate. As in the Uccello, the illustrative pretext is at variance with the design which it serves; and as in the Uccello, the design itself, the scaffolding of the architectonic structure, is really what counts.

DÜRER AND HIS CONTEMPORARIES

IT is a habit of the human mind to make to itself symbols in order to abbreviate its admiration for a class. So Dürer has come to stand for German art somewhat as Raphael once stood for Italian. Such symbols attract to themselves much of the adoration which more careful worshippers would distribute throughout the Pantheon, and it becomes difficult to appreciate them justly without incurring the charge of iconoclasm. But this, in Dürer's case, is the more difficult because, whatever one's final estimate of his art, his personality is at once so imposing and so attractive, and has been so endeared to us by familiarity, that something of this personal attachment has transferred itself to our aesthetic judgment.

The letters from Venice and the Diary of his journey in the Netherlands, which form the matter of this volume,[1] are indeed the singularly fortunate means for this pleasant discourse with the man himself. They reveal Dürer as one of the distinctively modern men of the Renaissance: intensely, but not arrogantly, conscious of his own personality; accepting with a pleasant ease the universal admiration of his genius – a personal admiration, too, of an altogether modern kind; careful of his fame as one who foresaw its immortality. They show him as having, though in a far less degree, something of Leonardo da Vinci's scientific interest, certainly as having a quick, though naïve curiosity about the world and a quite modern freedom from superstition. It is clear that his dominating, and yet kindly personality, no less than his physical beauty and distinction, made him the centre of interest wherever he went. His easy and humorous good-fellowship, of which the letters to Pirkheimer[2] are eloquent, won for him the admiring friendship of the best men of his time. To all these characteristics we must add a deep and sincere religious feeling, which led him to side with the leaders of the

Reformation, a feeling that comes out in his passionate sense of loss when he thinks that Luther is about to be put to death, and that prompted him to write a stirring letter to Erasmus, in which he urged him to continue the work of reform. For all that, there is no trace in him of either Protestantism or Puritanism. He was perhaps fortunate – certainly as an artist he was fortunate – in living at a time when the line of cleavage between the Reformers and the Church was not yet so marked as to compel a decisive choice. The symbolism of the Church still had for him its old significance, as yet quickened and not discredited by the reformer's energy. But intense as Dürer's devotion was, his religious feeling found its way to effective artistic expression only upon one side, namely, the brooding sense which accompanied it, of the imminence and terror of death. How much more definite is the inspiration in the drawing of *Death on a Horse* – in the British Museum, – in the *Knight, Death and the Devil*, and in the allied *Melancholia*,[3] than it is in his renderings of the Virgin or indeed of any of the scenes of Christian legend! It is this feeling, too, which gives to his description of his mother's death its almost terrible literary beauty and power.[4] Nor in the estimate of Dürer's character must one leave out the touching affection and piety which the family history written by him in 1524 reveals.

So much that is attractive and endearing in the man cannot but react upon our attitude to his work – has done so, perhaps, ever since his own day; and it is difficult to get far enough away from Dürer the man to be perfectly just to Dürer the artist. But if we make the attempt, it becomes clear, I think, that Dürer cannot take rank in the highest class of creative geniuses. His position is none the less of great importance and interest for his relation on the one hand to the Gothic tradition of his country, and on the other to the newly perceived splendours of the Italian Renaissance.

Much must depend on our estimate of his last work, the *Four Apostles*, at Munich. In that he summed up all that the patient and enthusiastic labour of a lifetime had taught him. If we regard that as a work of the highest beauty, if we can conscientiously put it beside the figures of the Sistine Chapel, beside the

Saints of Mantegna, or Signorelli, or Piero della Francesca, then indeed Dürer's labour was crowned with success; but if we find in it rather a careful exposition of certain theoretical principles, if we find that the matter is not entirely transfused with the style, if we find a conflict between a certain naïve crudity of vision and a straining after the grand manner, then we have to say that Dürer's art was the outcome of a magnificent and heroic but miscalculated endeavour.

It is one of the ironies of history that the Romans, the only Philistine people among Mediterranean races, should have been the great means of transmitting to the modern world that culture which they themselves despised, and that the Germans should have laboured so long and hard to atone for the heroism of their ancestors in resisting that beneficent loss of liberty. Nuremberg of the fifteenth century was certainly given over to the practice of fine art with a pathetic enthusiasm, and it remains as a sad but instructive proof of how little good-will and industry avail by themselves in such matters. The worship of mere professional skill and undirected craftsmanship is there seen pushed to its last conclusions, and the tourist's wonder is prompted by the sight of stone carved into the shapes of twisted metal, and wood simulating the intricacies of confectionery, his admiration is canvassed by every possible perversion of technical dexterity. Not 'What a thing is done!' but, 'How difficult it must have been to do it!' is the exclamation demanded.

Of all that perverted technical ingenuity which flaunts itself in the wavering stonework of a Kraft[5] or the crackling woodwork of a Storr,[6] Dürer was inevitably the heir. He grew up in an atmosphere where the acrobatic feats of technique were looked on with admiration rather than contempt. Something of this clung to him through life, and he is always recognised as the prince of craftsmen, the consummate technician. In all this side of Dürer's art we recognise the last over-blown efflorescence of the mediaeval craftsmanship of Germany, of the apprentice system and the 'master' piece; but that Gothic tradition had still left in it much that was sound and sincere. Drawing still retained something of the blunt, almost brutal frankness of statement, together with the sense of the characteristic which marked its earlier period. And it is perhaps this inheritance of Gothic directness of statement, this Gothic realism, that accounts for what is ultimately of most value in Dürer's work. There exists in the Kunsthistorisches Akademie at Vienna a painting of a man, dated 1394, which shows how much of Dürer's portraiture was already implicit in the Nuremberg school. In this remarkable work, executed, if we may trust the date, nearly a century before Dürer, there is almost everything that interests us in Dürer's portraits. Indeed, it has to an even greater extent that half-humorous statement of the characteristic, that outrageous realism that makes the vivid appeal of the Oswold Krell,[7] and the absence of which in Dürer's last years makes the Holtschuer[8] such a tiresome piece of brilliant delineation.

Dürer was perhaps the greatest infant prodigy among painters, and the drawing of himself at the age of twelve shows how early he had mastered that simple and abrupt sincerity of Gothic draughtsmanship. One is inclined to say that in none of his subsequent work did he ever surpass this in all that really matters, in all that concerns the essential vision and its adequate presentment. He increased his skill until it became the wonder of the world and entangled him in its seductions; his intellectual apprehension was indefinitely heightened, and his knowledge of natural appearances became encyclopaedic.

What, then, lies at the root of Dürer's art is this Gothic sense of the characteristic, already menaced by the professional bravura of the late Gothic craftsman. The superstructure is what Dürer's industry and intellectual acquisitiveness, acting in the peculiar conditions of his day, brought forth. It is in short what distinguishes him as the pioneer of the Renaissance in Germany. This new endeavour was in two directions, one due mainly to the trend of native ideas, the other to Italian influence. The former was concerned mainly with a new kind of realism. In place of the older Gothic realism with its naïve and self-confident statement of the salient characteristic of things seen, this new realism strove at complete representation of appearance by means of perspective, at a more searching and complete investigation of form, and a fuller relief in light and shade.

To some extent these aims were followed also by the Italians, and with even greater scientific ardour: all the artists of Europe were indeed striving to master the complete power of representation. But in Italy this aim was never followed exclusively; it was constantly modified and controlled by the idea of design, that is to say, of expression by means of the pure disposition of contours and masses, and by the perfection and ordering of linear rhythm. This notion of design as something other than representation was indeed the common inheritance of European art from the mediaeval world, but in Italy the principles of design were more profoundly embedded in tradition, its demands were more clearly felt, and each succeeding generation was quite as deeply concerned with the perfection of design as with the mastery of representation. In the full Renaissance, indeed, this idea of design became the object of conscious and deliberate study, and the decadence of Italian art came about, not through indifference to the claims of artistic expression, but through a too purely intellectual and conscious study of them. The northern and especially the Teutonic artists, who had not inherited so strongly this architectonic sense, made indeed heroic efforts to acquire it, sometimes by the futile method of direct imitation of a particular style, sometimes – and this is the case with Dürer – by a serious effort of aesthetic intelligence. But on the whole the attempt must be judged to have failed, and northern art has drifted gradually towards the merely photographic vision.

Dürer strove strenuously in both these directions. He unquestionably added immensely to the knowledge of actual form and to the power of representation, but his eagerness led him to regard quantity of form rather than its quality. With him drawing became a means of making manifest the greatest possible amount of form, the utmost roundness of relief, and his studies in pure design failed to keep pace with this. In the end he could not use to significant purpose the increased material at his disposal, and from the point of view of pure design his work actually falls short of that of his predecessor, Martin Schongauer,[9] who indeed was benefited by lacking Dürer's power of representation.[10]

From this point of view it may be worth while to examine in some detail Dürer's relations to Italian art. The earliest definite example of his study of Italian art is in 1494, when he was probably in Venice for the first time. It is a copy in pen and ink of an engraving of the *Death of Orpheus* by some follower of Mantegna. The engraving is not the work of a great artist, and Dürer's copy shows his superior skill in the rendering of form; but even here he has failed to realise the beauty of spatial arrangement in the original, and his desire to enrich the design with many skilfully drawn and convincing details results in a distinct weakening of the dramatic effect. Again, in the same year we have two drawings from engravings, this time by Mantegna himself.[11] It is easy to understand that of all Italians, Mantegna should have been the most sympathetic to Dürer, and that he should have regretted more than any other ill-fortune of his life, – more even than the similar fate that prevented his meeting Schongauer, – Mantegna's death just when he was setting out to Mantua to learn from the great master. What Dürer saw in Mantegna was his clear decision of line and his richly patterned effect. In his pen-and-ink copies he tries to surpass the original in both these ways, and indeed the effect is of greater complexity, with more fullness and roundness of form. Where Mantegna is content with a firm statement of the generalised contour of a limb, Dürer will give a curve for each muscle. There is in Dürer's copies a mass of brilliant detail; each part is in a sense more convincingly real; but in doing this something of the unity of rhythm and the easy relations of planes has been lost, and on the whole the balance is against the copyist. It is curious that when in time Rembrandt came to copy Mantegna he took the other way, and actually heightened the dramatic effect by minute readjustments of planning, and by a wilful simplification of the line.

Dürer evidently felt a profound reverence for Mantegna's designs, for he has altered them but little, and one might well imagine that even Dürer could scarcely improve upon such originals. But it is even more instructive to study his work upon the so-called Tarocchi engravings.[12] Here the originals were not executed by an artist of first-rate ability, though the designs have much of Cossa's[13] splendid style. Dürer seems, therefore, to have felt no particular constraint about altering them. His alterations show us clearly what it was that he saw in the originals and what he missed. In all these figures Dürer gives increased verisimilitude: his feet are like actual feet, not the schematic abstract of a foot that contents the Italian engraver; his poses are more casual, less formal and symmetrical; and his draperies are more ingeniously disposed; but none the less, from the point of view of the expression of imaginative truth, there is not one of Dürer's figures which equals the original, not one in which some essential part of the idea is not missed or at least less clearly stated. In general the continuity of the contour is lost sight of and the rhythm frittered away. In the Pope,[14] for instance, Dürer loses all the grave sedateness of the original by breaking the symmetry of the pose, its squareness and immovable aplomb. And with this goes, in spite of the increased verisimilitude, the sense of reality. In the *Knight and Page*[15] not only is the movement of the knight missed by correcting a distortion in the original, but the balance of the composition is lost by displacing the page. In the *Primum Mobile* (Plate V) the ecstatic rush of the figure is lost by slight corrections of the pose and by giving to the floating drapery too complicated a design.[16] It would be tedious to go through these copies in detail, but enough has been said to show how hard it was for Dürer, absorbed by his new curiosity in representation, to grasp those primary and elemental principles of design which were inherent in the Italian tradition.

About the same time we find Dürer studying both Pollaiuolo and Lorenzo di Credi.[17] The copy of Pollaiuolo is not a good example of Dürer's art; it certainly misses the tension and inner life of Pollaiuolo's nudes. The Lorenzo di Credi, as might be expected, is in many ways more than adequate to the original, though as compared even with Credi, Dürer has not a clear sense of the correlation of linear elements in the design.

The next stage in Dürer's connection with Italian art is his intimacy with Jacopo de' Barbari, who was settled in Nuremberg. From 1500 to 1505 this influence manifests itself clearly in Dürer's work. Unfortunately Barbari was too second-rate an artist to help him much in the principles of design, though he doubtless stimulated him to pursue those scientific investigations into the theory of human proportions which held out the delusive hope of reducing art to a branch of mathematics.

It was not, however, until his second visit to Venice that Dürer realised the inferiority, at all events, of Barbari, and it was then that, through his amiable relations with Giovanni Bellini, he came nearer than at any other moment of his life to penetrating the mysteries of Italian design. It is in the letters from Venice, written at this time, that his connection with the Venetian artists is made clear, and a study of those writings will be found to illuminate in a most interesting way Dürer's artistic consciousness, and help to answer the question of how he regarded his own work when seen in comparison with the Venetians, and in what manner the Venetians regarded this wonder worker from the north.

EL GRECO

✱

Mr holmes[1] has risked a good deal in acquiring for the nation the new El Greco.[2] The foresight and understanding necessary to bring off such a *coup* are not the qualities that we look for from a Director of the National Gallery. Patriotic people may even be inclined to think that the whole proceeding smacks too much of the manner in which Dr Bode in past ages built up the Kaiser-Friedrich-Museum,[3] largely at the expense of English collections. Even before the acquisition of the El Greco there were signs that Mr Holmes did not fully understand the importance of 'muddling through'. And now with the El Greco (Plate VIII.1) he has given the British public an electric shock. People gather in crowds in front of it, they argue and discuss and lose their tempers. This might be intelligible enough if the price were known to be fabulous, but, so far as I am aware, the price has not been made known, so that it is really about the picture that people get excited. And what is more, they talk about it as they might talk about some contemporary picture, a thing with which they have a right to feel delighted or infuriated as the case may be – it is not like most old pictures, a thing classified and museumified, set altogether apart from life, an object for vague and listless reverence, but an actual living thing, expressing something with which one has got either to agree or disagree. Even if it should not be the superb masterpiece which most of us think it is, almost any sum would have been well spent on a picture capable of provoking such fierce aesthetic interest in the crowd.

That the artists are excited – never more so – is no wonder, for here is an old master who is not merely modern, but actually appears a good many steps ahead of us, turning back to show us the way. Immortality if you like! But the public – what is it that makes them 'sit up' so surprisingly, one wonders. What makes this El Greco 'count' with them as surely no Old Master ever did within memory? First, I suspect, the extraordinary completeness of its realisation. Even the most casual spectator, passing among pictures which retire discreetly behind their canvases, must be struck by the violent attack of these forms, by a relief so outstanding that by comparison the actual scene, the gallery and one's neighbours are reduced to the key of a Whistlerian Nocturne. Partly, for we must face the fact, the melodramatic apparatus; the 'horrid' rocks, the veiled moon, the ecstatic gestures. Not even the cinema star can push expression further than this. Partly, no doubt, the clarity and the balanced rhythm of the design, the assurance and grace of the handling; for, however little people may be conscious of it, formal qualities do affect their reaction to a picture, though they may pass from them almost immediately to its other implications. And certainly here, if anywhere, formal considerations must obtrude themselves even on the most unobservant. The extraordinary emphasis and amplitude of the rhythm, which thus gathers up into a few sweeping diagonals the whole complex of the vision, is directly exciting and stimulating. It affects one like an irresistible melody, and makes that organisation of all the parts into a single whole, which is generally so difficult for the uninitiated, an easy matter for once. El Greco, indeed, puts the problem of form and content in a curious way. The artist, whose concern is ultimately and, I believe, exclusively with form, will no doubt be so carried away by the intensity and completeness of the design, that he will never even notice the melodramatic and sentimental content which shocks or delights the ordinary man. It is none the less an interesting question, though it is rather one of artists' psychology than of aesthetics, to inquire in what way these two things, the melodramatic expression of a high-pitched religiosity and a peculiarly intense feeling for plastic unity and rhythmic amplitude, were combined in El Greco's work; even to ask whether there can have been any casual connection between them in the workings of El Greco's spirit.

Strange and extravagantly individual as El Greco seems, he was not really an isolated figure, a miraculous and monstrous apparition thrust into the even current of artistic movement. He really takes his place alongside of Bernini[4] as a great exponent of the Baroque idea in figurative art. And the Baroque idea goes back to Michelangelo. Formally, its essence both in art and architecture was the utmost possible enlargement of the unit of design. One can see this most easily in architecture. To Bramante[5] the façade of a palace was made up of a series of storeys, each with its pilasters and windows related proportionally to one another, but each a co-ordinate unit of design. To the baroque architect a façade was a single storey with pilasters going the whole height, and only divided, as it were, by an afterthought into subordinate groups corresponding to the separate storeys. When it came to sculpture and painting the same tendency expressed itself by the discovery of such movements as would make the parts of the body, the head, trunk, limbs, merely so many subordinate divisions of a single unit. Now to do this implied extremely emphatic and marked poses, though not necessarily violent in the sense of displaying great muscular strain. Such poses correspond as expression to marked and excessive mental states, to conditions of ecstasy, or agony or intense contemplation. But even more than to any actual poses resulting from such states, they correspond to a certain accepted and partly conventional language of gesture. They are what we may call rhetorical poses, in what they are not so much the result of the emotions as of the desire to express these emotions to the onlooker.

When the figure is draped the Baroque idea becomes particularly evident. The artists seek voluminous and massive garments which under the stress of an emphatic pose take heavy folds passing in a single diagonal sweep from top to bottom of the whole figure. In the figure of Christ in the National Gallery[6] picture El Greco has established such a diagonal, and has so arranged the light and shade that he gets a statement of the same general direction twice over, in the sleeve and in the drapery of the thigh.

Bernini was a consummate master of this method of amplifying the unit, but having once set up the great wave of rhythm which held the figure in a single sweep, he gratified his florid taste by allowing elaborate embroidery in the subordinate divisions, feeling perfectly secure that no amount of exuberance would destroy the firmly established scaffolding of his design.

Though the psychology of both these great rhetoricians is infinitely remote from us, we tolerate more easily the gloomy and terrible extravagance of El Greco's melodrama than the radiant effusiveness and amiability of Bernini's operas.

But there is another cause which accounts for our profound difference of feeling towards these two artists. Bernini undoubtedly had a great sense of design, but he was also a prodigious artistic acrobat, capable of feats of dizzying audacity, and unfortunately he loved popularity and the success which came to him so inevitably. He was not fine enough in grain to distinguish between his great imaginative gifts and the superficial virtuosity which made the crowd, including his Popes, gape with astonishment. Consequently he expressed great inventions in a horribly impure technical language. El Greco, on the other hand, had the good fortune to be almost entirely out of touch with the public – one picture painted for the king was sufficient to put him out of court for the rest of his life. And in any case he was a singularly pure artist, he expressed his idea with perfect sincerity, with complete indifference to what effect the right expression might have on the public. At no point is there the slightest compromise with the world; the only issue for him is between him and his idea. Nowhere is a violent form softened, nowhere is the expressive quality of brushwork blurred in order to give verisimilitude of texture; no harshness of accent is shirked, no crudity of colour opposition avoided, wherever El Greco felt such things to be necessary to the realisation of his idea. It is this magnificent courage and purity, this total indifference to the expectations of the public, that bring him so near to us today, when more than ever the artist regards himself as working for ends unguessed at by the mass of his contemporaries. It is this also which accounts for the fact that while nearly every one shudders involuntarily at Bernini's sentimental sugariness, very few artists of today have ever realised for a moment how unsympathetic to them is the literary content of an El Greco. They simply fail to notice what his pictures are about in the illustrative sense.

But to return to the nature of Baroque art. The old question here turns up. Did the dog wag his tail because he was pleased, or was he pleased because his tail wagged? Did the Baroque artists choose ecstatic subjects because they were excited about a certain kind of rhythm, or did they elaborate the rhythm to express a feeling for extreme emotional states? There is yet another fact which complicates the matter. Baroque art corresponds well enough in time with the Catholic reaction and the rise of Jesuitism, with a religious movement which tended to dwell particularly on these extreme emotional states, and, in fact, the Baroque artists worked in entire harmony with the religious leaders.

This would look as though religion had inspired the artists with a passion for certain themes, and the need to express these had created Baroque art.

I doubt if it was as simple as that. Some action and reaction between the religious ideas of the time and the artists' conception there may have been, but I think the artists would have elaborated the Baroque idea without this external pressure. For one thing, the idea goes back behind Michelangelo to Signorelli, and in his case, at least, one can see no trace of any preoccupation with those psychological states, but rather a pure passion for a particular kind of rhythmic design. Moreover, the general principle of the continued enlargement of the unit of design was bound to occur the moment artists recovered from the debauch of naturalism of the fifteenth century and became conscious again of the demands of abstract design.

In trying thus to place El Greco's art in perspective, I do not in the least disparage his astonishing individual force. That El Greco had to an extreme degree the quality we call genius is obvious, but he was neither so miraculous nor so isolated as we are often tempted to suppose.

The exuberance and abandonment of Baroque art were natural expressions both of the Italian and Spanish natures, but they were foreign to the intellectual severity of the French genius, and it was from France, and in the person of Poussin,[7] that the counterblast came. He, indeed, could tolerate no such rapid simplification of design. He imposed on himself endless scruples and compunctions, making artistic unity the reward of a long process of selection and discovery. His art became difficult and esoteric. People wonder sometimes at the diversity of modern art, but it is impossible to conceive a sharper opposition than that between Poussin and the Baroque. It is curious, therefore, that modern artists should be able to look back with almost equal reverence to Poussin and to El Greco. In part, this is due to Cézanne's influence, for, from one point of view, his art may be regarded as a synthesis of these two apparently adverse conceptions of design. For Cézanne consciously studied both, taking from Poussin his discretion and the subtlety of his rhythm, and from El Greco his great discovery of the permeation of every part of the design with a uniform and continuous plastic theme. The likeness is indeed sometimes startling. One of the greatest critics of our time, von Tschudi[8] – of Swiss origin, I hasten to add, and an enemy of the Kaiser – was showing me El Greco's *Laocoon*, which he had just bought for Munich, when he whispered to me, as being too dangerous a doctrine to be spoken aloud even in his private room, 'Do you know why we admire El Greco's handling so much? Because it reminds us of Cézanne.'

No wonder, then, that for the artist of today the new El Greco is of capital importance. For it shows us the master at the height of his powers, at last perfectly aware of his personal conception and daring to give it the completest, most uncompromising expression. That the picture is in a marvellous state of preservation and has been admirably cleaned adds greatly to its value. Dirty yellow varnish no longer interposes here its hallowing influence between the spectator and the artist's original creation. Since the eye can follow every stroke of the brush, the mind can recover the artist's gesture and almost the movements of his mind. For never was work more perfectly transparent to the idea, never was an artist's intention more deliberately and precisely recorded.

THREE PICTURES IN TEMPERA BY WILLIAM BLAKE

*

BLAKE's finished pictures have never received the same attention nor aroused the same admiration as his wash-drawings, his wood-cuts, or his engravings. It is difficult to account for this comparative neglect, since they not only show command of a technique which admits of the completest realisation of the idea, but they seem actually to express what was personal to Blake in a purer form than many of his other works, with less admixture of those unfortunate caprices which the false romantic taste of his day imposed too often even on so original and independent a genius. The explanation may perhaps lie in the fact that to most people Blake, for all his inimitable gifts, appears as a divinely inspired amateur rather than as a finished master of his art, and they are willing to tolerate what they regard as his imperfect control of form in media which admit only of hints and suggestions of the artist's vision.

There assuredly never was a more singular, more inexplicable phenomenon than the intrusion, as though by direct intervention of Providence, of this Assyrian spirit into the vapidly polite circles of eighteenth-century London. The fact that, as far as the middle classes of England were concerned, Puritanism had for a century and a half blocked every inlet and outlet of poetical feeling and imaginative conviction save one, may give us a clue to the causes of such a phenomenon. It was the devotion of Puritan England to the Bible, to the Old Testament especially, that fed such a spirit as Blake's directly from the sources of the most primeval, the vastest and most abstract imagery which we possess. Brooding on the vague and tremendous images of Hebrew and Chaldaean poetry, he arrived at such indifference to the actual material world, at such an intimate perception of the elemental forces which sway the spirit with immortal hopes and infinite terrors when it is most withdrawn from its bodily conditions, that what was given to his internal vision became incomparably more definite, more precisely and more clearly articulated, than anything presented to his senses. His forms are the visible counterparts to those words, like *the deep, many waters, firmanent, the foundations of the earth, pit* and *host*, whose resonant overtones blur and enrich the sense of the Old Testament. Blake's art moves us, if at all, by a similar evocation of vast elemental forces. He deals directly with these spiritual sensations, bringing in from external nature the least possible content which will enable him to create visible forms at all. But though he pushed them to their furthest limits, even he could not transcend the bounds which beset pictorial language; even he was forced to take something of external nature with him into his visionary world, and his wildest inventions are but recombinations and distorted memories of the actual objects of sense.

By the strangest irony, too, the forms which came to his hand as the readiest means of expressing his stupendous conceptions were in themselves the least expressive, the least grandiose, that ever art has dealt with. It was with the worn-out rags of an effete classical tradition long ago emptied of all meaning, and given over to turgid rhetorical display, that Blake had to piece together the visible garments of his majestic and profound ideas. The complete obsession of his nature by these ideas in itself compelled him to this: he was entirely without curiosity about such trivial and ephemeral things as the earth contained. His was the most anti-Hellenic temperament; he had no concern, either gay or serious, with phenomena; they were too transparent to arrest his eye, and that patient and scientific quarrying from his infinite possibilities of nature of just the appropriate forms to convey his idea was beyond the powers with which nature and the poor traditions of his day supplied him. Tintoretto, who had in some respects a similar temperament, who felt a similar need of conveying directly the revelations of his internal vision, was more happily situated. He was, by comparison, a trivial and vulgar seer, but the richness and expressive power of the forms which lay to his hand in Titian's and Michelangelo's art enabled him to attain a more unquestionable achievement.

But, allowing for circumstances, what Blake did was surely more considerable and implied a greater sheer lift of imaginative effort. That it was an attempt which remained almost without consequences, isolated and incomplete – married, too, by a certain incoherence and want of reasonable co-ordination – must be allowed, and may perhaps explain why Blake is not universally admitted among our greatest.

The Byzantine style, he declares, was directly and divinely revealed to him; and whether this were so, or whether he obtained it by the dim indications of Ottley's prints,[1] or through illuminated manuscripts, the marvellous fact remains that he did succeed in recovering for a moment that pristine directness and grandeur of expression which puts him beside the great Byzantine designers as the only fit interpreter of Hebrew mythology. His *Flight into Egypt*[2] will at once recall Giotto's treatment of the subject in the Arena chapel at Padua; but the likeness is, in a sense, deceptive, for Giotto was working away from Byzantinism as fast as Blake was working towards it, and the two pass one another on the road. For there is here but little of Giotto's tender human feeling, less still of his robust rationalism; what they have in common, what Blake rediscovered and Giotto inherited, is the sentiment of supernatural dignity, the hieratic solemnity and superhuman purposefulness of the gestures. Even more than in Giotto's version, the Virgin here sits on the ass as though enthroned in monumental state, her limbs fixed in the rigid symmetry which oriental art has used to express complete withdrawal from the world of sense. No less perfect in its expressiveness of the strange and exalted mood is the movement, repeated with such impressive monotony, in the figures of Joseph and the archangel. It is absurd, we think, to deny to the man who discovered the lines of these figures the power of draughtsmanship. Since Giotto's day scarcely any one has drawn thus – simplification has been possible only as the last effort of consummate science refining away the superfluous: but here the simplification of the forms is the result of an instinctive passionate reaching out for the direct symbol of the idea.

Blake's art indeed is a test case for our theories of aesthetics. It boldly makes the plea for art that it is a language for conveying impassioned thought and feeling, which takes up the objects of sense as a means to this end, owing them no allegiance and accepting from them only the service that they can render for this purpose. 'Poetry', says Blake, 'consists in bold, daring, and masterly conceptions; and shall painting be confined to the sordid drudgery of facsimile representations of merely mortal and perishing substances, and not be, as poetry and music are, elevated into its own proper sphere of invention and visionary conception?'[3] The theory that art appeals solely by the associated ideas of the natural objects it imitates is easily refuted when we consider music and architecture; in those at least the appeal to the spirit is made directly in a language which has no other use than that of conveying its own proper ideas and feelings. But in pictorial art the fallacy that nature is the mistress instead of the servant seems almost ineradicable, and it is difficult to convince people that increased scientific investigation of phenomena, increased knowledge of how things present themselves to our sight, changes the mode but does not necessarily increase the power, of pictorial expression. The Byzantine artists, with a knowledge of appearances infinitely less than that of the average art student of today, could compass the expression of imaginative truths which our most accomplished realists dare not attempt. The essential power of pictorial as of all other arts lies in its use of a fundamental and universal symbolism, and whoever has the instinct for this can convey his ideas, though possessed of only the most rudimentary knowledge of the actual forms of nature; while he who has it not can by no accumulation of observed facts add anything to the spiritual treasure of mankind. Of this language of symbolic form in which the spirit communicates its most secret and indefinable impulses Blake was an eloquent and persuasive master. He could use it, too, to the most diverse ends; and though the sublimity which is based upon dread came most readily to his mind, he could express, as we have seen in the *Flight into Egypt* , the sublimity of divine introspection. In the *David and Bathsheba*[4] he touches a different note, and he shows his true power of symbolic expression in this, that it is not by the treatment of the figure itself, not by any ordinary sensual enticements, that he gives the atmosphere of voluptuous abandonment. It is rather in the extravagant tropical flowers, in the architecture which itself blossoms with oriental exuberance, in the fiery orange of the clouds seen behind trees preternaturally virid,[5] that the spirit is bewildered with anticipations of extravagant bliss. The picture might be described in Blake's own terminology as the mental abstract of voluptuousness.

All art gives us an experience freed from the disturbing conditions of actual life. Blake's art more concentrated than most, gives us an experience which is removed more entirely from bodily and physiological accompaniments, and our experience has the purity, the intensity, and the abstraction of a dream.

CLAUDE

⁕

In spite of all the attacks of critics, in spite of the development of emphasis and high flavour in modern romantic landscape, which might well have spoilt us for his cool simplicity, Claude[1] still lives, not, indeed, as one of the gods of the saleroom, but in the hearts of contemplative and undemonstrative people. This is surely an interesting and encouraging fact. It means that a very purely artistic and poetical appeal still finds its response in the absence of all subsidiary interests and attractions. The appeal is, indeed, a very limited one, touching only certain highly self-conscious and sophisticated moods, but it is, within its limits, so sincere and so poignant that Claude's very failings become, as it were, an essential part of its expression. These failings are, indeed, so many and so obvious that it is not to be wondered at if, now and again, they blind even a sensitive nature like Ruskin's to the fundamental beauty and grandeur of Claude's revelation. But we must be careful not to count as failings qualities which are essential to the particular kind of beauty that Claude envisages, though, to be quite frank, it is sometimes hard to make up one's mind whether a particular characteristic is a lucky defect or a calculated negation. Take, for instance, the peculiar *gaucherie* of his articulations. Claude knows less, perhaps, than any considerable landscape painter – less than the most mediocre of modern landscapists – how to lead from one object to another. His foregrounds are covered with clumsily arranged leaves which have no organic growth, and which, as often as not, lie on the ground instead of springing from it. His trees frequently isolate themselves helplessly from their parent soil. In particular, when he wants a *repoussoir*[2] in the foreground at either end of his composition he has recourse to a clumsily constructed old bare trunk, which has little more meaning than a stage property. Even in his composition there are *naïvetés* which may or may not be intentional: sometimes they have the happiest effect, at others they seem not childlike but childish. Such, for instance, is his frequent habit of dividing spaces equally, both vertically and horizontally, either placing his horizontal line half-way up the picture, or a principal building on the central vertical line. At times this seems the last word of a highly subtilised simplicity, of an artifice which conceals itself; at others one cannot be sure that it is not due to incapacity. There is, in fact, a real excuse for Ruskin's exaggerated paradox that Claude's drawings look like the work of a child of ten.[3] There is a whole world of beauty which one must not look for at all in Claude. All that beauty of the sudden and unexpected revelation of an unsuspected truth which the Gothic and Early Renaissance art provides is absent from Claude. As the eye follows his line it is nowhere arrested by a sense of surprise at its representative power, nor by that peculiar thrill which comes from the communication of some vital creative force in the artist. Compare, for instance, Claude's drawing of mountains, which he knew and studied constantly, with Rembrandt's. Rembrandt had probably never seen mountains, but he obtained a more intimate understanding by the light of his inner vision than Claude could ever attain to by familiarity and study. We need not go to Claude's figures, where he is notoriously feeble and superficially Raphaelesque, in order to find how weak was his hold upon character, whatever the object he set himself to interpret. In the British Museum there is a most careful and elaborate study of the rocky shores of a stream.[4] Claude has even attempted here to render the contorted stratification of the river-bed, but without any of that intimate imaginative grasp of the tension and stress which underlie the appearance and which Turner could give in a few hurried scratches. No one, we may surmise, ever loved trees more deeply than Claude, and we know that he prided himself on his careful observation of the difference of their specific characters; and yet he will articulate their branches in the most haphazard, perfunctory manner. There is nothing in all Claude's innumerable drawings which reveals the inner life of the tree itself, its aspirations towards air and light, its struggle with gravitation and wind, as one little drawing by Leonardo da Vinci does.

All these defects might pass more easily in a turbulent romanticist, hurrying pell mell to get expressed some moving and dramatic scene, careless of details so long as the main movement were ascertained, but there is none of this fire in Claude. It is with slow ponderation and deliberate care that he places before us his perfunctory and generalised statements, finishing and polishing them with relentless assiduity, and not infrequently giving us details that we do not desire and which add nothing but platitude to the too prolix statement.

All this and much more the admirer of Claude will be wise to concede to the adversary, and if the latter ask wherein the beauty of a Claude lies he may with more justice than in any other case fall back on the reply of one of Du Maurier's aesthetes, 'in the picture'.[5] For there is assuredly a kind of beauty which is not only compatible with these defects but perhaps in some degree depends on them. We know and recognise it well enough in literature. To take a random instance. Racine makes Titus say in *Bérénice*: 'De mon aimable erreur je suis désabusé.'[6] This may be a dull, weak, and colourless mode of expression, but if he had said with Shakespeare, 'Now old desire doth in his death-bed lie, and young affection gapes to be his heir',[7] we should feel that it would destroy the particular kind of even and unaccented harmony at which Racine aimed. Robert Bridges, in his essay on Keats, very aptly describes for literature the kind of beauty which we find in Shakespeare: 'the power of concentrating all the far-reaching resources of language on one point, so that a single and apparently effortless expression rejoices the aesthetic imagination at the moment when it is most expectant and exacting.'[8] That, *ceteris paribus*,[9] applies admirably to certain kinds of design. It corresponds to the nervous touch of a Pollaiuolo or a Rembrandt. But Claude's line is almost nerveless and dull. Even when it is most rapid and free it never surprises us by any intimate revelation of character, any summary indications of the central truth. But it has a certain inexpressive beauty of its own. It is never elegant, never florid, and, above all, never has any ostentation of cleverness. The beauty of Claude's work is not to be sought primarily in his drawing; it is not a beauty of expressive parts but the beauty of a whole. It corresponds in fact to the poetry of his century – to Milton or Racine. It is in the cumulative effect of the perfect co-ordination of parts none of which is by itself capable of absorbing our attention or fascinating our imagination that the power of a picture by Claude lies. It is the unity and not the content that affects us. There is, of course, content, but the content is only adequate to its purpose and never claims our attention on its own account. The objects he presents to us have no claim on him but as parts of a scheme. They have no life and purpose of their own, and for that very reason it is right that they should be stated in vague and general terms. He wishes a tree to convey to the eye only what the word 'tree' might suggest at once to the inner vision. We think first of the mass of waving shade held up against the brilliance of the sky, and this, even with all his detailed elaboration, is about where Claude, whether by good fortune or design, leaves us. It is the same with his rocks, his water, his animals. They are all made for the mental imagery of the contemplative wanderer, not of the acute and ardent observer. But where Claude is supreme is in the marvellous invention with which he combines and recombines these abstract symbols so as to arouse in us more purely than nature herself can the mood of pastoral delight. That Claude was deeply influenced by Virgil one would naturally suppose from his antiquarian classicism, and a drawing in the British Museum shows that he had the idea of illustrating the Aeneid.[10] In any case his pictures translate into the language of painting much of the sentiment of Virgil's Eclogues, and that with a purity and grace that rival his original. In his landscapes Meliboeus always leaves his goats to repose with Daphnis under the murmuring shade, waiting till his herds come of themselves to drink at the ford, or in sadder moods of passionless regret one hears the last murmurs of the lament for Gallus as the well-pastured goats turn homewards beneath the evening star.

Claude is the most ardent worshipper that ever was of the *genius loci.* Of his landscapes one always feels that 'some god is in this place'. Never, it is true, one of the greater gods: no mysterious and fearful Pan, no soul-stirring Bacchus or all-embracing Demeter; scarely, though he tried more than once deliberately to invoke them, Apollo and the Muses, but some mild local deity, the inhabitant of a rustic shrine whose presence only heightens the glamour of the scene.

It is the sincerity of this worship, and the purity and directness of its expression, which makes the lover of landscape turn with such constant affection to Claude, and the chief means by which he communicates it is the unity and perfection of his general design; it is not by form considered in itself, but by the planning of his tone divisions, that he appeals, and here, at least, he is a past master. This splendid architecture of the tone masses is, indeed, the really great quality in his pictures; its perfection and solidity are what enables them to bear the weight of so meticulous and, to our minds, tiresome an elaboration of detail without loss of unity, and enables us even to accept the enamelled hardness and tightness of his surface. But many people of today, accustomed to our more elliptical and quick-witted modes of expression, are so impatient of these qualities that they can only appreciate Claude's greatness through the medium of his drawings, where the general skeleton of the design is seen without its adornments, and in a medium which he used with perfect ease and undeniable beauty. Thus to reject the pictures is, I think, an error, because it was only when a design had been exposed to constant correction and purification that Claude got out of it its utmost expressiveness, and his improvisations steadily grow under his critical revision to their full perfection. But in the drawings, at all events, Claude's great powers of design are readily seen, and the study of the drawings has this advantage also, that through them we come to know of a Claude whose existence we could never have suspected by examining only his finished pictures.

In speaking of the drawings it is well to recognise that they fall into different classes with different purposes and aims. We need not, for instance, here consider the records of finished compositions in the *Liber Veritatis*.[11] There remain designs for paintings in all stages of completeness, from the first suggestive idea to the finished cartoon and the drawings from nature. It is, perhaps, scarcely necessary to remark that it would have been quite foreign to Claude's conception of his art to have painted a picture from nature. He, himself, clearly distinguished sharply between his studies and his compositions. His studies, therefore, were not incipient pictures, but exercises done for his own pleasure or for the fertility they gave to his subsequent invention, and they have the unchecked spontaneity and freedom of hand that one would expect in such unreflecting work. These studies again fall into two groups: first, studies of detail, generally of foliage or of tree forms, and occasionally of rocks and flowers; and secondly, studies of general effects. Of the studies of detail I have already said something. They have the charm of an easy and distinguished calligraphy, and of a refined selection of the decorative possibilities of the things seen, but without any of that penetrating investigation of their vital nature which gives its chief beauty to the best work of this kind.

It is, indeed, in the second group of studies from nature that we come from time to time upon motives that startle and surprise us. We find in these a susceptibility to natural charms which, in its width of range and freedom from the traditional limitations of the art of landscape, is most remarkable. Here we find not only Claude the prim seventeenth-century classic, but Claude the romanticist, anticipating the chief ideas of Corot's later development,* and Claude the impressionist, anticipating Whistler and the discovery of Chinese landscape, as, for instance, in the marvellous *aperçu* of a mist effect, in the British Museum.†[12] Or, again, in a view which is quite different from any of these, but quite as remote from the Claude of the oil-paintings, in the great view of the Tiber, a masterpiece of hurried, almost unconscious planning of bold contrasts of transparent gloom and dazzling light on water and plain.[13]

The impression one gets from looking through a collection of Claude's drawings like that at the British Museum is of a man without any keen feeling for objects in themselves, but singularly open to impressions of general effects in nature, watching

* As, for instance, in a wonderful drawing, *On the Banks of the Tiber*, in Mr Heseltine's collection.[14]

† It is not impossible that Claude got the hint for such a treatment as this from the impressionist efforts of Graeco-Roman painters. That he studied such works we know from a copy of one by him in the British Museum.[15]

always for the shifting patterns of foliage and sky to arrange themselves in some beautifully significant pattern and choosing it with fine and critical taste. But at the same time he was a man with vigorous ideas of the laws of design and the necessity of perfectly realised unity, and to this I suppose one must ascribe the curious contrast between the narrow limits of his work in oil as compared with the wide range, the freedom and the profound originality of his work as a draughtsman. Among all these innumerable effects which his ready susceptibility led him to record he found but a few which were capable of being reduced to that logical and mathematical formula which he demanded before complete realisation could be tolerated. In his drawings he composes sometimes with strong diagonal lines, sometimes with free and unstable balance. In his pictures he has recourse to a regular system of polarity, balancing his masses carefully on either side of the centre, sometimes even framing it in like a theatrical scene with two *repoussoirs* pushed in on either side. One must suppose, then, that he approached the composition of his pictures with a certain timidity, that he felt that safety, when working on a large scale, could only be secured by a certain recognised type of structure, so that out of all the various moods of nature to which his sensitive spirit answered only one lent itself to complete expression. One wishes at times that he had tried more. There is in the British Museum a half-effaced drawing on blue paper, an idea for treating the *Noli me tangere*[16] which, had he worked it out, would have added to his complete mastery of bucolic landscape a masterpiece of what one may call tragic landscape. It is true that here, as elsewhere, the figures are in themselves totally inadequate, but they suggested an unusual and intense key to the landscape. On the outskirts of a dimly suggested wood the figures meet and hold converse; to the right the mound of Calvary glimmers pale and ghostlike against the night sky, while over the distant city the first pink flush of dawn begins. It is an intensely poetical conception. Claude has here created a landscape in harmony with deeper, more mystical aspirations than elsewhere, and, had he given free rein to his sensibilities, we should look to him even more than we do now as the greatest inventor of the motives of pure landscape. As it is, the only ideas to which he gave complete though constantly varied expression are those of pastoral repose.

Claude's view of landscape is false to nature in that it is entirely anthropocentric. His trees exist for pleasant shade; his peasants to give us the illusion of pastoral life, not to toil for a living. His world is not to be lived in, only to be looked at in a mood of pleasing melancholy or suave reverie. It is, therefore, as true to one aspect of human desire, as it is false to the facts of life. It may be admitted that this is not the finest kind of art – it is the art of a self-centred and refined luxury which looks on nature as a garden to its own pleasure-house – but few will deny its genial and moderating charm, and few of us live so strenuously as never to feel a sense of nostalgia for that Saturnian reign to which Virgil and Claude can waft us.

AUBREY BEARDSLEY'S DRAWINGS

✱

MESSRS. CARFAX have on view the most complete collection of Beardsley's drawings that has hitherto been shown. The development of his precocious and eccentric genius can here be studied in typical examples. We have the drawings of his childhood – drawings inspired by Dicky Doyle and Robida,[1] but in which is already apparent his proclivity to the expression of moral depravity. We pass at a leap from these crude and artistically feeble works to the astonishing *Siegfried*,[2] in which he is already a complete and assured master of an entirely personal style.

From this time onwards, for the remaining six years of his life, Beardsley kept on producing with the fertility of those artists whom the presage of an early death stimulates to a desperate activity. His style was constantly changing in accidentals, but always the same in essentials. He was a confirmed eclectic, borrowing from all ages and all countries. And true eclectic and genuine artist as he was, he converted all his borrowings to his own purposes. It mattered nothing what he fed on; the strange and perverse economy of his nature converted the food into a poison. His line is based upon that of Antonio Pollaiuolo.[3] Again and again in his drawings of the nude we see how carefully he must have copied that master of structural and nervous line. But he uses it for someting quite other than its original purpose; he converts it from a line expressive of muscular tension and virile force into one expressive of corruption and decay. Mantegna,[4] too, was a favourite with Beardsley, who seems to have had a kind of craving for the opposites to his own predominant qualities; and from Mantegna, the most austere of Italians, he derived again and again motives for his illustrations of depravity. The eighteenth century, China, Japan, even the purest Greek art, were all pressed into his service; the only thing he could do nothing with was nature itself. Here he was entirely at a loss, and whenever he yielded to the pressure of contemporary fashions and attempted to record impressions of things seen, as in the topical illustrations of plays which he contributed to the *Pall Mall Magazine*, he failed to be even mediocre. Everything that was to be in the least expressive had to come entirely from within, from the nightmares of his own imagination.

His amazing gift of hand is perhaps the quality which most obviously attracts attention, the quality which endeared him most to publishers and process-block makers. It was the one indisputable quality he possessed, not to be denied by the most adverse critic, and yet in itself it is no more than thousands of journeymen artists – engravers, die-cutters, and such like – have always possessed. Nor, to be perfectly frank, is the quality of his line of a very high order; its precision is not unfrequently mechanical. Whistler called him the last of the writing-masters, and there was a truth in this, if we may add that the style of writing which he favoured was degenerate. His long, meandering flourishes ending in sharp spikes and dots, however firm and precise the line, are often mean in intention and poor in quality. What is deserving of real admiration is the fertility of his invention, the skill with which he finds the formula which corresponds, in his peculiar language, with what he wants to describe. As an instance, one may take the garden background to the *Platonic Lament* in the Salome series,[5] where the rose trellis and cut yew-tree behind are brilliant examples of this kind of epitomised description. Still more important artistically, and closely connected with this power of invention, is the real beauty of his spacing, the admirable planning of masses of black and white. At times, as in the *Dancer's Reward*, he rises almost to the height of the great Greek vase-painters in this respect, though, if we look even at this in detail, the line has an intricacy, a *mesquinerie*,[6] which is the very opposite of the Greek ideal of draughtsmanship.

No less remarkable is his success in the decorative planning of three tones, of black, white, and grey, and he divides these with such subtle skill that for once it is not a mere false analogy to talk of the colour effect of designs in black and white; for he so disposes the three tones, getting the grey by an evenly distributed network of fine black lines, that each tone produces the sensation of something as distinct from the others as do flat washes of different tints. The *Frontispiece to Salome* is an excellent example of this.

Beardsley had, then, in an extraordinary degree the decorative impulse, the motive which made the mediaeval scribe flourish his pen all over the margins of his vellum page; and, spurred by this impulse, he had the patience of an Indian craftsman, covering whole sheets with minute dots and scarcely perceptible lines. This instinct in its purest form rarely makes for the finest art; it is only when controlled by a larger, more genial sentiment for architectural mass that it becomes ennobled, and with Beardsley, in spite of the bold oppositions of his blacks and whites, in spite of his occasional wilful simplification, this rarely occurred. One might even argue that to some extent Beardsley's moral perversity actually prevented him, in spite of his extraordinary specific talent for design, from ever becoming a great designer. It was just this *mesquinerie* of line, this littleness and intricacy of the mere decorator, this love of elegance rather than beauty, which on purely artistic grounds one finds to be his great failing, that he cherished as a means of expressing his diabolism. But if Beardsley was corrupt, he was certainly sincere in his corruption. There is no suggestion in his work, as in that of some modern artists, like Señor Zuloaga,[7] that corruption is an affectation taken up in order to astonish the *bourgeoisie*. Beardsley is never funny or amusing or witty; his attempts in this direction are contemptible; still less is he voluptuous or seductive; he is very serious, very much in earnest. There is even a touch of hieratic austerity and pomp in his style, as becomes the archpriest of a Satanic cultus. He has, indeed, all the stigmata of the religious artist – the love of pure decoration, the patient elaboration and enrichment of surface, the predilection for flat tones and precision of contour, the want of the sense of mass and relief, the extravagant richness of invention. It is as the Fra Angelico of Satanism that his work will always have an interest for those who are curious about this recurrent phase of complex civilisations. But if we are right in our analysis of his work, the finest qualities of design can never be appropriated to the expression of such morbid and perverted ideals; nobility and geniality of design are attained only by those who, whatever their actual temperament, cherish these qualities in their imagination.

THE FRENCH POST-IMPRESSIONISTS

✱

WHEN the first Post-Impressionist Exhibition was held in these Galleries two years ago[1] the English public became for the first time fully aware of the existence of a new movement in art, a movement which was the more disconcerting in that it was no mere variation upon accepted themes but implied a reconsideration of the very purpose and aim as well as the methods of pictorial and plastic art. It was not surprising, therefore, that a public which had come to admire above everything in a picture the skill with which the artist produced illusion should have resented an art in which such skill was completely subordinated to the direct expression of feeling. Accusations of clumsiness and incapacity were freely made, even against so singularly accomplished an artist as Cézanne. Such darts, however, fall wide of the mark, since it is not the object of these artists to exhibit their skill or proclaim their knowledge, but only to attempt to express by pictorial and plastic form certain spiritual experiences; and in conveying these, ostentation of skill is likely to be even more fatal than downright incapacity.

Indeed, one may fairly admit that the accusation of want of skill and knowledge, while ridiculous in the case of Cézanne is perfectly justified as regards one artist represented – for the first time in England – in the present Exhibition, namely, Rousseau.[2] Rousseau was a custom-house officer who painted without any training in the art. His pretensions to paint made him the butt of a great deal of ironic wit, but scarcely any one now would deny the authentic quality of his inspiration or the certainty of his imaginative conviction. Here then is one case where want of skill and knowledge do not completely obscure, though they may mar, expression. And this is true of all perfectly naïve and primitive art. But most of the art here seen is neither naïve nor primitive. It is the work of highly civilised and

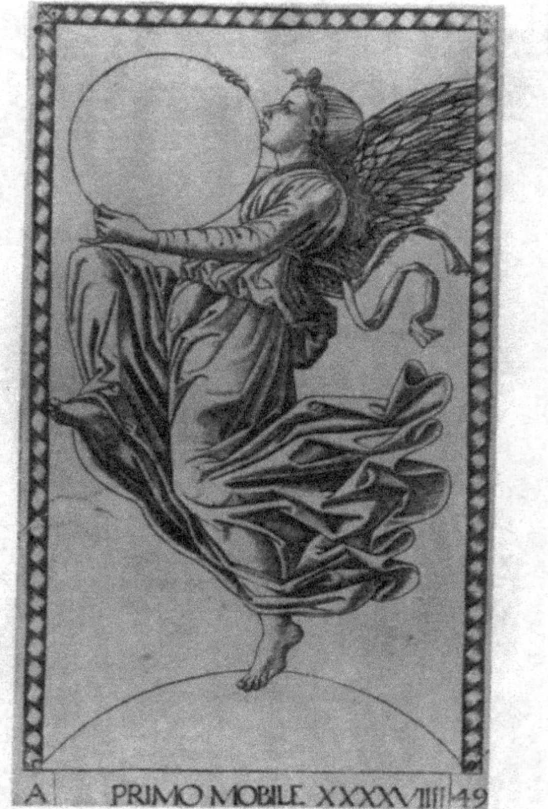

V.1 'Tarocchi print', Primum Mobile. 17.9 × 10 cm.

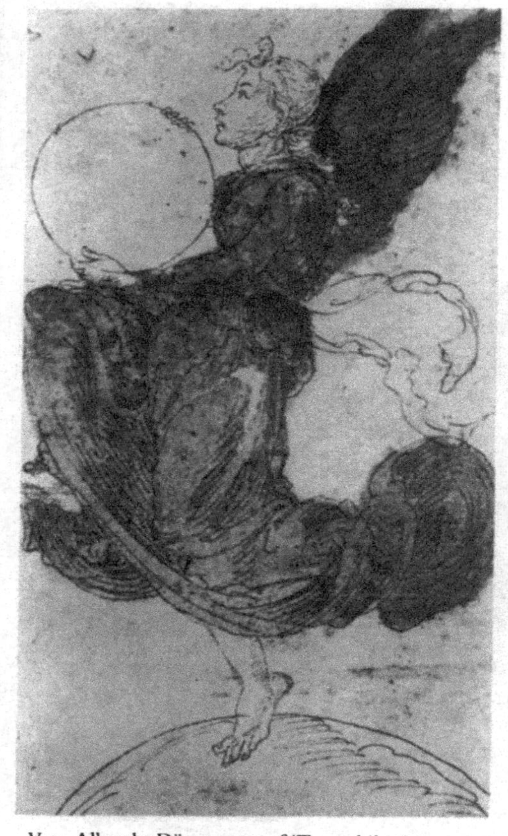

V.2 Albrecht Dürer: copy of 'Tarocchi' print. 1494. Pen and ink: 19 × 10.6 cm.

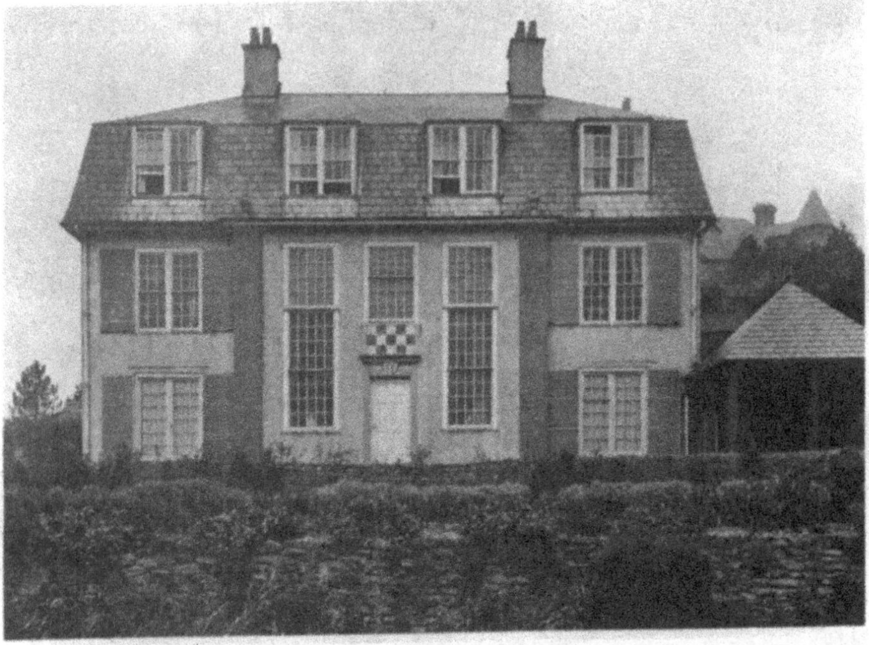

VI.1 'Durbins', front elevation. *Vogue*, March 1918.

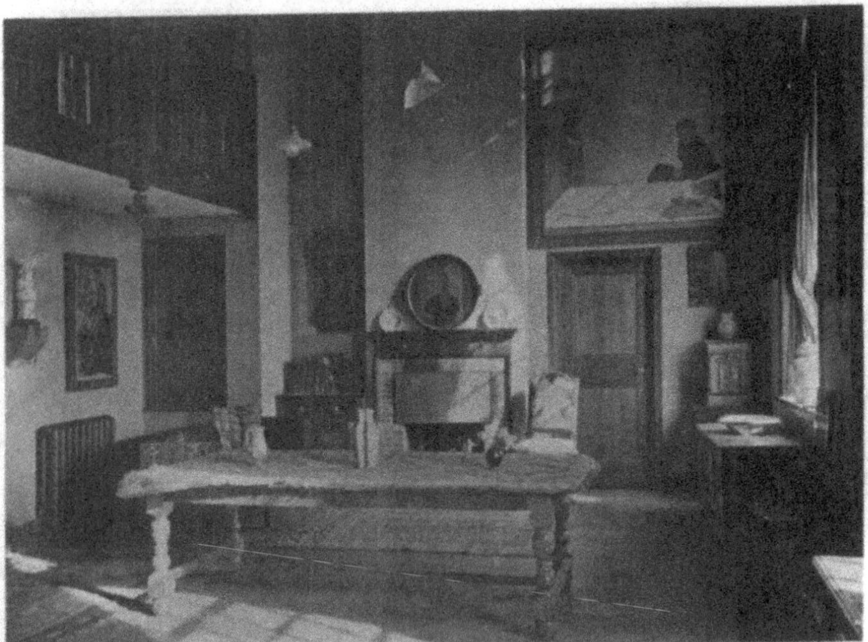

VI.2 'Durbins', living room. *Vogue*, March 1918.

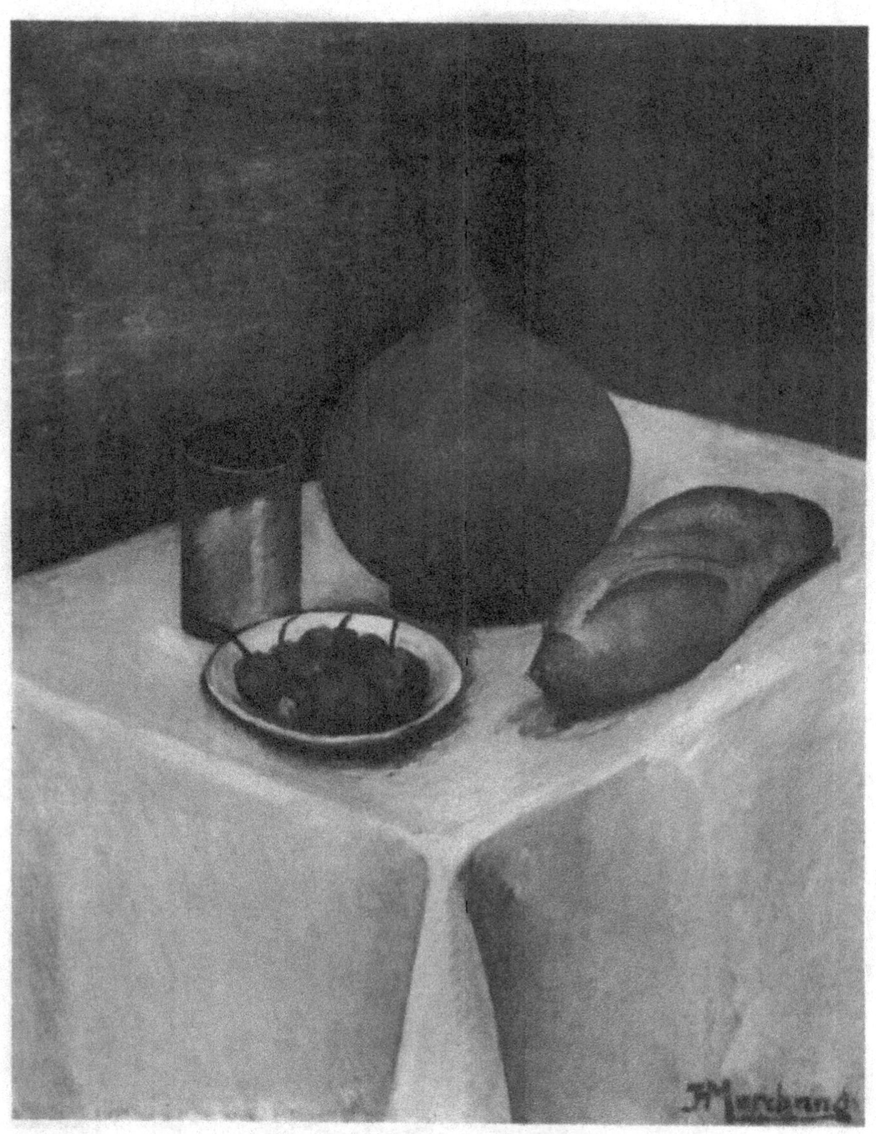

VII Jean Marchand: Still Life, n.d. Oil on canvas: 65.1 × 53.4 cm.

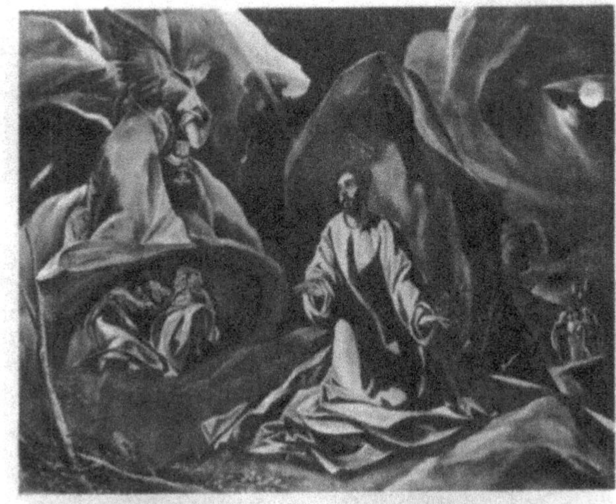

VIII.1 El Greco: The Agony in the Garden. *c.*1590. Oil on canvas: 102 × 131 cm.

VIII.2 Raphael: The Transfiguration. 1518–20. Oil on panel: 405 × 278 cm.

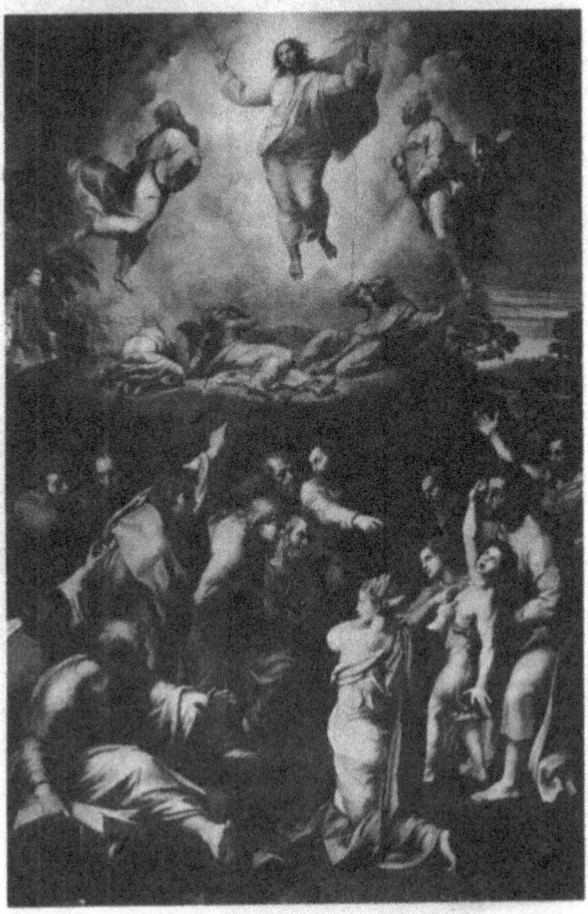

modern men trying to find a pictorial language appropriate to the sensibilities of the modern outlook.

Another charge that is frequently made against these artists is that they allow what is merely capricious, or even what is extravagant and eccentric, in their work – that it is not serious, but an attempt to impose on the good-natured tolerance of the public. This charge of insincerity and extravagance is invariably made against any new manifestation of creative art. It does not of course follow that it is always wrong. The desire to impose by such means certainly occurs, and is sometimes temporarily successful. But the feeling on the part of the public may, and I think in this case does, arise from a simple misunderstanding of what these artists set out to do. The difficulty springs from a deep-rooted conviction, due to long-established custom, that the aim of painting is the descriptive imitation of natural forms. Now, these artists do not seek to give what can, after all, be but a pale reflex of actual appearance, but to arouse the conviction of a new and definite reality. They do not seek to imitate form, but to create form; not to imitate life, but to find an equivalent for life. By that I mean that they wish to make images which by the clearness of their logical structure, and by their closely-knit unity of texture, shall appeal to our disinterested and contemplative imagination with something of the same vividness as the things of actual life appeal to our practical activities. In fact, they aim not at illusion but at reality.

The logical extreme of such a method would undoubtedly be the attempt to give up all resemblance to natural form, and to create a purely abstract language of form – a visual music; and the later works of Picasso[3] show this clearly enough. They may or may not be successful in their attempt. It is too early to be dogmatic on the point, which can only be decided when our sensibilities to such abstract forms have been more practised than they are at present. But I would suggest that there is nothing ridiculous in the attempt to do this. Such a picture as Picasso's *Head of a Man*[4] would undoubtedly be ridiculous if, having set out to make a direct imitation of the actual model, he had been incapable of getting a better likeness. But Picasso did nothing of the sort. He has shown in his *Portrait of Mlle L. B.*

that he could do so at least as well as any one if he wished, but he is here attempting to do something quite different.

No such extreme abstraction marks the work of Matisse. The actual objects which stimulated his creative invention are recognisable enough. But here, too, it is an equivalence, not a likeness, of nature that is sought. In opposition to Picasso, who is pre-eminently plastic, Matisse aims at convincing us of the reality of his forms by the continuity and flow of his rhythmic line, by the logic of his space relations, and, above all, by an entirely new use of colour. In this, as in his markedly rhythmic design, he approaches more than any other European to the ideals of Chinese art. His work has to an extraordinary degree that decorative unity of design which distinguishes all the artists of this school.

Between these two extremes we may find ranged almost all the remaining artists. On the whole the influence of Picasso on the younger men is more evident than that of Matisse. With the exception of Braque none of them push their attempts at abstraction of form so far as Picasso, but simplification along these lines is apparent in the work of Derain, Herbin, Marchand, and L'Hote.[5] Other artists, such as Doucet and Asselin,[6] are content with the ideas of simplification of form as existing in the general tradition of the Post-Impressionist movement, and instead of feeling for new methods of expression devote themselves to expressing what is most poignant and moving in contemporary life. But however various the directions in which different groups are exploring the newly-found regions of expressive form they all alike derive in some measure from the great originator of the whole idea, Cézanne. And since one must always refer to him to understand the origin of these ideas, it has been thought well to include a few examples of his work in the present Exhibition, although this year it is mainly the moderns, and not the old masters, that are represented. To some extent, also, the absence of the earlier masters in the exhibition itself is made up for by the retrospective exhibition of Monsieur Druet's admirable photographs. Here Cézanne, Gauguin, and Van Gogh can be studied at least in the main phases of their development.

Finally, I should like to call attention to a distinguishing characteristic of the French artists seen here, namely, the markedly Classic spirit of their work. This will be noted as distinguishing them to some extent from the English, even more perhaps from the Russians, and most of all from the great mass of modern painting in every country. I do not mean by Classic, dull, pedantic, traditional, reserved, or any of those similar things which the word is often made to imply. Still less do I mean by calling them Classic that they paint 'Visits to Aesculapius' or 'Nero at the Colosseum'.[7] I mean that they do not rely for their effect upon associated ideas, as I believe Romantic and Realistic artists invariably do.

All art depends upon cutting off the practical responses to sensations of ordinary life, thereby setting free a pure and as it were disembodied functioning of the spirit; but in so far as the artist relies on the associated ideas of the objects which he represents, his work is not completely free and pure, since romantic associations imply at least an imagined practical activity. The disadvantage of such an art of associated ideas is that its effect really depends on what we bring with us: it adds no entirely new factor to our experience. Consequently, when the first shock of wonder or delight is exhausted the work produces an ever lessening reaction. Classic art, on the other hand, records a positive and disinterestedly passionate state of mind. It communicates a new and otherwise unattainable experience. Its effect, therefore, is likely to increase with familiarity. Such a classic spirit is common to the best French work of all periods from the twelfth century onwards, and though no one could find direct reminiscences of a Nicolas Poussin here, his spirit seems to revive in the work of artists like Derain. It is natural enough that the intensity and singleness of aim with which these artists yield themselves to certain experiences in the face of nature may make their work appear odd to those who have not the habit of contemplative vision, but it would be rash for us, who as a nation are in the habit of treating our emotions, especially our aesthetic emotions, with a certain levity, to accuse them of caprice or insincerity. It is because of this classic concentration of feeling (which by no means implies abandonment) that the French merit our serious attention. It is this that makes their art so difficult on a first approach but gives it its lasting hold on the imagination.

NOTE – At least one French artist of great merit was unrepresented at the Post-Impressionist Exhibitions – Georges Rouault,[8] a fellow-pupil with Matisse of Gustave Moreau.[9] He stands alone in the movement as being a visionary, though, unlike most visionaries, his expression is based on a profound knowledge of natural appearances. (1920.)

DRAWINGS AT THE BURLINGTON FINE ARTS CLUB

✱

THE Burlington Fine Arts Club have arranged a most interesting collection of drawings by dead masters. Abandoning the club's usual method of taking a particular period or country, the committee have this time allowed their choice to range over many periods and countries, excluding only living artists, and admitting one so recently dead as Degas.[1] This variety of material naturally stimulates one to hazard some general speculations on the nature of drawing as an art. 'H.T.', who writes the preface to the catalogue, already points the way in this direction by some *obiter dicta*. He points out that the essence of drawing is not the line, but its content. He says:

A single line may mean nothing beyond a line; add another alongside and both disappear, and we are aware only of the contents, and a form is expressed. The beauty of a line is in its result in the form which it helps to bring into being.[2]

Here the author has undoubtedly pointed out the most essential quality of good drawing. I should dispute, rather by way of excessive caution, his first statement, 'A single line may mean nothing beyond a line', since a line is always at least the record of a gesture, indicating a good deal about its maker's personality, his tastes and even probably the period when he lived; but I entirely agree that the main point is always the effect which two lines have of evoking the idea of a certain volume having a certain form. When 'H. T.' adds that 'Draughtsmen know this, but writers on art do not seem to',[3] he seems to be too sweeping. Even so bad a writer on art as Pliny had picked up the idea from a Greek art critic, for in describing the drawing of Parrhasios[4] he says:

By the admission of artists he was supreme in contour. This is the last subtlety of painting; for to paint the main body and centres of objects is indeed something of an achievement, but one in which many have been famous, but to paint the edges of bodies and express the disappearing planes is rare in the history of art. For the contour must go round itself and so end that it promises other things behind and shows that which it hides.*

This is an admirable account, since it gives the clue to the distinction between descriptive drawing and drawing in which the contour does not arrest the form, but creates plastic relief of the whole enclosed volume. Now, this plastic drawing can never be attained by a mere *description* of the edges of objects. Such a description, however exact, can at the utmost do no more than recall vividly the original object; it cannot enable the spectator to realise its plastic volume more clearly than the original object would. Now, when we look at a really good drawing we do get a much more vivid sense of a plastic volume than we get from actual objects.

Unfortunately this is a very severe test to apply, and would, I think, relegate to an inferior class the vast majority of drawings, even those in the present exhibition. The vast majority of drawings even by the celebrated masters do appeal mainly by other more subsidiary qualities, by the brightness of their descriptive power, and by the elegance and facility of their execution. There is an undoubted pleasure in the contemplation of mere skill, and there are few ways of demonstrating sheer skill of hand more convincingly than the drawing of a complex series of curves with perfect exactitude and great rapidity. And when the curves thus brilliantly drawn describe vividly some object in life towards which we have pleasing associations we

* I have had to paraphrase this passage, but add the original. Whether my paraphrase is correct in detail or not, I think there can be little doubt about the general meaning.

Plin., *Nat. Hist.*, xxxv. 67: 'Parrhasius... confessione artificum in liniis extremis palmam adeptus. Haec est picturae summa sublimitas; corpora enim pingere et media rerum est quidem magni operis, sed in quo multi gloriam tulerint. Extrema corporum facere et desinentis picturae modum includere rarum in successu artis invenitur. Ambire enim debet se extremitas ipsa, et sic desinere ut promittat alia post se ostendatque etiam quae occultat.'

get a complex pleasure which is only too likely to be regarded as an aesthetic experience when it is in fact nothing of the kind.

The author of the preface has quite clearly seen that this element of brilliance in the execution of the line does frequently come into play, and he considers this calligraphic quality to be always a sign of lowered aesthetic purpose, citing Tiepolo[5] quite rightly as a great master of such qualities. And he quite rightly points out that with the deliberate pursuit of calligraphy there is always a tendency to substitute type forms for individual forms. On the other hand, all good drawing also tends to create types, since a type results from the synthetic unity of the design. The real question here would seem to be the fullness or emptiness of the type created, and it would be fair to say that the calligraphic draughtsman accepted most readily an empty type. For instance, one would have to admit that Ingres created a type, and repeated it as much as Tiepolo, only Ingres continually generated his type of form upon actual material, whereas Tiepolo tended merely to repeat his without enriching it with fresh material.

The exhibition has been to some extent arranged around Ingres, and as many of his drawings as possible have been collected. Ingres has long been accepted in the schools as *par excellence* the great modern master of drawing. His great saying, '*Le dessin c'est la probité de l'art*',[6] has indeed become a watchword of the schools and an excuse for indulgence in a great deal of gratuitous and misplaced moral feeling. It has led to the display of all kinds of pedagogic folly. Art is a passion or it is nothing. It is certainly a very bad moral gymnasium. It is useless to try to make a kind of moral parallel bars out of the art of drawing. You will certainly spoil the drawing, and it is doubtful if you will get the morals. Drawing is a passion to the draughtsman just as much as colour is to the colourist, and the draughtsman has no reason to feel moral superiority because of the nature of his passion. He is fortunate to have it, and there is an end of the matter. Ingres himself had the passion for draughtsmanship very intensely, though perhaps one would scarcely guess it from the specimens shown in this exhibition. These unfortunately are, with a few exceptions, taken from the large class of drawings which he did as a young man in Rome. He was already married, and was poor. He was engaged on some of his biggest and most important compositions, on which he was determined to spare no pains or labour; consequently he found himself forced to earn his living by doing these brilliant and minutely accurate portraits of the aristocratic tourists and their families, who happened to pass through Rome. These drawings bear the unmistakable mark of their origins. They are commissions, and they are done to satisfy the sitter. Anything like serious research for form is out of the question; there is little here but Ingres's extreme facility and a certain negative good taste. Probably the only drawing here which shows Ingres's more serious powers is the tight, elaborate and rather repellent study for the *Apotheosis of Napoleon,*[7] which is a splendid discovery of composition within a round. But the real fact is, I believe, that Ingres's power as a draughtsman hardly ever comes out fully in his drawings; one must turn to his paintings to see how great and sincere a researcher he was. In his drawings he was too much preoccupied with the perfect description of facts; when he came to the painting he began that endless process of readjustment and balance of contours which make him so great and original a designer. If one places his drawings and studies from the nude for, say, his *Venus Anadyomene*[8] beside the photograph of the picture one gets some idea of the tireless and passionate research for the exact correspondence of the contours on either side of the figure which Ingres undertook. He throws over one by one all the brilliant notations of natural form in the studies, and arrives bit by bit at an intensely abstract and simplified statement of the general relations. But though the new statement is emptied of its factual content, it has now become far more compact, far more intense in its plasticity. Here and there among Ingres's innumerable drawings one may find a nude study in which already this process of elimination and balance has taken place, but the examples are rare, and if one would understand why Ingres is one of the great masters of design, one must face the slightly repellent quality of his oil paintings rather than allow oneself to be seduced by the elegance and ease of his drawings.

It would, I think, be possible to show that very few great

designers have attained to full expression in line. I suspect indeed, that the whole tradition of art in Europe, since about the end of the fifteenth century, has been against such complete expression. If we compare the great masterpieces of pure drawing such as the drawings of figures on Persian pots of the twelfth and thirteenth centuries, and the few remaining examples of drawings by the Italian primitives of the fourteenth and early fifteenth centuries, with the vast mass of European drawings subsequent to that date, we see, I think, the contrast of aims and purpose of the two groups. Somewhere about the time of Filippino Lippi there was formulated an idea of drawing which has more or less held the field ever since in art schools.

As most drawing has centred in the human figure we may describe it in relation to that, the more so that this view of drawing undoubtedly came in with the study of anatomy. The general principle is that there are certain cardinal facts about the figure, or points of cardinal importance in the rendering of structure – the artist is trained to observe these with special care, since they become the *points de repère* for his drawing. And since they are thus specially observed they are noted with a special accent. When once the artist has learned to grasp the relations of these *points de repère* firmly he learns also to pass from one to the other with great ease and rapidity, not to say with a certain indifference as to what happens in the passage. By this method the essentials of structure and movement of a figure are accurately given and the whole statement can be made with that easy facility and rapidity of line which gives a peculiar pleasure. Such drawing has the merit of being at once structurally accurate and more or less calligraphically pleasing. The most admired masters, such as Vandyke, Watteau, even to some extent Rubens, all exhibit the characteristics of such a conception. Now in the earlier kind of drawing there were no recognised *points de repère*, no particular moments of emphasis; the line was so drawn that at every point its relation to the opposed contour was equally close, the tension so to speak was always across the line and not along its direction. The essential thing was the position of the line, not its quality, so that there was the less inclination to aim at that easy rapidity which marks the later draughtsmanship. Essentially, then, this earlier drawing was less descriptive and more purely evocative of form. It may well be that the demands made upon the artist by the closer study of nature brought in by the Renaissance became an almost insuperable barrier to artists in the attempt to find any such completely synthetic vision of form as lay to hand for their predecessors. We see, for instance, in Albert Dürer's *Beetle*[9] an example of purely descriptive and analytic drawing with no attempt at inner coherence of form. On the other hand, of course, all the great formalists made deliberate efforts to come through the complex of phenomena to some abstract synthesis. Fra Bartolomeo and Raphael clearly made such abstraction a matter of deliberate study, but as I have pointed out in the case of Ingres, the obsession of fact has generally forced the artist to such a long series of experiments towards the final synthetic form that it is only in the finished picture that it emerges fully.

On the other hand, some modern masters have also found their way through, more or less completely, and from this point of view few drawings in the exhibition are as remarkable as the drawing of a seated woman by Corot. Here one supposes it may be a kind of *naïveté* of vision rather than the exhaustive process of an Ingres, that has led Corot to this vividly realised plasticity of form. I find the essentials of good drawing more completely realised here than in almost any other drawing in the exhibition, and yet how little of a professional draughtsman Corot was. It is hard to speak here of Degas's works as drawings. With one exception they are pastels and essentially paintings, but they are of great beauty and show him victorious over his own formidable cleverness, his unrivalled but dangerous power of witty notation.

At the opposite pole to Corot's drawing with its splendid revelation of plastic significance we must put Menzel[10] with his fussy preoccupation with undigested fact. It is hard indeed to see quite how Menzel's drawings found their way into this good company, except perhaps as drunken helots, for they are conspicuously devoid of any aesthetic quality whatever. They are without any rhythmic unity, without any glimmering of a sense of style, and style though it be as cheap as Rowlandson's is still victorious over sheer misinformed literalness. Somewhere between Menzel and Corot we must place Charles Keane,[11] and I fear, in spite of the rather exaggerated claims made for him in the preface, he is nearer to Menzel, though even so, how much better! The early Millais drawing is of course an astounding attempt by a man of prodigious gift and no sensibility to pretend that he had the latter. It is a pity there are no Rossettis here to show the authentic inspiration of which this is the echo.

I come now to the Rembrandts, of which there are several good examples. Rembrandt always intrigues one by the multiplicity and diversity of his gifts and the struggle between his profound imaginative insight and his excessive talents. The fact is, I believe that Rembrandt was never a linealist, that he never had the conception of contour clearly present to him. He was too intensely and too inveterately a painter and chiaroscurist. The last thing he saw was a contour, and more than anything else it eluded his vision. His vision was in fact so intensely fixed on the interplay of planes, their modulation into one another, and on the balance of directions, that with him the drawn line has a quite peculiar and personal meaning. It is used first to indicate directions of stress and movement, as, for instance, a straight line will be dashed down to indicate, not the contour of a limb, but its direction, the line along which stress of action takes place. He seems almost to dread the contour, to prefer to make strokes either inside or outside of it, and to trust to the imagination to discover its whereabouts, anything rather than a final definite statement which would arrest the interplay of planes. The line is also used to suggest very vaguely and tentatively the division of planes; but almost always when he comes to use wash on top of the line his washes go across the lines, so that here too one can hardly say the line indicates the division so much as the approximate position of a plane.

In conclusion I would suggest that the art of pure contour is comparatively rare in modern art. For what I should cite as great and convincing examples of that art I would ask the reader to turn to the 'Morgan Byzantine Enamels', the 'Manafi-i-Heiwan', and to Vignier, 'Persian Pottery',[12] while other examples might be found among Byzantine and Carolingian miniaturists.

Now, this art depends upon a peculiarly synthetic vision and a peculiar system of distortion, without which the outline would arrest the movement of planes too definitely. There indeed is the whole crux of the art of line drawing; the line generates a volume, but it also arrests the planes too definitely: that is why in some great modern artists, as we saw in the case of Rembrandt, there is a peculiar kind of dread of the actual contour. It is felt by those who are sensitive to the interplay and movement of planes that the line must in some way, by its quality or its position, or by breaks or repetitions, avoid arresting the imagination by too positive a statement. It was almost a peculiarity of the early art that I have cited that it was able to express a form in a quite complete, evenly drawn contour without this terrible negative effect of the line. I say almost a peculiarity, because I think a few quite modern artists, such as Matisse and perhaps Modigliani,[13] have recovered such a power, but in the great mass of post-Renaissance drawing the art of the pure contour in line has broken down, and the essential qualities even of the great linealists are only to be seen fully in their paintings; the drawn line itself has had to take on other functions.

PAUL CÉZANNE

In a society which is as indifferent to works of art as our modern industrialism it seems paradoxical that artists of all kinds should loom so large in the general consciousness of mankind – that they should be remembered with reverence and boasted of as national assets when statesmen, lawyers, and soldiers are forgotten. The great mass of modern men could rub along happily enough without works of art or at least without new ones, but society would be sensibly more bored if the artist died out altogether. The fact is that every honest bourgeois, however sedate and correct his life, keeps a hidden and scarce-admitted yearning for that other life of complete individualism which hard necessity or the desire for sucess has denied him. In contemplating the artist he tastes vicariously these forbidden joys. He regards the artist as a strange species, half idiot, half divine, but above all irresponsibly and irredeemably himself. He seems equally strange in his outrageous egoism and his superb devotion to an idea.

Also in a world where the individual is squeezed and moulded and polished by the pressure of his fellow-men the artist remains irreclaimably individual – in a world where every one else is being perpetually educated the artist remains ineducable – where others are shaped, he grows. Cézanne realised the type of the artist in its purest, most unmitigated form, and M. Vollard has had the wit to write a book about Cézanne and not about Cézanne's pictures. The time may come when we shall require a complete study of Cézanne's work, a measured judgment of his achievement and position – it would probably be rash to attempt it as yet. Meanwhile we have M. Vollard's portrait, at once documented and captivating.[1] Should the book ever become as well known as it deserves there would be, one guesses, ten people fascinated by Cézanne for one who would walk down the street to see his pictures.

The art historian may sometimes regret that Vasari did not give us more of the aesthetics of his time; but Vasari knew his business, knew, perhaps, that the aesthetics of an age are quickly superseded but that the human document remains of perennial interest to mankind. M. Vollard has played Vasari to Cézanne and done so with the same directness and simplicity, the same narrative ease, the same insatiable delight in the oddities and idiosyncrasies of his subject. And what a model he had to paint! Every word and every gesture he records sticks out with the rugged relief of a character in which everything is due to the compulsion of inner forces, in which nothing has been planed down or smoothed away by external pressure – not that external pressure was absent but that the inner compulsion – the inevitable bent of Cézanne's temperament, was irresistible. In one very important detail Cézanne was spared by life – he always had enough to live on. The thought of a Cézanne having to earn his living is altogether too tragic. But if life spared him in this respect his temperament spared him nothing – for this rough Provençal countryman had so exasperated a sensibility that the smallest detail of daily life, the barking of a dog, the noise of a lift in a neighbouring house, the dread of being touched even by his own son might produce at any moment a nervous explosion. At such times his first relief was in cursing and swearing, but if this failed the chances were that his anger vented itself on his pictures – he would cut one to pieces with his palette knife, or failing that roll it up and throw it into the stove. M. Vollard describes with delightful humour the tortures he endured in the innumerable sittings which he gave Cézanne for his portrait – with what care he avoided any subject of conversation which might lead to misunderstanding. But with all his adroitness there were one or two crises in which the portrait was threatened with the dreaded knife – fortunately Cézanne always found some other work on which to vent his indignation, and the portrait survived, though after a hundred and fifteen sittings, in which Cézanne exacted the immobility of an apple, the portrait was left incomplete. 'I am not displeased with the shirt front,' was Cézanne's characteristic appreciation.[2]

Two phrases continually recur in Cézanne's conversation

which show his curious idiosyncrasies. One the often-quoted one of his dread that any one might '*lui jetter le grappin dessus*'[3] and the other '*moi qui suis faible dans la vie*'.[4] They express his constant attitude of distrust of his kind – for him all women were '*des veaux et des calculatrices*'[5] – his dread of any possible invasion of his personality, and his sense of impotence in face of the forces of life.

None the less, though he pathetically exaggerated his weakness he never seems to have had the least doubt about his supreme greatness as an artist; what troubled and irritated him was his incapacity to express his 'sensation' in such terms as would make its meaning evident to the world. It was for this reason that he struggled so obstinately and hopelessly to get into the 'Salon de M. Bouguereau'.[6] His attitude to conventional art was a strange mixture of admiration at its skill and of an overwhelming horror of its emptiness – of its so 'horrible resemblance'.

The fact is that Cézanne had accepted uncritically all the conventions in the pathetic belief that it was the only way of safety for one 'so feeble in life'. So he continued to believe in the Catholic Church not from any religious conviction but because 'Rome was so strong' – so, too, he believed in the power and importance of the 'Salon de Bouguereau' which he hated as much as he feared. So, too, with what seems a paradoxical humility he let it be known, when his fame had already been established among the intelligent, that he would be glad to have the Legion of Honour. But here, too, he was destined to fail. The weighty influence and distinguished position of his friends could avail nothing against the undisguised horror with which any official heard the dreaded name of Cézanne. And it appeared that Cézanne was the only artist in France for whom this distinction was inaccessible, even through 'influence'. Nothing is stranger in his life than the contrast between the idea the public formed of Cézanne and the reality. He was one of those men destined to give rise to a legend which completely obscured the reality. He was spoken of as the most violent of revolutionaries – Communard and Anarchist were the favourite epithets – and all the time he was a timid little country gentleman of immaculate respectability who subscribed wholeheartedly to any reactionary opinion which might establish his 'soundness'. He was a timid man who really believed in only one thing, 'his little sensation'; who laboured incessantly to express this peculiar quality and who had not the faintest notion of doing anything that could shock the feelings of any mortal man or woman. No wonder then that when he looked up from his work and surveyed the world with his troubled and imperfect intellectual vision he was amazed and perturbed at the violent antagonism which he had all unconsciously provoked. No wonder that he became a shy, distrustful misanthrope, almost incapable of any association with his kind.

I have suggested that Cézanne was the perfect realisation of the type of the artist – I doubt whether in the whole of Vasari's great picture gallery there is a more complete type of 'original'. But in order to accept this we must banish from our mind the conventional idea of the artist as a man of flamboyant habits and calculated pose. Nothing is less possible to the real artist than pose – he is less capable of it than the ordinary man of business because more than any one else his external activities are determined from within by needs and instinct which he himself barely recognises.

On the other hand the imitation artist is a past master of pose, he poses as the sport of natural inclinations whilst he is really deliberately exploiting his caprices; and as he has a natural instinct for the limelight this variety of the 'Cabotin'[7] generally manages to sit for the portrait of the artist. Cézanne then, though his external life was that of the most irreproachable of country gentlemen, though he went to mass every Sunday and never willingly left the intimacy of family life, was none the less the purest and most unadulterated of artists, the most narrowly confined to his single activity, the most purely disinterested and the most frankly egoistic of men.

Cézanne had no intellectual independence. I doubt if he had the faintest conception of intellectual truth, but this is not to deny that he had a powerful mind. On the contrary he had a profound intelligence of whatever came within his narrow outlook on life, and above all he had the gift of expression, so that however fantastic, absurd, or naïve his opinions may have been, they were always expressed in such racy and picturesque language that they become interesting as revelations of a very human and genuine personality.

One of the tragi-comedies of Cézanne's life was the story of his early friendship with Zola, followed in middle life by a gradual estrangement, and at last by a total separation. It is perhaps the only blot in M. Vollard's book that he has taken too absolutely Cézanne's point of view, and has hardly done justice to Zola's goodness of heart. The cause of friction, apart from Cézanne's habitual testiness and ill-humour, was that Zola's feeling for art, which had led him in his youth to a heroic championship of the younger men, faded away in middle life. His own practice of literature led him further and further away from any concern with pure art, and he failed to recognise that his own early prophecy of Cézanne's greatness had come true, simply because he himself had become a popular author, and Cézanne had failed of any kind of success. Unfortunately Zola, who had evidently lost all real aesthetic feeling, continued to talk about art, and worse than that he had made the hero of *L'Œuvre*[8] a more or less recognisable portrait of his old friend. Cézanne could not tolerate Zola's gradual acquiescence in worldly ideals and ways of life, and when the Dreyfusard question[9] came up not only did his natural reactionary bias make him a vehement anti-Dreyfusard but he had no comprehension whatever of the heroism of Zola's actions; he found him merely ridiculous, and believed him to be engaged in an ill-conceived scheme of self-advertisement. But for all his contempt of Zola his affection remained deeper than he knew, and when he hthe news of Zola's death Cézanne shut himself up alone in his studio, and was heard sobbing and groaning throughout the day.

Cézanne's is not the only portrait in M. Vollard's entertaining book – there are sketches of many characters, among them the few strange and sympathetic men who appreciated and encouraged Cézanne in his early days. Of Cabaner the musician M. Vollard has collected some charming notes. Cabaner was a 'philosopher', and singularly indifferent to the chances of life.[10]

During the siege of Paris he met Coppée, and noticing the shells which were falling he became curious. 'Where do all these bullets come from?' Coppée: 'It would seem that it is the besiegers who send them.' Cabaner, after a silence: 'Is it always the Prussians?' Coppée, impatiently: 'Who on earth could it be?' Cabaner: 'I don't know . . . other nations!'[11] But the book is so full of good stories that I must resist the temptation to quote.

Fortunately M. Vollard has collected also a large number of Cézanne's *obiter dicta* on art. These have all Cézanne's pregnant wisdom and racy style. They often contain a whole system of aesthetics in a single phrase, as, for instance: 'What's wanted is to do Poussin over again from Nature.'[12]

They show, moreover, the natural bias of Cézanne's feelings and their gradual modification as his understanding became more profound. What comes out clearly, and it must never be forgotten in considering his art, is that his point of departure was from Romanticism. Delacroix was his god and Ingres, in his early days, his devil – a devil he learned increasingly to respect, but never one imagines really to love, '*Ce Dominique est très fort mais il m'emm——*.'[13] That Cézanne became a supreme master of formal design every one would nowadays admit, but there is some excuse for those contemporaries who complained of his want of drawing. He was not a master of line in the sense in which Ingres was. 'The contour escapes me,' as he said.[14] That is to say he arrived at the contour by a study of the interior planes; he was always plastic before he was linear. In his early works, such, for instance, at the *Scène de plein air*,[15] he is evidently inspired by Delacroix; he is almost a romanticist himself in such work, and his design is built upon the contrasts of large and rather loosely drawn silhouettes of dark and light. In fact it is the method of Tintoretto, Rubens, and Delacroix.

In the *Bathers resting*,[16] painted in 1877, there is already a great change. It is rather by the exact placing of plastic units than by continuous flowing silhouettes and the design holds. Giorgione perhaps, is behind this, but no longer Tintoretto, and, above all, Poussin has intervened.

In later works, such as the portrait of *Mme Cézanne in a greenhouse*,[17] the plasticity has become all-important, there is no longer any suggestion of a romantic *décor*; all is reduced to the purest terms of structural design.

These notes on Cézanne's development are prompted by the illustrations in Vollard's book. These are numerous and excellent, and afford a better opportunity for a general study of Cézanne's *œuvre* than any other book. In fact, when the time comes for the complete appreciation of Cézanne, M. Vollard's book will be the most important document existing. It should, however, have a far wider appeal than that. I hope that after the war M. Vollard will bring out a small cheap edition – it should become a classic biography. To say, as I would, that M. Vollard's book is a monument worthy of Cézanne himself is to give it the highest praise.

RENOIR

WHAT a lover of the commonplace Renoir was! It is a rare quality among artists. A theoretically pure artist exists no more than a Euclidean point, but if such a being could exist, every possible actual sight would be equally suitable as a point of departure for his artistic vision. Everything would stir in him the impulse to creation. He would have no predilections, no tastes for this or that kind of thing. In practice every artist is set going by some particular kind of scene in nature, and for the most part artists have to search out some unusual or unexplored aspect of things. Gauguin, for instance, had to go as far as Tahiti. When Renoir heard of this, he said, in a phrase which revealed his own character: 'Pourquoi? On peint si bien a Batignolles.'[1] But there are plenty of artists who paint more or less well at Batignolles or Bloomsbury and yet are not lovers of the commonplace. Like Walter Sickert, for instance, they find their Tahiti in Mornington Crescent.[2] Though they paint in commonplace surroundings, they generally contrive to catch them at an unexpected angle. Something odd or exotic in their taste for life seems to be normal to artists. The few artists or writers who have shared the tastes of the average man have, as a rule, been like Dickens – to take an obvious case – very imperfect and very impure artists, however great their genius. Among great artists one thinks at once of Rubens as the most remarkable example of a man of common tastes, a lover of all that was rich, exuberant and even florid. Titian, too, comes nearly up to the same standard, except that in youth his whole trend of feeling was distorted by the overpowering influence of Giorgione, whose tastes were recondite and strange. Renoir in the frankness of his colour harmonies, in his feeling for design and even in the quality of his pigment, constantly reminds us of these two. Now it is easier to see how an artist of the sixteenth or seventeenth century could develop commonplace tastes than one of our own times. For with the nineteenth century came in a gradual process of differentiation of the artist from the average man. The modern artist finds himself so little understood by the crowd, in his aims and methods, that he tends to become distinct in his whole attitude to life.

What, then, is so peculiar about Renoir is that he has this perfectly ordinary taste in things and yet remains so intensely, so purely, an artist. The fact is perhaps that he was so much an artist that he never had to go round the corner to get his inspiration; the immediate, obvious, front view of everything was more than sufficient to start the creative impulse. He enjoyed instinctively, almost animally, all the common good things of life, and yet he always kept just enough detachment to feel his delight aesthetically – he kept, as it were, just out of reach of appetite.

More than any other great modern artist Renoir trusted implicitly to his own sensibility; he imposed no barrier between his own delight in certain things and the delight which he communicates. He liked passionately the obviously good things of life, the young human animal, sunshine, sky, trees, water, fruit; the things that every one likes; only he liked them at just the right distance with just enough detachment to replace appetite by emotion. He could rely on this detachment so thoroughly that he could dare, what hardly any other genuine modern has dared, to say how much he liked even a pretty sight. But what gives his art so immediate, so universal an appeal is that his detachment went no further than was just necessary. His sensibility is kept at the exact point where it is transmuted into emotion. And the emotion, though it has of course the generalised aesthetic feeling, keeps something of the fullness and immediacy of the simpler attitude. Not that Renoir was either naïve or stupid. When he chose he showed that he was capable of logical construction and vigorous design. But for his own pleasure he would, as he himself said, have been satisfied to make little isolated records of his delight in the detail of a flower or a lock of hair. With the exception of *Les Parapluies* at the National Gallery[3] we have rarely seen his more deliberate compositions in England. But in all his work alike Renoir remains the man who could trust recklessly his instinctive reaction to life.

Let me confess that these characteristics – this way of keeping, as it were, just out of reach of appetite – makes Renoir to me, personally, a peculiarly difficult artist. My taste for exotic artists such as Cosima Tura[4] and his kin amounts at times to a vice. Consequently, I am sometimes in danger of not doing Renoir justice, because at the first approach to one of his pictures I miss the purely accessory delight of an unexpected attitude. The first approach to one of his pictures may indeed remind one of pictures that would be the delight of the servants' hall, so unaffectedly simple is his acceptance of the charm of rosy-cheeked girls, of pretty posies and dappled sunlight. And yet one knows well enough that Renoir was as 'artful' as one could wish. Though he had not the biting wit of a Degas, he had a peculiar love of mischievous humour; he was anything but a harmless or innocent character. All his simplicity is on the surface only. The longer one looks, the deeper does Renoir retire behind veil after veil of subtlety. And yet, compared with some modern artists, he was, after all, easy and instinctively simple. Even his plastic unity was arrived at by what seems a more natural method than, say, Cézanne's. Whereas Cézanne undertook his indefatigable research for the perspective of the receding planes, Renoir seems to have accepted a very simple general plastic formula. Whatever Cézanne may have meant by his celebrated saying about cones and cylinders,[5] Renoir seems to have thought the sphere and cylinder sufficient for his purpose. The figure presents itself to his eye as an arrangement of more or less hemispherical bosses and cylinders, and he appears generally to arrange the light so that the most prominent part of each boss receives the highest light. From this the planes recede by insensible gradations towards the contour, which generally remains the vaguest, least ascertained part of the modelling. Whatever lies immediately behind the contour tends to become drawn into its sphere of influence, to form an undefined recession enveloping and receiving the receding planes. As the eye passes away from the contour, new but less marked bosses form themselves and fill the background with repetitions of the general theme. The picture tends thus to take the form of a bas-relief[6] in which the recessions are not into the profound distances of pictorial space, but only back, as it were to the block out of which the bossed reliefs emerge, though, of course, by means of atmospheric colour the eye may interpret these recessions as distance. This is clearly in marked contrast to Cézanne's method of suggesting endless recessions of planes with the most complicated interwoven texture.

Renoir's drawing takes on the same fundamental simplicity. An Ingres arrived at the simplified statement necessary for great design by a process of gradual elimination of all the superfluous sinuosities which his hand had recorded in the first drawing from nature. Renoir seems never to have allowed his eye to accept more than the larger elements of mass and direction. His full, rounded curves embrace the form in its most general aspect. With advancing years and continually growing science he was able, at last, to state this essential synthesis with amazing breadth and ease. He continually increased the amplitude of his forms until, in his latest nudes, the whole design is filled with a few perfectly related bosses. Like Titian's, Renoir's power of design increased visibly up to the very end of his life. True, he was capable at all periods of conceiving large and finely co-ordinated compositions, such as *Les Parapluies* and the *Charpentier family*;[7] but at the end even the smallest studies have structural completeness.

A POSSIBLE DOMESTIC ARCHITECTURE

⁕

HOUSES are either builders' houses or architects' houses. Not that speculative builders do not employ architects, but they generally employ architects who efface themselves behind the deadly conventionality and bewildering fantasy of their façades. Architects' houses are generally built to the order of a gentleman who wishes his house to have some distinctive character, to stand out from the common herd of houses, either by its greater splendour or its greater discretion. The builders' house, like the dresses of the lower middle class, is generally an imitation of the gentleman's, only of a fashion that has just gone out of date and imitated badly in cheaper materials. No one defends it. It is made so because you must make a house somehow, and bought because it is the usual and therefore inevitable thing. No one enjoys it, no one admires it, it is accepted as part of the use and wont of ordinary life. The gentleman's and architect's house is different. Here time and thought, and perhaps great ingenuity and taste are employed in giving to the house an individual character. Unfortunately this individual character is generally terribly conscious of its social aspect, of how the house will look, not to those who live in it so much as to those who come to visit. We have no doubt outlived the more vulgar forms of this social consciousness, those which led to the gross display of merely expensive massiveness and profusion. Few modern houses would satisfy Mr Podsnap.[1] But its subtler forms are still apparent. They generally make themselves felt in the desire to be romantic. As it requires much too much imagination to find romance in the present, one looks for it in the past, and so a dive is made into some period of history, and its monuments studied and copied, and finally 'adapted' to the more elaborate exigencies of modern life. But, alas, these divers into the past seem never to have been able to find the pearl of romance, for, ever since the craze began in the eighteenth century, they have been diving now here, now there, now into Romanesque, now into Gothic, now into Jacobean, now into Queen Anne. They have brought up innumerable architectural 'features' which have been duly copied by modern machinery, and carefully glued on to the houses, and still the owners and the architects, to do them justice, feel restless, and are in search of some new 'old style' to try. The search has flagged of late, people know it is useless, and here and there architects have set to work merely to build so well and with such a fine sense of the material employed that the result should satisfy the desire for comeliness without the use of any style. I am thinking of some of Mr Blow's earlier works[2] where a peculiar charm resulted from the unstinting care with which every piece of material had been chosen and the whole fitted together almost as though the stones had been precious stones instead of flints or bricks.

But on the whole the problem appears to be still unsolved, and the architects go on using styles of various kinds with greater or less degrees of correctness. This they no longer do with the old zest and hope of discovery, but rather with a languid indifference and with evident marks of discouragement.

Now style is an admirable thing, it is the result of ease and coherence of feeling, but unfortunately a borrowed style is an even stronger proof of muddled and befogged emotions than the total absence of style. The desire for a style at all costs, even a borrowed style, is part of that exaggerated social consciousness which in other respects manifests itself as snobbery. What if people were just to let their houses be the direct outcome of their actual needs, and of their actual way of life, and allow other people to think what they like. What if they behaved in the matter of houses as all people wish to behave in society without any undue or fussy self-consciousness. Wouldn't such houses have really a great deal more character, and therefore interest for others, than those which are deliberately made to look like something or other. Instead of looking like something, they would then be something.

The house which I planned and built for myself (Plate VI. 1)[3] was the result of certain particular needs and habits. I had originally no idea of building a house: I had so often heard the proverb that 'Fools build houses for wise men to live in', that I had come to believe it, but I required a house of a certain size for my family within easy reach of London. I looked at a great many houses and found that those which had a sufficient number of rooms were all gentlemen's establishments, with lodge, stabling, and greenhouses. Now it was characteristic of my purse that I could not afford to keep up a gentleman's establishment and of my tastes that I could not endure to. I was a town dweller, and I wanted a town house and a little garden in the country. As I could not find what I wanted, the idea came into my head that I must build it or go without. The means at my disposal were definitely limited; the question was therefore whether I could build a house of the required size with that sum. I made a plan containing the number of rooms of the sizes I required, and got an estimate. It was largely in excess of the sum I possessed for the purpose. I feared I must give up my scheme when I met a friend who had experimented in building cheap cottages on his estate, and learned from him that the secret of economy was concentration of plan. I also discovered in discussing my first estimate that roofs were cheaper than walls. I thereupon started on a quite different plan, in which I arranged the rooms to form as nearly as possible a solid block, and placed a number of the rooms in a hipped or Mansard roof. It will be seen that, so far, the planning of the house was merely the discovery of a possible equation between my needs and the sum at my disposal.[4]

But in trying to establish this equation I had found it necessary to make the rooms rather smaller than I should have liked, and having a great liking for large and particularly high interiors – I hate Elizabethan rooms with their low ceilings in spite of their prettiness, and I love the interiors of the baroque palaces of Italy – I determined to have one room of generous dimensions and particularly of great height (Plate VI. 2).[5] This large room surrounded by small rooms was naturally made into a general living-place, with arrangements by means of a lift to enable it to be used as a dining hall if there were more in the house than could be accommodated in the small breakfast room.

The estimate for this new concentrated plan, in spite of the large dimensions of the living-place, came to little more than half the estimate for the former plan, and made my project feasible, provided that I could calculate all details and did not run into extras.

So far then there has been no question of architecture; it has been merely solving the problem of personal needs and habits, and of cost, and if architecture there is to be, it should, I think, come directly out of the solution of these problems. The size and disposition of the plan having thus been fixed, the elevations are given in outline, and the only question is how the rectangle of each elevation is to be treated. Doors and windows are the elements of the design, and here again something will already be determined by needs or tastes. There is need of a certain amount of light, and my own taste is to have as much as possible, so that the windows had to be large rectangles. But when all these things are determined by need there is still a wide margin of choice – the size of the panes in the windows, the depth of recess of the windows within the wall, the flatness or relief of each element. All these and many more are still matters of choice, and it is through the artist's sense of proportion and his feeling for the plastic relief of the whole surface that a work of mere utility may become a work of art. In the case of the main elevation of my house I found that when all the windows, including the long windows of the high living-place, were duly arranged, there was a want of unity owing to the nearly equal balance between the horizontal and vertical members. I therefore underlined the slight projection of the central part – a projection enforced by by-laws – by varying the material, replacing at this point the plaster of the walls by two bands of red brick. In this way the vertical effect of the central part was made to dominate the whole façade. The artistic or architectural part of this house was confined, then, merely to the careful choice of proportions within certain fixed limits defined by needs, and neither time, money, nor thought was expended on giving the house the appearance of any particular style.

I have gone thus at length into the history of my own house merely as an example of the way in which, I think, a genuine architecture, and in the end, no doubt, an architectural style, might arise. It requires a certain courage or indifference to public opinion on the part of the owner. My own house is neighboured by houses of the most gentlemanly picturesqueness, houses from which tiny gables with window slits jut out at any unexpected angle, and naturally it is regarded as a monstrous eyesore by their inhabitants. Indeed, when I first came here it was supposed that the ugliness of my house was so apparent that I myself could not be blind to it, and should not resent its being criticised in my presence. They were quite right, I did not resent it; I was only very much amused.

To arrive at such a genuine domestic architecture as I conceive, requires, then, this social indifference to surrounding snobbishness on the part of the owner, and it requires a nice sense of proportion and a feeling for values of plastic relief on the part of the artist who designs the house, but it does not require genius or even any extraordinary talent to make a genuine and honest piece of domestic architecture which will continue to look distinguished when the last 'style' but one having just become *démodé* already stinks in the nostrils of all cultured people.

JEAN MARCHAND

✱

THERE are some thirty pictures by M. Jean Marchand now on view at the Carfax Gallery in Bury Street. This gives one an occasion for reviewing the work of this comparatively young artist. M. Marchand belongs, of course, to the revolutionary movement of this century in that he derives the general principles of his art from Cézanne, but he is the most traditional of revolutionaries. Not by the wildest stretch of the imagination could one conceive of M. Marchand deliberately or consciously doing anything to astonish the public. It is quite true that no genuine artist ever did, but some artists have found an added piquancy in the thought that inventions that occurred to them would in point of fact have this adventitious charm. But with M. Marchand such possibilities seem more remote than with most of his compeers. An extreme simplicity and directness of outlook and a touching sincerity in all that he does are the most prominent characteristics of his work. Not that he makes one suppose him to be too naïve to play tricks with his art; on the contrary, one sees that he is highly self-conscious and intellectual, but that he knows the utter futility of any deliberate emphasis on the artist's part. He knows that any effect of permanent value must flow directly from the matter in hand; that it is useless to make anything appear more interesting or impressive than it is; that, whatever his vision is, it must be accepted literally, and without any attempt to add to its importance or effectiveness.

In short, M. Marchand is a classic artist – one might almost in these days say a French artist, and count it as synonymous, but that one remembers that the French, too, have had their orgies of romantic emphasis, and have always ready to hand a convention of coldly exaggerated rhetoric. Moreover, if one thinks of a nearly allied painter such as Derain,[1] whose work is so terribly *interesting*, one sees that to a quite peculiar degree M. Marchand exemplifies the sentimental honesty of the French. I leave the question open whether this is a moral trait, or is not rather the result of a clearer perception than we often attain to of the extreme futility of lying where art is concerned.

Certainly one can imagine the temptations for a man of M. Marchand's great technical ability to choose some slightly wilful or fantastic formula of vision and to exploit it for what it might bring out; for M. Marchand was handicapped in any competition for notoriety by the very normality and sanity of his vision. Compared to the descriptions of sketches in *Jane Eyre*[2] his pictures would be judged to be entirely lacking in imagination. He never tries to invent what he has not actually seen. Almost any of the ordinary things of life suffice for his theme – a loaf of bread or a hat left on the table, a rather vulgar French château restored by Viollet-le-Duc[3] with a prim garden and decorous lake, a pot of aspidistra in a suburban window. These and the like are the subjects of his pictures, and he paints the objects themselves in all their vulgar everydayness. They do not become excuses for abstract designs; they retain in his pictures all their bleak commonplaceness.

Any one unfamiliar with his pictures who read such an account of his work might think M. Marchand was a dull literalist, whose mere accomplishment it is to render the similitude of objects. But such a conclusion would be entirely wrong. However frankly M. Marchand accepts the forms of objects, however little his normal vision distorts or idealises them, however consciously and deliberately he chooses the arrangement, he does build up by sheer method and artistic science a unity which has a singularly impressive quality. I heard some one say, in front of a still life (Plate VII) which represented a white tablecloth, a glass tumbler, an earthenware water-bottle and a loaf of bread, that it was like Buddha. With such a description as I give of the picture the appreciation sounds precious and absurd; before the picture it seems perfectly just. For M. Marchand has attained the reward of his inflexible honesty; his construction is so solid and unfaltering, he builds up his designs with such massive and direct handling, that without the slightest suggestion of emphasis, without any underlining, the effect comes through; the material becomes expressive; he becomes a creator, and not a mere adapter of form.

For the understanding of his personality it is interesting to consider his Cubist period, since Marchand's reaction to Cubism is typical of his nature. Cubism, like S. Paul, has been all things to all men – at least to almost all artists of the present generation. To some it has been a doctrine and a revelation; to some it has been a convenient form of artistic journalism; to some it has been a quick road to notoriety, to some an aid to melodramatic effect. To M. Marchand it was just a useful method and a gymnastic. He used it for just what it could give him as an exercise in the organisation of form. It was to him like a system of notation to a mathematician, a means of handling quantities which without it would have been too elusive and too infinite to grasp. By means of Cubism the infinity of a sphere could be reduced to half a dozen planes, each of which he could learn to relate to all the other planes in the picture; and the singular ease and directness of his plastic construction seem to be due to his early practice of Cubist methods. Having once learned by this process of willed and deliberate analysis how to handle complex forms, he has been able to throw away the scaffolding and to construct palpably related and completely unified designs with something approaching the full complexity of natural forms, though the lucid statement and the ease of handling which it actuates testify to the effect of his apprenticeship in Cubism. Such a use of a theory – as a method, not as a doctrine – seems to me typical of M. Marchand's balanced judgment, of his alert readiness to use any and every means that could conduce to his slow and methodical development, and hold out hopes of a continued growth.

M. Marchand, so assured, so settled an artist, is still young. In the landscapes which he did in the South of France just before the war he explored a peculiarly persuasive and harmonious scheme of colour, based on warm ochres, earth reds, and dull blues. These pictures have the envelopment and the sonorous harmony of some early Italian masters in spite of the frank oppositions and the vigorous scaffolding of modern design. In the later work done in the last years he shows a new sense of colour, a new sharpness and almost an audacity, if one can imagine so well-balanced a nature capable of audacity. He uses dull neutral colours, the dirty white of a cloudy sky, harsh dull greens and blacks, the obvious and unattractive colours that so frequently occur in nature; but he uses them in such combinations, and with such accents of tone and such subtly prepared accordances and oppositions, that these obvious dull colours strike one as fascinating discoveries. This is the height of artistic science, so to accept the obvious and commonplace that it gives one the pleasant shock of paradox. It seems hardly rash to foretell for him a solid and continually growing fame.

RETROSPECT

THE work of re-reading and selecting from the mass of my writings as an art critic has inevitably brought me up against the question of its consistency and coherence. Although I do not think that I have republished here anything with which I entirely disagree, I cannot but recognise that in many of these essays the emphasis lies in a different place from where I should now put it. Fortunately I have never prided myself upon my unchanging constancy of attitude, but unless I flatter myself I think I can trace a certain trend of thought underlying very different expressions of opinion. Now since that trend seems to me to be symptomatic of modern aesthetic, and since it may perhaps explain much that seems paradoxical in the actual situation of art, it may be interesting to discuss its nature even at the cost of being autobiographical.

In my work as a critic of art I have never been a pure Impressionist, a mere recording instrument of certain sensations. I have always had some kind of aesthetic. A certain scientific curiosity and a desire for comprehension have impelled me at every stage to make generalisations, to attempt some kind of logical co-ordination of my impressions. But, on the other hand, I have never worked out for myself a complete system such as the metaphysicans deduce from *a priori* principles. I have never believed that I knew what was the ultimate nature of art. My aesthetic has been a purely practical one, a tentative expedient, an attempt to reduce to some kind of order my aesthetic impressions up to date. It has been held merely until such time as fresh experiences might confirm or modify it. Moreover, I have always looked on my system with a certain suspicion. I have recognised that if it ever formed too solid a crust it might stop the inlets of fresh experience, and I can count various occasions when my principles would have led me to condemn, and when my sensibility has played the part of Balaam[1] with the effect of making temporary chaos of my system. That has, of course, always re-arranged itself to take in the new experience, but with each such cataclysm it has suffered a loss of prestige. So that even in its latest form I do not put forward my system as more than a provisional induction from my own aesthetic experiences.

I have certainly tried to make my judgment as objective as possible, but the critic must work with the only instrument he possesses – namely, his own sensibility with all its personal equations. All that he can consciously endeavour is to perfect that tool to its utmost by studying the traditional verdicts of men of aesthetic sensibility in the past, and by constant comparison of his own reactions with those of his contemporaries who are specially gifted in this way. When he has done all that he can in this direction – and I would allow him a slight bias in favour of agreement with tradition – he is bound to accept the verdict of his own feelings as honestly as he can. Even plain honesty in this matter is more difficult to attain than would be supposed by those who have never tried it. In so delicate a matter as the artistic judgment one is liable to many accidental disturbing influences, one can scarcely avoid temporary hypnotisms and hallucinations. One can only watch for and try to discount these, taking every opportunity to catch one's sensibility unawares before it can take cover behind prejudices and theories.

When the critic holds the result of his reaction to a work of art clearly in view he has next to translate it into words. Here, too, distortion is inevitable, and it is here that I have probably failed most of accuracy, for language in the hands of one who lacks the mastery of a poet has its own tricks, its perversities and habits. There are things which it shies at and goes round, there are places where it runs away and, leaving the reality which it professes to carry tumbled out at the tail of the cart, arrives in a great pother, but without the goods.

But in spite of all these limitations and the errors they entail it seems to me that the attempt to attain objective judgments has not altogether failed, and that I seem to myself to have been always groping my way towards some kind of a reasoned and practical aesthetic. Many minds have been engaged alongside of mine in the same pursuit. I think we may claim that partly as a result of our common efforts a rather more intelligent attitude exists in the educated public of today than obtained in the last century.

Art in England is sometimes insular, sometimes provincial. The pre-Raphaelite movement was mainly an indigenous product. The dying echoes of this remarkable explosion reverberated through the years of my nonage, but when I first began to study art seriously the vital movement was a provincial one. After the usual twenty years of delay, provincial England had become aware of the Impressionist movement in France, and the younger painters of promise were working under the influence of Monet. Some of them even formulated theories of naturalism in its most literal and extreme form. But at the same time Whistler, whose Impressionism was of a very different stamp, had put forward the purely decorative idea of art, and had tried in his 'Ten o'clock',[2] perhaps too cavalierly, to sweep away the web of ethical questions, distorted by aesthetic prejudices, which Ruskin's exuberant and ill-regulated mind had spun for the British public.

The Naturalists made no attempt to explain why the exact and literal imitation of nature should satisfy the human spirit, and the 'Decorators'[3] failed to distinguish between agreeable sensations and imaginative significance.

After a brief period during which I was interested in the new possibilities opened up by the more scientific evaluation of colour which the Impressionists practised, I came to feel more and more the absence in their work of structural design. It was an innate desire for this aspect of art which drove me to the study of the Old Masters and, in particular, those of the Italian Renaissance, in the hope of discovering from them the secret of that architectonic idea which I missed so badly in the work of my contemporaries. I think now that a certain amount of 'cussedness' led me to exaggerate what was none the less a genuine personal reaction. Finding myself out of touch with my generation I took a certain pleasure in emphasising my isolation. I always recognised fully that the only vital art of the day was that of the Impressionists whose theories I disbelieved, and I was always able to admit the greatness of Degas and Renoir. But many of my judgments of modern art were too much affected by my attitude. I do not think I ever praised Mr Wilson Steer or Mr Walter Sickert as much as they deserved, and I looked with too great indulgence on some would-be imitators of the Old Masters. But my most serious lapse was the failure to discover the genius of Seurat, whose supreme merits as a designer I had every reason to acclaim.[4] I cannot even now tell whether I ever saw his work in the exhibitions of the early nineties, but if I did his qualities were hidden from me by the now transparent veil of pointillism – a pseudo-scientific system of atmospheric colour notation in which I took no interest.

I think I can claim that my study of the Old Masters was never much tainted by archaeological curiosity. I tried to study them in the same spirit as I might study contemporary artists, and I always regretted that there was no modern art capable of satisfying my predilections. I say there was no modern art because none such was known to me, but all the time there was one who had already worked out the problem which seemed to me insoluble of how to use the modern vision with the constructive design of the older masters.[5] By some extraordinary ill luck I managed to miss seeing Cézanne's work till some considerable time after his death.[6] I had heard of him vaguely from time to time as a kind of hidden oracle of ultra-impressionism, and, in consequence, I expected to find myself entirely unreceptive to his art. To my intense surprise I found myself deeply moved. I have discovered the article in which I recorded this encounter,[7] and though the praise I gave would sound grudging and feeble today – for I was still obsessed by ideas about the content of a work of art – I am glad to see that I was so ready to scrap a long-cherished hypothesis in face of a new experience.

In the next few years I became increasingly interested in the art of Cézanne and of those like Gauguin and van Gogh who at that time represented the first effects of his profound influence on modern art, and I gradually recognised that what I had hoped for as a possible event of some future century had already occurred, that art had begun to recover once more the language of design and to explore its so long neglected possibilities. Thus it happened that when at the end of 1910 by a curious series of chances, I was in a position to organise an exhibition at the Grafton Galleries, I seized the opportunity to bring before the English public a selection of works conforming to the new direction. For purposes of convenience it was necessary to give these artists a name, and I chose, as being the vaguest and most non-committal, the name of Post-Impressionist.[8] This merely stated their position in time relatively to the Impressionist movement. In conformity with my own previous prejudices against Impressionism, I think I underlined too much their divorce from the parent stock. I see now more clearly their affiliation with it, but I was none the less right in recognising their essential difference, a difference which the subsequent development of Cubism has rendered more evident. Of late the thesis of their fundamental opposition has been again enforced in the writings of M. Lhote.[9]

If I may judge by the discussions in the press to which this exhibition gave rise, the general public failed to see that my position with regard to this movement was capable of a logical explanation, as the result of a consistent sensibility. I tried in vain to explain what appeared to me so clear, that the modern movement was essentially a return to the ideas of formal design which had been almost lost sight of in the fervid pursuit of naturalistic representation. I found that the cultured public which had welcomed my expositions of the works of the Italian Renaissance now regarded me as either incredibly flippant or, for the more charitable explanation was usually adopted, slightly insane. In fact, I found among the cultured who had hitherto been my most eager listeners the most inveterate and exasperated enemies of the new movement. The accusation of anarchism was constantly made. From an aesthetic point of view this was, of course, the exact opposite of the truth, and I was for long puzzled to find the explanation of so paradoxical an opinion and so violent an enmity. I now see that my crime had been to strike at the vested emotional interests. These people felt instinctively that their special culture was one of their social assets. That to be able to speak glibly of Tang and Ming,[10] of Amico di Sandro[11] and Baldovinetti, gave them a social standing and a distinctive cachet. This showed me that we had all along been labouring under a mutual misunderstanding, *i.e.* that we had admired the Italian primitives for quite different reasons. It was felt that one could only appreciate Amico di Sandro when one had acquired a certain considerable mass of erudition and given a great deal of time and attention, but to admire a Matisse required only a certain sensibility. One could feel fairly sure that one's maid could not rival one in the former case, but might by a mere haphazard gift of Providence surpass one in the second. So that the accusation of revolutionary anarchism was due to a social rather than an aesthetic prejudice. In any case the cultured public was determined to look upon Cézanne as an incompetent bungler, and upon the whole movement as madly revolutionary. Nothing I could say would induce people to look calmly enough at these pictures to see how closely they followed tradition, or how great a familiarity with the Italian primitives was displayed in their work. Now that Matisse has become a safe investment for persons of taste, and that Picasso and Derain have delighted the miscellaneous audience of the London Music Halls with their designs for the Russian Ballet, it will be difficult for people to imagine the vehemence of the indignation which greeted the first sight of their works in England.

In contrast to its effect on the cultured public the Post-Impressionist exhibition aroused a keen interest among a few of the younger English artists and their friends. With them I began to discuss the problems of aesthetic that the contemplation of these works forced upon us.

But before explaining the effects of these discussions upon my aesthetic theory I must return to consider the generalisations which I had made from my aesthetic experiences up to this point.

In my youth all speculations on aesthetic had revolved with wearisome persistence around the question of the nature of beauty. Like our predecessors we sought for the criteria of the beautiful, whether in art or nature. And always this search led to a tangle of contradictions or else to metaphysical ideas so vague as to be inapplicable to concrete cases.

It was Tolstoy's genius that delivered us from this *impasse*, and I think that one may date from the appearance of *What is Art?* the beginning of fruitful speculation in aesthetic.[12] It was not indeed Tolstoy's preposterous valuation of works of art that counted for us, but his luminous criticism of past aesthetic systems, above all, his suggestions that art had no special or necessary concern with what is beautiful in nature, that the fact that Greek sculpture had run prematurely to decay through an extreme and non-aesthetic admiration of beauty in the human figure afforded no reason why we should for ever remain victims of their error.

It became clear that we had confused two distinct uses of the word beautiful, that when we used beauty to describe a favourable aesthetic judgment on a work of art we meant something quite different from our praise of a woman, a sunset or a horse as beautiful. Tolstoy saw that the essence of art was that it was a means of communication between human beings. He conceived it to be *par excellence* the language of emotion. It was at this point that his moral bias led him to the strange conclusion that the value of a work of art corresponded to the moral value of the emotion expressed. Fortunately he showed by an application of his theory to actual works of art what absurdities it led to. What remained of immense importance was the idea that a work of art was not the record of beauty already existent elsewhere, but the expression of an emotion felt by the artist and conveyed to the spectator.

The next question was, Of what kind of emotions is art the expression? Is love poetry the expression of the emotion of love, tragedy the expression of pity and fear, and so forth? Clearly the expression in art has some similarity to the expression of these emotions in actual life, but it is never identical. It is evident that the artist feels these emotions in a special manner, that he is not entirely under their influence, but sufficiently withdrawn to contemplate and comprehend them. My 'Essay in Aesthetics' here reprinted, elaborates this point of view, and in a course of unpublished lectures[13] I endeavoured to divide works of visual art according to the emotional point of view, adopting the classification already existing in poetry into Epic, Dramatic, Lyric, and Comedic.

I conceived the form of the work of art to be its most essential quality, but I believed this form to be the direct outcome of an apprehension of some emotion of actual life by the artist, although, no doubt, that apprehension was of a special and peculiar kind and implied a certain detachment. I also conceived that the spectator in contemplating the form must inevitably travel in an opposite direction along the same road which the artist had taken, and himself feel the original emotion. I conceived the form and the emotion which it conveyed as being inextricably bound together in the aesthetic whole.

About the time I had arrived at these conclusions the discussion of aesthetic stimulated by the appearance of Post-Impressionism began. It became evident through these discussions that some artists who were peculiarly sensitive to the formal relations of works of art, and who were deeply moved by them, had almost no sense of the emotions which I had supposed them to convey. Since it was impossible in these cases to doubt the genuineness of the aesthetic reaction it became evident that I had not pushed the analysis of works of art far enough, had not disentangled the purely aesthetic elements from certain accompanying accessories.

It was, I think, the observation of these cases of reaction to pure form that led Mr Clive Bell in his book, *Art*,[14] to put forward the hypothesis that however much the emotions of life might appear to play a part in the work of art, the artist was really not concerned with them, but only with the expression of a special and unique kind of emotion, the aesthetic emotion. A work of art had the peculiar property of conveying the aesthetic emotion, and it did this in virtue of having 'significant form'. He also declared that representation of nature was entirely irrelevant to this and that a picture might be completely non-representative.

This last view seemed to me always to go too far since any, even the slightest suggestion, of the third dimension in a picture must be due to some element of representation. What I think has resulted from Mr Clive Bell's book, and the discussions which it has aroused on this point is that the artist is free to choose any degree of representational accuracy which suits the expression of his feeling. That no single fact, or set of facts, about nature can be held to be obligatory for artistic form. Also one might add as an empirical observation that the greatest art seems to concern itself most with the universal aspects of natural form, to be the least preoccupied with particulars. The greatest artists appear to be most sensitive to those qualities of natural objects which are the least obvious in ordinary life precisely because, being common to all visible objects, they do not serve as marks of distinction and recognition.

With regard to the expression of emotion in works of art I think that Mr. Bell's sharp challenge to the usually accepted view of art as expressing the emotions of life has been of great value. It has led to an attempt to isolate the purely aesthetic feeling from the whole complex of feelings which may and generally do accompany the aesthetic feeling when we regard a work of art.

Let us take as an example of what I mean Raphael's *Transfiguration* (Plate VIII. 2), which a hundred years ago was perhaps the most admired picture in the world, and twenty years ago was one of the most neglected. It is at once apparent that this picture makes a very complex appeal to the mind and feelings. To those who are familiar with the Gospel story of Christ it brings together in a single composition two different events which occurred simultaneously at different places, the Transfiguration of Christ and the unsuccessful attempt of the Disciples during His absence to heal the lunatic boy. This at once arouses a number of complex ideas about which the intellect and feelings may occupy themselves. Goethe's remark on the picture is instructive from this point of view. 'It is remarkable', he says, 'that any one has ever ventured to query the essential unity of such a composition. How can the upper part be separated from the lower? The two form one whole. Below the suffering and the needy, above the powerful and helpful – mutually dependent, mutually illustrative.'[15]

It will be seen at once what an immense complex of feelings interpenetrating and mutually affecting one another such a work sets up in the mind of a Christian spectator, and all this merely by the content of the picture, its subject, the dramatic story it tells.

Now if our Christian spectator has also a knowledge of human nature he will be struck by the fact that these figures, especially in the lower group, are all extremely incongruous with any idea he is likely to have formed of the people who surrounded Christ in the Gospel narrative. And according to his prepossessions he is likely to be shocked or pleased to find instead of the poor and unsophisticated peasants and fisherfolk who followed Christ, a number of noble, dignified, and academic gentlemen in improbable garments and purely theatrical poses. Again the representation merely as representation will set up a number of feelings and perhaps of critical thoughts dependent upon innumerable associated ideas in the spectator's mind.

Now all these reactions to the picture are open to any one who has enough understanding of natural form to recognise it when represented adequately. There is no need for him to have any particular sensibility to form as such.

Let us now take for our spectator a person highly endowed with the special sensibility to form, who feels the intervals and relations of forms as a musical person feels the intervals and relations of tones, and let us suppose him either completely ignorant of, or indifferent to, the Gospel story. Such a spectator will be likely to be immensely excited by the extraordinary power of co-ordination of many complex masses in a single inevitable whole, by the delicate equilibrium of many directions of line. He will at once feel that the apparent division into two parts is only apparent, that they are co-ordinated by a quite peculiar power of grasping the possible correlations. He will almost certainly be immensely excited and moved, but his emotion will have nothing to do with the emotions which we have discussed hitherto, since in this case we have supposed our spectator to have no clue to them.

It is evident then that we have the possibility of infinitely diverse reactions to a work of art. We may imagine, for instance, that our pagan spectator, though entirely unaffected by the story, is yet conscious that the figures represent men, and that their gestures are indicative of certain states of mind and, in consequence, we may suppose that according to an internal bias his emotion is either heightened or hindered by the recognition of their rhetorical insincerity. Or we may suppose him to be so absorbed in purely formal relations as to be indifferent even to this aspect of the design as representation. We may suppose him to be moved by the pure contemplation of the spatial relations of plastic volumes. It is when we have got to this point that we seem to have isolated this extremely elusive aesthetic quality which is the one constant quality of all works of art, and which seems to be independent of all the prepossessions and associations which the spectator brings with him from his past life.

A person so entirely preoccupied with the purely formal meaning of a work of art, so entirely blind to all the overtones and associations of a picture like the *Transfiguration* is extremely rare. Nearly every one, even if highly sensitive to purely plastic and spatial appearances, will inevitably entertain some of those thoughts and feelings which are conveyed by implication and by reference back to life. The difficulty is that we frequently give wrong explanations of our feelings. I suspect, for instance, that Goethe was deeply moved by the marvellous discovery of design, whereby the upper and lower parts cohere in a single whole, but the explanation he gave of this feeling took the form of a moral and philosophical reflection.

It is evident also that owing to our difficulty in recognising the nature of our own feelings we are liable to have our aesthetic reaction interfered with by our reaction to the dramatic overtones and implications. I have chosen this picture of the Transfiguration precisely because its history is a striking example of this fact. In Goethe's time rhetorical gesture was no bar to the appreciation of aesthetic unity. Later on in the nineteenth century, when the study of the Primitives had revealed to us the charm of dramatic sincerity and naturalness, these gesticulating figures appeared so false and unsympathetic that even people of aesthetic sensibility were unable to disregard them, and their dislike of the picture as illustration actually obliterated or prevented the purely aesthetic approval which they would probably otherwise have experienced. It seems to me that this attempt to isolate the elusive element of the pure aesthetic reaction from the compounds in which it occurs has been the most important advance of modern times in practical aesthetic.

The question which this simile suggests is full of problems; do these form chemical compounds, as it were, in the case of the normal aesthetically gifted spectator, or are they merely mixtures due to our confused recognition of what goes on in the complex of our emotions? The picture I have chosen is also valuable, just at the present time, from this point of view. Since it presents in vivid opposition for most of us a very strong positive (pleasurable) reaction on the purely aesthetic side, and a violently negative (painful) reaction in the realm of dramatic association.

But one could easily point to pictures where the two sets of emotions seem to run so parallel that the idea that they reinforce one another is inevitably aroused. We might take, for instance, Giotto's *Pietà*. In my description of that (p.116), it will be seen that the two currents of feeling ran so together in my own mind that I regarded them as being completely fused. My emotion about the dramatic idea seemed to heighten my emotion about the plastic design. But at present I should be inclined to say that this fusion of two sets of emotion was only apparent and was due to my imperfect analysis of my own mental state.

Probably at this point we must hand over the question to the experimental psychologist. It is for him to discover whether this fusion is possible, whether, for example, such a thing as a song really exists, that is to say, a song in which neither the meaning of the words nor the meaning of the music predominates; in which music and words do not merely set up separate currents of feeling, which may agree in a general parallelism, but really fuse and become indivisible. I expect that the answer will be in the negative.

If on the other hand such a complete fusion of different kinds of emotion does take place, this would tend to substantiate the ordinary opinion that the aesthetic emotion has greater value in highly complicated compounds than in the pure state.

Supposing, then, that we are able to isolate in a work of art this purely aesthetic quality to which Mr Clive Bell gives the name of 'significant form'. Of what nature is it? And what is the value of this elusive and – taking the whole mass of mankind – rather uncommon aesthetic emotion which it causes? I put these questions without much hope of answering them, since it is of the greatest importance to recognise clearly what are the questions which remain to be solved.

I think we are all agreed that we mean by significant form something other than agreeable arrangements of form, harmonious patterns, and the like. We feel that a work which possesses it is the outcome of an endeavour to express an idea rather than to create a pleasing object. Personally, at least, I always feel that it implies the effort on the part of the artist to bend to our emotional understanding by means of his passionate conviction some intractable material which is alien to our spirit.

I seem unable at present to get beyond this vague adumbration of the nature of significant form. Flaubert's 'expression of the idea' seems to me to correspond exactly to what I mean, but, alas! he never explained, and probably could not, what he meant by the 'idea'.

As to the value of the aesthetic emotion – it is clearly infinitely removed from those ethical values to which Tolstoy would have confined it. It seems to be as remote from actual life and its practical utilities as the most useless mathematical theory. One can only say that those who experience it feel it to have a peculiar quality of 'reality' which makes it a matter of infinite importance in their lives. Any attempt I might make to explain this would probably land me in the depths of mysticism. On the edge of that gulf I stop.

NOTES

ART AND LIFE

From notes given to the Fabian Society, 1917. This society held a summer school in August 1917 and it is possible that Fry gave his lecture there.

1 A style named after Jeanne Bécu, comtesse du Barry (1743–93), patroness of the arts.

2 Fry is probably thinking of his former employer John Pierpont Morgan (1837–1913), whose financial empire was matched only by his huge collection of art works.

3 Salimbeni's chronicle: G.G. Coulton, *From St Francis to Dante, a translation of all that is of interest in the chronicle of the Franciscan Salimbene, 1221–88* (1906).

4 St Bernard of Clairvaux (1090–1153).

5 Paray le Monial is in east central France in the department of Saône-et-Loire. The Benedictine priory was founded in the tenth century.

6 Michelangelo Merisi da Caravaggio (1573–1610).

7 Jacques-Louis David (1748–1825).

8 Whistler's 'Ten O'Clock Lecture' was given in London on 20 Feb. 1885 and published in his *The Gentle Art of Making Enemies* (1890). Whistler tried to establish the autonomy of art and nature and to defend himself against the critical abuse of Ruskin. In 1878 Ruskin and Whistler had gone to law about Ruskin's remarks in *Fors Glavigera* which denigrated Whistler's painting *The Falling Rocket*.

9 William Robertson Smith, *Lectures on the Religion of the Semites* (Edinburgh, 1899).

10 John Singer Sargent (1856–1925), painter of highly sophisticated aristocratic portraits.

AN ESSAY IN AESTHETICS

First published in the *New Quarterly*, 2 (April 1909), pp.171–90.

1 In *A Manual of Oil Painting* (1886), John Collier wrote: 'This representation of natural objects by means of pigments on a flat surface is a very definite matter and most people are competent to judge of the truth or falsehood of such a representation ...' (p.3). John Collier (1850–1934) was

a painter of portraits and subject pictures. He studied at the Slade and was encouraged by Fry's *bêtes noires* Edward Poynter and Alma-Tadema. Collier's definition of art is similar to that given by G.P. Lomazzo in his *Trattato dell'arte della pittura* (Milan, 1585) where he wrote that 'pittura è Arte laquale con linee proportionate, e con colori simili à la natura de le cose, seguitando il lume perspettivo imita talmente la natura de le cose corporee ...' (p.19).

2 'It is probable then, that if a man should arrive in our city, so clever as to be able to assume any character and imitate any object, and should propose to make a public display of his talents and his productions, we shall pay him reverence as a sacred, admirable, and charming personage, but we shall tell him that in our state there is no one like him ... and we shall send him away to another city ...' (*The Republic of Plato*, trans. J.L. Davies and D.J. Vaughan (Cambridge, 1866), iii, 92–3).

3 Tolstoy does not say precisely this but he condemns Beethoven's Ninth Symphony for being unable to unite 'all men in one common feeling'. (Leo Tolstoy, *What is Art?*, trans. Aylmer Maude, 3rd ed. (1898), p.173).

4 Bastien-Lepage (1850–84), leader of the *plein airiste* school in France and a strong influence on the New English Art Club in its early years in England.

5 In Tolstoy's story this is a wolf.

6 Denman Waldo Ross, *Theory of Pure Design, Harmony, Balance, Rhythm* (Boston and Cambridge, Mass., 1907).

7 Michelangelo's *Jeremiah* is in the Sistine Chapel.

8 i.e. the *Tondo Doni*.

9 'Le modelé humain a, chez eux, toute la beauté des lignes courbées de la fleur. Et les profiles sont fermes, amples comme ceux des grandes montagnes: c'est de l'architecture' (Gustave Coquiot, *Le Vrai Rodin*, 2nd ed. (Paris, 1913), p.226)

THE OTTOMAN AND THE WHATNOT

First published as 'The Ottoman and the Whatnot', *Athenaeum*, 27 June 1919, pp.529–30.

1 Antimacassar: a covering for the back of chairs to prevent staining from greasy hair. It was invented in the nineteenth century and Fry is using it as a symbol for Victorian attitudes.

2 Mr Podsnap's rhetoric: from Dickens's *Our Mutual Friend* (1864–5). Podsnap epitomises Victorian conservatism, narrowness and complacency.

3 'the young person': i.e. Podsnap's daughter, Georgina. One of his tests

of propriety was 'Would it bring a blush of shame to the cheeks of a young person?'

4 Ojibbeways and Waramunga: tribes of North American Indians.

5 The Ottoman: a couch with a head but no back, the body of which is 'stuffed over' so that no wood is visible.

6 a traitor: because the Ottoman (i.e. Turk) is a foreigner.

7 the Whatnot: a series of pillars holding shelves for china ornaments, and in this case the works of Tennyson and Whittier.

8 Tennyson and John Greenleaf Whittier: poets who represented, for Fry, Victorian propriety and moral rectitude. Whittier (1807–92) was an American Quaker.

9 'Distance ... the view': Thomas Campbell, *Pleasures of Hope* (1799), pt. i, l.7.

10 A Limoges casket: produced between the twelfth and the fourteenth centuries in south western France.

11 A cassone is a marriage coffer. It is often highly decorated and has large feet in the shape of claws. The panels on it are frequently painted with mythological subjects or with fables.

12 Boccaccian freedom: a reference to the bawdy tales which make up the *Decameron* of Giovanni Boccaccio (1313–75).

13 Caffieri: after Jacques Caffieri (1678–1755), a French worker in metal.

14 Riesener: after Jean Henri Riesener (1734–1806), a French cabinet-maker of the Louis XVI period.

15 a Louis XV tabatière: a French rococo snuff box.

16 *Stimmung*: mood.

17 Leech's drawings: John Leech (1817–64) was a cartoonist for *Punch* from 1847.

18 crewel-work: embroidery in which a design is worked in worsted on a background of linen or cloth.

19 *le style coco*: not a term in general use, but probably a diminutive or variant of *le style rococo*.

20 a future article: i.e. 'The Artist's Vision' which follows in *Vision and Design*.

THE ARTIST'S VISION

First published as 'The Artist's Vision', *Athenaeum*, 11 July 1919, pp.594–5.

ART AND SOCIALISM

First published as 'The Artist in the Great State' in *Socialism and the Great State*, ed. H.G. Wells *et al.* (1912), pp.251–72. The passage 'This question

. . . upon all this?' (pp.49–51) was added by Fry when the article was revised for *Vision and Design*.

1 Frances, Countess of Warwick (1861–1938), was a well-known socialist who founded various colleges and homes for children; Sir George Chiozza Money (1870–1944) was of Italian extraction and was Labour M.P. for E. Northants.; Sir Edwin Ray Lankester (1847–1929) was Professor of Zoology at London University; H.G. Wells (1866–1946) the novelist, was an active social campaigner. They all contributed essays to *Socialism and the Great State*.

2 Sir Ray Lankester says this in 'The Making of New Knowledge', *Socialism and the Great State*, pp.137–9.

3 The Art Treasures Exhibition at Manchester in 1857 was organised by George Schàrff, the first secretary of the National Portrait Gallery, and was seen by 1,050,000 people.

4 Two lectures delivered in Manchester in 1857.

5 The writing on the wall at Belshazzar's feast (Dan. 5:25): premonition of doom.

6 Marble quarried from Mount Pentelicus near Athens.

7 This was probably a speech given by Shaw as the closing address of the *Liverpool Courier* Book Exhibition on Saturday 14 Nov. 1908.

8 See note 4 above.

9 Fry was organising the Omega Workshop at the time of writing this essay (see Introduction, p.xix).

10 A wall covering invented by the linoleum manufacturer F. Walton in 1877. It was used to imitate wood panelling and stamped leather.

11 guilloche pattern: a continuous scroll formed by two or more bands twisted to create a plait.

12 anthemion: honeysuckle pattern in the form of a palmette. Actually the Greek word for 'flower'.

13 Fry is thinking, of course, of Cézanne.

14 The Kaiser-Friedrich-Museum, later the Bode Museum, was built by Ernst Eberhard von Ihne between 1897 and 1903. William II, who wished to promote the museum as an object of national prestige, came into conflict with Hugo von Tschudi, the director,who wanted to include Impressionist painting. See note on von Tschudi, 'El Greco', p.227.

15 'In the Mean State that is, the waste of work is so grievous that it is but the minority of the working population which is engaged in material production . . .'. (Leo Money, 'Work in the Great State', in *Socialism and the Great State*, p.75.)

16 The 'shop' or workshop of an artist where he painted with his apprentices.

17 'the adult units of our people . . . could probably do all that is now usefully done in not more than five hours a day.' (Leo Money, *Socialism and the Great State*, p.104.)

18 'In the Great State of the future, as in the life of the more prosperous classes of today, the greater proportion of occupations and activities will be private and free.' (H.G. Wells, 'The Past and the Great State', *Socialism and the Great State*, p.42.)

ART AND SCIENCE

First published as 'Art and Science' in the *Athenaeum*, 6 June 1919, pp.434–5.

1 *Athenaeum*, 11 April 1919, pp.176–7.

2 'The Justification of the Scientific Method', *Athenaeum*, 2 May 1919, pp.274–5.

3 Both of these aspects . . . and this becomes for the time being a universe: this long passage was first written for the *Burlington Fine Arts Club Catalogue of an Exhibition of Florentine Painting Before 1500* (1919). It was removed from the essay 'The Art of Florence' and placed in 'Art and Science' when the two were reprinted in *Vision and Design*.

THE ART OF THE BUSHMEN

First published as 'Bushman Paintings', *Burlington Magazine*, 16 (March 1910), pp.334–8.

1 Emmanuel Loewy, *The Rendering of Nature in Early Greek Art*, trans. J. Fothergill (1907) [Fry's note].

2 Loewy, p.5.

3 *Bushman Drawings*, copied by M. Helen Tongue, intro. Henry Balfour (Oxford, 1909) [Fry's note].

4 Henry Balfour was the author of *The Evolution of Decorative Art. An Essay upon its origin and development as illustrated by the art of modern races of mankind* (1893). Balfour points out that the serious study of decorative art went back to George Harris, *The Theory of the Arts* (1869).

5 *Bushman Drawings*, p.9.

6 Henry Head (1861–1940) was a neurologist and editor of *Brain*. He was brought up, like Fry, a Quaker and like Fry, too, he combined an objective scientific view of things with a preoccupation with mysticism. He was consulted by Leonard Woolf after Virginia Woolf's breakdown in 1913.

7 Dorothea F. Bleek was the author of numerous works on Bushman and South African rock-painting.

NEGRO SCULPTURE

First published in the *Athenaeum*, 16 April 1920, p.516.

1 *galbe*: the contour or outline.

ANCIENT AMERICAN ART

First published as 'American Archeology', *Burlington Magazine* 33 (Nov. 1918), pp.155–7.

1 Thomas A. Joyce, *South American Archeology* (1912); *Mexican Archeology* (1914); *Central American Archeology* (1916).

2 Lord Kingsborough's monumental work: Augustine Aglio, *Antiquities of Mexico*, ed. Edward King, Viscount Kingsborough, 9 vols. (1830–48).

3 C.H. Read, 'Ancient Peruvian Pottery', *Burlington Magazine* 17 (April 1910), p.22 [Fry's note].

4 Gauguin copied Aztec sculpture at the Exposition of 1889, according to Robert Goldwater in *Primitivism in Modern Art* (New York, 1938, revised ed. 1967), p.66.

5 Tiahuanaco gateway: Tiahuanaco is now in Bolivia, some 21 kilometres from Lake Titicaca. It consists of a group of buildings begun 1000 BC of which the 'Gate of the Sun' is the most important. It is constructed of a single block of Andesite 3 × 3.75m.

6 Truxillo pottery: pottery from the Chicama Valley, Truxillo, Peru. It is discussed and illustrated in the article mentioned in note 3.

7 Walter Lehmann was the Keeper of the Royal Ethnographic Museum at Berlin.

8 The Shang dynasty collapsed in 1050 BC and was superseded by the Chou dynasty which prevailed until 256 BC.

9 a history of the Mormons published in 1851: Fry is probably thinking of J.W. Gunnison, *The Mormons; or Latter-Day Saints . . . a History* (London and Philadelphia, 1852).

10 Brigham Young was a Mormon leader in the mid-nineteenth century after the death of Adam Smith. He was the founder of Salt Lake City.

THE MUNICH EXHIBITION OF MOHAMMEDAN ART

This was first published in the *Burlington Magazine* 17 (Aug. 1910), pp.283–90 and 17 (Sept. 1910), pp.327–33. Fry also wrote a review of the exhibition for the *Morning Post*, 29 July 1910, p.9.

1 Sassanid: the Sassanian period (AD 226–637) saw the creation of a new style of abstract, pseudo-floral ornament. It was one of the most brilliant periods of Islamic art.

2 Aurel Stein, Albert von Le Coq, Albert Grunwedel, Paul Pelliot were all contemporary archaeologists and collectors. They are mentioned in Jeanette Mirsky, *Sir Aurel Stein* (Chicago, 1977).

3 cloisonnée enamel: enamel poured into *cloisons* or compartments formed by a network of metal bands on the surface of an object.

4 Orthokid enamel: this was probably a mirror dedicated to Abdoul Fadl Orotk Chah and is mentioned in a work of reference which Fry used: Gaston Migeon, *Manuel d'art musulman* (Paris, 1907), ii, 234.

5 Limoges enamels: enamel painting which began in the mid-twelfth century in the Abbey of Solignac near Limoges. It flourished until the fourteenth century.

6 There seems to be no reference to this in the work of Babelon, but the cut glass is illustrated in Migeon, ii, 374–5.

7 Friedrich Sarre was a prolific writer on Islamic art and an archaeologist. He excavated Samarra on the Tigris above Baghdad. He was one of the editors of the huge three-volume catalogue produced for the exhibition – *Die Ausstellung von Meisterwerken Mohammedanischer Kunst in München, 1910*.

8 Sapor or Bishapur: Shapur I (AD 3) commemorated his victories over Rome by a series of bas-reliefs carved on the rock-face of Fars and in the gorge of Bishapur.

9 The relief of Chosroes is at Taq-i-Bostan in Kurdistan. Chosroes I (AD 531–78) was a king of the Sassanid dynasty and was known as 'the Blessed'.

10 repoussé: relief or decoration on metal, especially silver or copper, by hammering from the underside.

11 Khorsabad is a late eighth–early seventh century BC royal palace near Mousul.

12 Coptic: the Copts were Christian Egyptians who broke away from the Church after the Council of Chalcedon in AD 451. They developed an artistic style which, though derived initially from Hellenistic and Byzantine art, and later influenced by Islamic art, is nevertheless unique and individual.

13 Most of Prince Bobrinsky's collection is now in the Hermitage.

14 Assurbanipal or Ashurbanipal was King of Nineveh in 668 BC and Sennacherib was King of Assyria, assassinated in 680 BC. The history of the latter is recorded in a number of cuneiform inscriptions.

15 Rhages or Rayy: the most important potting town of the Seljuk period (twelfth and thirteenth centuries) and a cultural centre of the first rank, near Tehran. Here the most advance methods were carried on until the mid-thirteenth century, producing luxury wares such have rarely been equalled since.

16 Mossoul or Mosul (now in N. Iraq) was a renowned centre for the production of finely engraved and inlaid brass from the time of the Seljuks.

17 aquamanile: a medieval bronze ewer for ablutions at table, often in the shape of an animal.

18 The bronze griffin in the Campo Santo, Pisa, is a Fatimid sculpture of the eleventh century. It is illustrated in *The Legacy of Islam*, ed. T. Arnold and A. Guillaume (Oxford, 1931), fig. 18.

19 An aquamanile bronze in the form of a peacock and an incense burner in the form of a parrot, both in the Louvre, are illustrated in Migeon, *Manuel*, ii, 225–7.

20 palmette: a fan-shaped decorative motif resembling a palmated leaf or a panicle of flowers.

21 *intreccie*: interlacery or plaitwork.

22 Gaston Migeon, 'Notes d'archéologie musulmane', *Gazette des Beaux-Arts* 33 (June 1905), pp.441–55 and *Manuel*, i, 226.

23 Mariano Fortuny y Madrazo, born in 1871 in Granada, the son of the painter Mariano Fortuny y Carbó. He lived and worked in Venice.

24 This was the 'Exhibition of the Fayence of Persia and the Nearer East', 1908.

25 Ibn Tulun: an early mosque (built AD 876–9) in Cairo.

26 Abdullah ben el-Fadhl or Abdallāh ibn al-Fadl was a Persian miniaturist.

27 Rakka or Raqqa is on the Euphrates near Aleppo. Elaborate faience techniques were developed there in the twelfth century.

28 Fouquet: lived in Cairo and his huge collection of Coptic and Egypto-Arabic ceramic work was sold in 1922.

29 Charles V (1338–80).

GIOTTO

First published as 'Giotto', *Monthly Review*, i (Dec. 1900), pp.139–57 and *Monthly Review*, ii (Feb. 1901), pp.96–121. It was the second part of a much longer piece and came immediately after Fry's 'Art Before Giotto', *Monthly Review*, i (Oct. 1900), pp.126–51.

1 Sigismondo Pandolfo Malatesta (1417–68), despot of Rimini, whose prowess on the battlefield was matched by his patronage of the arts.

2 St Bonaventura's *Life* was known as the *Legenda Maior* and was written between 1260 and 1263 as an authoritative biography to dispel all the inaccurate stories that had grown up around the saint.

3 Bonaventura, *Legenda Maior* in *Opera Omnia*, ed. Quaracchi (Ad Claras

Aquas, 1882–1902), VIII. viii. 6. The extracts from the *Legenda* seem to correspond to no standard English translation, so are probably Fry's own.

4 See H. Thode, *Franz von Assisi und die Anfänge der Kunst der Renaissance in Italien* (Berlin, 1885) [Fry's note].

5 Jacopone da Todi (1220/30–1306) was a famous ascetic, mystic poet, and contemporary of Dante. He entered the Franciscan order but was excommunicated for opposing papal authority.

6 Pindar (518–438 BC) was noted for his splendour of language, rhythm and imagery.

7 Lorenzo Ghiberti, *Commentarii* (*c.*1450) was written in the last years of his life and contains observations on fourteenth-century Tuscan art. Giorgio Vasari, *Le Vite de' più eccellenti pittori, scultori et architettori*, 2nd ed. (1568), the major source of pre-Renaissance art-historical information.

8 This is a shortened version of Genesis and Fry is referring to the story of Joseph. Fry probably saw the twenty-four manuscript leaves reproduced in W. Ritter von Hartel and Franz Wickhoff, *Die Wiener Genesis herausgegeben* (Vienna, 1895).

9 triforium: an arcaded wall-passage facing on to the nave between the arcade and the clerestory.

10 This is *Esau's return from Hunting* in the Upper Church, by the Master of the Esau Fresco.

11 caryatid: a supporting pillar cast in female form.

12 spandrill or spandrell: the triangular space between the side of an arch or the surface between two arches in an arcade.

13 See note 10.

14 i.e. in his *Commentarii*.

15 Petrus Rudolphus: Pietro Ridolfi da Tossignano, *Historiam seraphicae religionis libri tres* (1578), ii, 185. For a more recent account of the historical evidence see Alastair Smart, *The Assisi Problem and the Art of Giotto* (1971).

16 Robert Browning, 'Old Pictures in Florence', xxiii from *Men and Women* (1855).

> But at any rate I have loved the season
> Of Art's spring-birth so dim and dewy;
> My sculptor is Nicolo the Pisan,
> My painter – who, but Cimabue?

17 Mr Punch: George Du Maurier created the caricature figure of Mrs Cimabue Brown as a parody of the female aesthete in the late 1870s and early 1880s.

18 a distinguished critic: J.P. Richter, *Lectures on the National Gallery* (1898), pp.6–8 [Fry's note].

19 C.F.L. Felix von Rumohr, *Italienische Forschungen*, 3 vols. (Berlin, 1827–31). This work was important for giving a historical basis to the taste for early Italian art in the 1830s.

20 Dante, *Purgatorio*, XI. xi. 94–6: 'Cimabue thought to hold the field in painting; and now it is Giotto's name that is on everybody's lips, so that the other's fame is obscured.' Quoted Smart, op.cit., p.48.

21 Cimabue (*c.*1240–1302), *Madonna of Sta Trinità*, now in the Uffizi.

22 *The Virgin with Angels*. There is some doubt as to whether it is entirely by Cimabue.

23 The Maesta or Virgin in Majesty was painted in 1311 to replace an older image on the high altar of Siena cathedral. It is now in the cathedral museum but some of the predella scenes are scattered outside Italy.

24 morbidezza: i.e. softness.

25 I have been unable to discover where Horne made this claim.

26 Caravaggio (1573–1610); Agostino Carracci (1557–1602), Annibale (1560–1609) and Lodovico (1555–1619) are representative of High Baroque painting in Rome. Most notable is the decoration of the Farnese Palace by Annibale Carracci, brother of Agostino.

27 Nicòla Pisano (active *c.*1258–78).

28 Frescoes by Consulus at the Sacro Speco Subiaco. The portrait of St Francis was painted at the time of his visit to the convent *c.*1210.

29 the Cosmati: a family of marble workers active in Rome from the beginning of the twelfth century to the end of the thirteenth. Their work was Byzantine but with strong classical influence. Fry mentions the way in which their work was 'brought to an untimely end by the political disasters of the fourteenth century' (*Macmillan's Guide to Italy* [1901], p.xxxvii).
Jacopo Torriti: active 1295 and known by only two mosaics in Rome – the apses of S. Giovanni in Laterano and Sta Maria Maggiore.
Filippo Rusutti: active 1300; known by mosaics above the portico of Sta Maria Maggiore.
Pietro Cavallini: active 1273–1308. Mosaics of the life of the Virgin in Sta Maria Trastevere, Rome, 1291 and the Last Judgment in Sta Cecilia in Trastevere, Rome, *c.*1293.

30 In 1900 Federico Hermann gained access to the nuns' choir to find the fresco of the Last Judgment partly covered.

31 'Doctors of the Church': mosaics on the ceiling of the nave in the Upper Church of San Francesco at Assisi. They were painted to celebrate the cult of the *doctores* promulgated in 1297.

32 Giovanni Pisano (active *c.*1265–1314), son of Nicòla.

33 i.e. the Baptistery at Pisa.

34 Presepio: the Christmas crib.

35 Jean François, Béraud (1849–1936). His *Magdalen at the House of the Pharisees* was shown at the exhibition of the Société des Beaux Arts in 1891 and illustrated on p.151 of the catalogue. It was described in the *Art Journal* n.s. 15 (Jan. 1895), pp.21–2.

36 Fry is using Mrs Gamp from Dickens's *Martin Chuzzlewit* (1843–4) to personify the commonplace. 'Ercles' vein' he uses to suggest the heroic: cf. Bottom, in a fit of bombast: 'This was lofty ... This is Ercles' vein, a tyrant's vein' (*A Midsummer Night's Dream*, I. ii. 42–3).

37 See note 29.

38 Albigensian crusade: the Albigensians were a heretical sect in southern France during the late twelfth and early thirteenth centuries. The cruel crusade conducted against them by Innocent III was led by Simon de Montfort.

39 Petrus Waldus or Waldo was the leader of a reforming body of Christians formed about 1170. They came from Piedmont, Dauphiné and Provence, joined the Reformation movement and were severely persecuted.

40 *Three Maries*: they are from the rear of the *Maestà*, Siena.

41 Bernard Berenson, 'The Central Italian Painters of the Renaissance' in *The Italian Painters of the Renaissance*, new ed. (1952), p.90. Berenson mentions the 'Three Maries' of Duccio, but the comparison between Giotto and Duccio is made later in the essay and not in connection with the *Three Maries*.

42 soffit: the underside of any architectural element.

43 *Legenda Maior*, xv, 3 and 5.

44 Cardinal Stefaneschi: died 1343.

45 The *Navicella* which was transferred from the old St Peter's to the portico of the new Basilica was so restored in the sixteenth and seventeenth centuries it is now considered to be a lost work.

46 This polytriptych, now thought to be by the followers of Giotto, is in the Pinacoteca, Vatican.

47 Melozzo da Forli (1438–94).

48 Scrovegni: In the *Inferno*, VII. xi. 65–73 it is Rinaldo dei Scrovegni who speaks to Dante.

49 the artist: his name was Bianchi. 'Faut-il se plaindre', says M. Maurice Denis in his *Théories*, 'qu'un Bianchi, plutôt que les laisser périr, ait ajouté un peu de la froidure de Flandrin aux fresques de Giotto à Santa Croce.' 'Les Elèves d'Ingres', *Théories* (1912), 4th ed. (Paris, 1920), p.103 [Fry's note].

50 Ambrogio and Pietro Lorenzetti were brothers, active in Siena in the early part of the fourteenth century.

51 Vasari relates how the Pope – probably Boniface VIII – sent a messenger

to Tuscany to find out how good a painter Giotto was and requesting 'a drawing, that he might send to his holiness. Giotto, who was very courteous, took a sheet of paper, and a pencil dipped in a red colour; then, resting his elbow on his side, to form a sort of compass, with one turn of the hand he drew a circle, so perfect and exact that it was a marvel to behold. This done, he turned, smiling to the courtier, saying, "Here is your drawing." ' (*Lives of the Most Eminent Painters ... etc.* trans. Mrs Jonathan Foster (1850), i, 102–3).

THE ART OF FLORENCE

First published as *Burlington Fine Arts Club Catalogue of an Exhibition of Florentine Painting Before 1500* (1919). A long extract from the text was removed for *Vision and Design* and inserted into the essay entitled 'Art and Science'. See notes to 'Art and Science', p.217.

1 Antonio Pisanello (*c.*1395–*c.*1455); Jacopo Bellini (*c.*1400–*c.*1470).

2 Fry probably alludes to Giotto's *Dormition of the Virgin* which is now in Berlin, and is perhaps the most important work of Giotto outside Italy. The Director of the National Gallery, Sir Charles Eastlake, missed it at an auction in London in 1863. Fry seems to have his dates wrong. See Cecil Gould, *One Hundred and Fifty Years of the National Gallery, 1824–1974* (1974), p.8.

3 Lady Jekyll's single figure of Christ: Giotto, *Salvator Mundi*. Half length, nearly life-size, bearded figure of the Saviour, seen in full-face gazing majestically out of the composition. He blesses in the Greek manner with the two first fingers of the right hand, and with His left holds against His breast the book of life. A patterned cruciform nimbus on a gold ground. The composition is placed within a geometrical design bounded by a circle. Purchased in Florence in 1876 by William Graham. Exhibited for the first time at the Grafton Galleries *Exhibition of Old Masters* (1911). Catalogue edited by Roger Fry and Maurice W. Brockwell (pp.3-4, ill. plate 2). In spite of the importance of this piece it seems to have disappeared. In 1957 it was noticed that it formed the top part of Giotto's Crucifix in the Tempio Malatestiano, Rimini (see Federico Zeri, 'Due appunte su Giotto', *Paragone* 8 (July 1957), pp.79-87). At that time it was thought to be in a private collection 'in the south of England' (Zeri, p.85).

4 Mr Harris's Bernardo Daddi: Daddi (*c.*1300–50), a Crucifixion. In the centre of the composition Christ is nailed to the cross, down which blood is trickling from the Saviour's wounds. On the left of the Cross stands the Virgin, and on the right St John. Gold tooled background. Lent to the exhibition by Henry Harris. Now in the Louvre, Paris.

5 Giovanni da Milano: (active 1345–70). *St James the Elder*. Three-quarter length of St James the Elder, in red robe and green-blue mantle, holding a pilgrim's staff in his right hand and a book in his left. Present

whereabouts unknown.

6 Mr Rickett's single figure: Masaccio (1401–28). Roundel, *God the Father*. Acquired by the National Gallery in 1922. Bought by Charles Ricketts from a shop in Bayswater in 1908 as a Russian icon. The attribution to Masaccio is disputed. See Martin Davies, *National Gallery Catalogue. The Early Italian Schools*, 2nd ed. (1961), p.189.

7 Filippo Brunelleschi (1377–1446); Donatello (1386–1466); Andrea del Castagno (1423–57); Paolo Uccello (1397–1475).

8 Piero della Francesca (1410/20–92); Luca Signorelli (1441–1523); Antonio del Pollaiuolo (1432–98).

9 Leonardo da Vinci (1452–1519).

10 Andrea del Verrocchio (1435–88).

11 Caravaggio: see note 6, p.213; Rembrandt van Rijn (1606–69).

12 These are the words of Michelangelo as quoted by the Portuguese painter Francesco d'Ollanda. See Charles Holroyd, *Michael Angelo Buonarroti* (1903), p.280. The actual words were: 'uma musica e uma melodia que somente o inteleito póde sentir, a grande deficuldade' (quoted Robert J. Clements, *Michelangelo's Theory of Art* (New York, 1961), p.18). Fry used this saying of Michelangelo's as an epigraph for his edition of the *Discourses of Sir Joshua Reynolds* (1905).

THE JACQUEMART-ANDRE COLLECTION

First published as 'Three Pictures in the Jacquemart-André Collection', *Burlington Magazine*, 25 (May 1919), pp.79-85.

1 The collection which belongs to the Institut de France was started by Edouard André (1833–94) and Nélie Jacquemart (1841–1912). André, the son of a banker, left the army in 1863 to devote himself to collecting works of art. Nélie Jacquemart abandoned her career as a painter when she married André and devoted her interest and talents to enriching the collection. The Hôtel André on Boulevard Haussmann was begun in 1869 and the museum inaugurated in 1875. The collection was a gift from Mme Jacquemart to the Institute.

2 *St George and the Dragon*: Catalogue suggests 'school of Uccello' (1397–1475). Tempera. Acquired for the collection in the Bardini sale, Florence, 1891.

3 Vasari says: 'Paolo Uccello would have proved himself the most original and inventive genius ever devoted to the art of painting, from the time of Giotto downwards, had he bestowed but half the labour on the delineation of men and animals that he lost and threw away over the minutiae of perspective.' (*Lives of the . . . Painters*, trans. Foster, i, 348.)

4 Jan van Eyck (*c.*1390–1441). W.P. Frith (1819–1909). Famous for

panoramas of Victorian life, e.g. *Ramsgate Sands* (1854), *Derby Day* (1858), and *The Railway Station* (1862).

5 the National Gallery battle-piece: i.e. *Niccolò Mauruzi da Tolentino at the Battle of San Romano*. Purchased for the National Gallery in 1857.

6 Alesso Baldovinetti (1425–99).

7 *Virgin and Child*: Tempera on canvas. Possibly a Church Banner. Acquired for the collection from the Bardini sale, Florence, 1891.

8 *Portrait of a Lady in Yellow*. The attribution to Baldovinetti first made by Fry in the *Burlington Magazine*, 18 (1911), pp.311 ff., is now generally accepted.

9 *The Most Holy Trinity with SS. Benedict and John Gualberto*: painted in 1471 and brought to the Accademia in 1810 from the Convent of S. Trinità where it originally adorned the main altar of the Church.

10 Luca Signorelli: see note 8, p.225.

DÜRER AND HIS CONTEMPORARIES

This is a shortened form of Fry's introduction to *Records of Journeys to Venice and the Low Countries by Albrecht Dürer* (Boston, 1913).

1 this volume: i.e. Dürer's *Records of Journeys*.

2 Wilibald Pirkheimer or Pirckheimer (1470–1530), an erudite German humanist.

3 *Melancholia*: engraving (1514). *Knight, Death and the Devil*: engraving (1513).

4 literary beauty and power: 'I saw also that Death smote her two great strokes to the heart' [Fry's note in *Records of Journeys*].

5 Adam Kraft or Krafft (*c.*1460–*c.*1508). One of the founders of the Nuremberg school. His most celebrated work is the Ciborium in the choir of St Lawrence, Nuremberg.

6 Niclaus Storr or Stör: died 1562 at Nuremberg.

7 Oswold Krell or Oswalt Krel: a merchant of Lindau. Dürer's portrait of him was painted in 1499 and is now in the Pinakothek, Munich.

8 Hieronymous Holtschuer or Holzschuher: his portrait was painted in 1526 and is in the Staatliche Museen, Berlin-Dahlem.

9 Martin Schongauer (*c.*1430–91).

10 representation: 'Nothing in Dürer's engraved work can compare for unity and expressive purposefulness of disposition with Schongauer's engraving of the Virgin and Child' [Fry's note in *Records of Journeys*].

11 *Death of Orpheus*: (Hamburg, Kunsthalle). *Bacchanal with Silenus* (Vienna, Albertina). *Battle of the Gods* (Vienna, Albertina).

12 the so-called Tarocchi engravings: These were once thought to be a pack of cards based on designs by Mantegna, but A.M. Hind in the *Catalogue of Early Italian Engravings... in the British Museum* (1910) says that the collection 'neither forms a pack of *tarocchi* nor bears any... definite relation to Mantegna' (p.217).

13 Francesco del Cossa (*c*.1435–*c*.1477). His paintings are to be found in Ferrara and Bologna.

14 the Pope: another of the Tarocchi engravings in the British Museum.

15 *Knight and Page*: no date (London, British Museum).

16 'It is only fair to state that in the Genius of Time the empty and inflated drapery over the chest in the original is greatly improved by Dürer, who gives the torso more plastic relief, but even here the relation of the body to the legs lacks the continuity of the Tarocchi engraving' [Fry's note in *Records of Journeys*].

17 Antonio del Pollaiuolo: see note 8, p.225. Lorenzo di Credi (1458–1537).

EL GRECO

First published as 'The New El Greco at the National Gallery', *Athenaeum*, 6 Feb. 1920, 170-2.

1 Charles John Holmes (1868–1936), painter, critic and administrator. He was a student of Charles Ricketts and from 1905 was a member of the New English Art Club where he exhibited his paintings. Between 1903 and 1909 he edited the *Burlington Magazine* and in 1910 he supported Fry in the first Post-Impressionist exhibition. In 1916 he became Director of the National Gallery and wrote a number of books on the history of art.

2 the new El Greco: see note 6 below.

3 Wilhelm von Bode joined the Berlin Museum in 1872 and became Director in 1905. He was an art historian of some distinction and massively extended the museum. In 1956 the Kaiser-Friedrich-Museum was renamed the Bode Museum.

4 Gian Lorenzo Bernini (1598–1680). El Greco (1541–1614).

5 Donato Bramante (1444–1514).

6 Christ in the National Gallery: El Greco, *The Agony in the Garden of Gethsemane*. Probably a workshop repetition of the same subject now at Toledo (Ohio). It was bought from the Convento de Las Salesas Nuevas, Madrid, by Lionel Harris in 1919 and from him for the National Gallery in November 1919.

7 Nicolas Poussin (1594–1665).

8 Hugo von Tschudi (1851–1911). In 1884 became assistant to Wilhelm von Bode with whom he published *Beschreibung der Bildwerke der Christlichen*

Epoche... etc. (Berlin, 1888). He became Director of the National Gallery, Berlin, in 1896 and in 1907, Director of the National Galleries of Munich. He was the author of many works on art and artists, but was chiefly known, together with Liebermann and Meier-Graefe, for having introduced the Impressionists into Germany. He came into conflict with Emperor William II over his policy on Impressionism.

THREE PICTURES IN TEMPERA BY WILLIAM BLAKE

First published with an extra final paragraph as 'Three Pictures in Tempera By William Blake', *Burlington Magazine*, 4 (March 1904), pp.204-6.

1 Ottley's prints: William Young Ottley, *The Italian Schools of Design: being a series of fac-similes of original drawings, by the most eminent painters and sculptors of Italy; with biographical notices of the artists, and observations on their work* (1823). This work did much to popularise early Italian art in England.

2 In 1920 this was in the possession of Graham Walford Robinson (1866–1948), the painter, poet and collector of Blake. In 1949 it was sold at Christies to George Goyder.

3 This is a quotation (with slight inaccuracies) from 'A Descriptive Catalogue of Pictures IV' in *The Complete Works of William Blake*, ed. Geoffrey Keynes (Oxford, 1966), p.576.

4 *Bathsheba at the Bath* was presented to the Tate Gallery by the National Art Collections Fund in 1914.

5 virid: i.e. green, blooming.

CLAUDE

First published in the *Burlington Magazine*, 11 (Aug. 1907), pp.267-98.

1 Claude Lorraine (1600–82).

2 *repoussoir*: a strong foreground passage.

3 Describing a sketch in the *Liber Veritatis* Ruskin wrote: 'Look only at the wretched archery, and consider if it would be possible for any child to draw the thing with less understanding, or more mistakes in the given compass.' (*Modern Painters III*, in the *Complete Works*, ed. E.T. Cook and Alexander Wedderburn (1903–12), v, 404.)

4 the rocky shores of a stream: there are many drawings of this kind by Claude but Fry is probably referring to BM no. Oo. 6-76, H. 63.

5 Du Maurier's aesthetes: a reference to cartoons which appeared in *Punch* between 1877 and 1883 when the 'aesthetic' craze was at its height. They often poked fun at the language of art-criticism. The words 'in the picture' are taken from a conversation between a Philistine and an aesthete in a

caption to a Du Maurier cartoon. It must have appealed to Fry since it was the kind of criticism that was made of his first Post-Impressionist exhibition in 1910. The conversation is as follows:

MODERN AESTHETICS

(*Ineffable Youth goes into ecstacies over an extremely Old Master – say,* Fra Porcinello Babaragianno, A.D. 1266–1281?)

Matter-of-Fact Party. 'But it's such a repulsive *subject!*'
Ineffable Youth. '"Subject" in Art is of no moment! The *Picktchah* is beautiful!'
Matter-of-Fact Party. 'But you'll own the *Drawing's* vile, and the *Colour's* beastly!'
Ineffable Youth. 'I'm Cullah-blind, and don't p'ofess to understand D'awing! The *Picktchah* is beautiful!'
Matter-of-Fact Party (getting warm). 'But it's all out of *Perspective*, hang it! and so abominably *untrue to Nature!*'
Ineffable Youth. 'I don't care about Naytchah, and hate Perspective! The *Picktchah* is *most* beautiful!'
Matter-of-Fact Party (losing all self-control). 'But, dash it all, Man! where the *Dickens* is the *beauty*, then?'
Ineffable Youth (quietly). 'In the Picktchah!'
[*Total defeat of Matter-of-Fact Party.*]

(*Punch*, 72 (10 Feb. 1877), p.51.)

6 This quotation is: 'De mon aimable erreur je fus désabusé' (*Bérénice*, II. ii. 461).

7 *Romeo and Juliet*, II. i. 1-2.

8 *Poems of John Keats*, ed. G. Thorn Drury, introduction by Robert Bridges (London and New York, 1896), I, xci.

9 *ceteris paribus*: other things being equal.

10 *Seacoast With the Landing of Aeneas in Latium.* BM no. Oo. 7-160, H. 275.

11 The *Liber Veritatis*: a personal record in the form of sketches of Claude's own paintings to guard against forgeries.

12 Possibly BM no. Oo. 6-87, H. 177.

13 There are a number of studies of the Tiber. This may be BM no. Oo. 6-8, H. 131.

14 Mr Heseltine's collection: John P. Heseltine (1843–1929) sold his collection of thirty-eight Claudes in 1912. They found their way to the Louvre in 1918.

15 Copy from an Antique Landscape. BM no. 7-239, H. 249. Marcel Roethlisberger writes: 'This extraordinary drawing copies exactly what must

have been the finest and largest antique landscape fresco known at the time. It had been found in 1624–25 "in hortis Barberini" during the excavation work for Palazzo Barberini on a wall of a funeral crypt. ... This is Claude's only copy from an antique picture' (*Claude Lorraine: The Drawings* [California, 1968], Catalog, p.322).

16 *Noli me tangere*: *Landscape with Christ and the Magdalen*. BM no. Oo. 8-256, H. 312. One of four preliminary drawings for a painting done in 1680–1 for Cardinal Spada.

AUBREY BEARDSLEY'S DRAWINGS

First published as an unsigned review in the *Athenaeum*, 5 Nov. 1904, pp.627-8.

1 Richard Doyle (1824–83). Book illustrator and painter of fairy subjects. Worked for *Punch* in 1840s.
Albert Robida (1848–1926). As a caricaturist he was associated with many Parisian journals after 1866.

2 *Siegfried* (1892–3). Illustration of Act II. Now in the Victoria and Albert Museum, London.

3 Antonio Pollaiuolo: see note 8, p.225.

4 Andrea Mantegna (1431–1506).

5 Salome series: formerly in the collection of John Lane.

6 *mesquinerie*: i.e. meanness.

7 Ignacio Zuloaga Zabaleta (1870–1945). Associated with the Symbolists and with Degas and Rodin.

THE FRENCH POST-IMPRESSIONISTS

First published as 'The French Group' in the *Catalogue of the Second Post-Impressionist Exhibition*, Grafton Galleries, 1912.

1 two years ago: i.e. in 1910.

2 Henri Rousseau (1844–1910).

3 By 'the later works of Picasso' Fry is referring to what we now call his early Cubist paintings.

4 *Head of a Man*: this picture (oil on paper) painted in the Spring of 1913 was then owned by Fry and is now in the collection of Mr Richard Zeisler.

5 André Derain (1880–1954). Associated with the Fauves in 1905. Showed Cubist influence in 1908. Illustrated Apollinaire, Jacob and Wilde.
Auguste Herbin (1882–1960). Came to Paris in 1901 as an Impressionist. Fully-fledged Cubist by 1909.

André Lhote (1885–1962). Influenced by Gauguin. Came to Paris in 1908. Had his first one-man show at the Galerie Druet in 1910.
Jean Marchand: see note to essay on Marchand, p.234 below.

6 Henri Doucet (1883–1915). Exhibited at Salon d'Automne in 1908 and Salon des Indépendents in 1911. Much praised by poet Charles Vildrac who was a close friend of Roger Fry.
Maurice Asselin (1882–1947). Member of the jury of the Salon d'Automne in 1910.

7 Probably a reference to the painting of Edward Poynter and Laurens Alma-Tadema. See Introduction, p.xvi.

8 Fry is wrong about Rouault. He was represented by eight drawings at the First Post-Impressionist exhibitior

9 Gustave Moreau (1826–1898), the leading late-nineteenth-century Symbolist painter.

DRAWINGS AT THE BURLINGTON FINE ARTS CLUB

First published with this title in the *Burlington Magazine*, 32 (Feb. 1919), pp.51–63.

1 Edgar Degas (1834–1917). There were two pictures by Degas in the exhibition.

2 Burlington Fine Arts Club, *Catalogue of a Collection of Drawings by Deceased Masters* (1917), p.8. The 'H.T.' of the catalogue is probably Henry Tonks who was on the exhibition committee and lent a drawing by Rowlandson.

3 Ibid., p.8.

4 Parrhasios (5th–4th century BC). Of the Ionic school. He worked in Athens and in Asia Minor.

5 Giovanni Battista Tiepolo (1696–1770). There were twelve drawings by Tiepolo in the exhibition.

6 A quotation from the so called 'Doctrine d'Ingres' in Maurice Denis, 'Les Elèves d'Ingres', in *Théories* (1912), 4th ed. (Paris, 1920), p.99. First published in *L'Occident*, July, Aug. and Sept., 1902. There were eight pictures by Ingres in the exhibition.

7 *Apotheosis of Napoleon*: the drawing which is signed 1824 was a sketch for the ceiling of the Grand Salle des Fêtes, Palais des Tuileries, Paris. The ceiling was destroyed by fire in 1871.

8 *Venus Anadyomene*: Chantilly, Musée Condé.

9 Dürer's *Beetle*: Stag-Beetle (*c.*1505). G. Tyser Collection, London. Thought by Panofsky to be by another hand. See *Albrecht Dürer* (Princeton Univ. Press, 1945), ii. 131.

10 Adolf Menzel (1815–1905). German painter of historical and genre scenes. Most of his works are in the National Gallery of Berlin. There were seven drawings by Menzel in the exhibition.

11 Charles Keene (1823–91). Cartoonist for *Punch*, *Illustrated London News* and *Once a Week*. There were six drawings by Keene in the exhibition.

12 O.M. Dalton 'Byzantine Enamels in Mr Pierpont Morgan's Collection', *Burlington Magazine*, 21 (April 1912), pp.3–10; (May 1912), pp.65–73; (June 1912), pp.127–8; (July 1912), pp.219–24; (Aug. 1912), p.290. Claude Anet, 'The "Manafi-i-Heiwan" – I', *Burlington Magazine*, 23 (July 1913), pp.224–31; II (Aug. 1913), p.261. Charles Vignier, 'New Excavations at Rhages', *Burlington Magazine*, 25 (July 1914), pp.211–18.

13 Henri Matisse (1869–1954); Amedeo Modigliani (1884–1920).

PAUL CEZANNE

First published as a review of *Paul Cézanne* by Ambroise Vollard in the *Burlington Magazine*, 31 (August 1917), pp.52–61.

1 i.e. Ambroise Vollard, *Paul Cézanne* (Paris, 1917). Vollard was a picture collector and friend of the Post-Impressionist painters. He was included in Maurice Denis's famous picture *Hommage à Cézanne* (1900). His portrait was painted not only by Cézanne (1900) but by Picasso, Rouault, Renoir and Bonnard. See *Recollections of a Picture Dealer*, trans. V.M. MacDonald (1936).

2 See Vollard, *Cézanne*, p.105.

3 i.e. 'take him over'. See Vollard, op. cit. p.101.

4 See Vollard, op. cit., pp.100, 114 and 119.

5 i.e. 'fawning and calculating'. See Vollard, op. cit., p.37.

6 'Son espoir était toujours le même: le salon de Bouguereau, en attendant le Louvre, qu'il regardait comme le seul abrit digne de son art' (Vollard, op. cit., p.98). Bouguereau (1825–1905) was the outstanding academic neo-classical painter of late-nineteenth-century France.

7 'Cabotin': i.e. a ham actor.

8 *L'Œuvre* by Emile Zola (1886). Claude Lantier, the hero, is often considered to be an amalgam of Manet and Cézanne. His revolutionary pictures create a *succès de scandale*, but he finally commits suicide.

9 the Dreyfusard question: a French political scandal between 1894 and 1914, centred on Alfred Dreyfus who was wrongly accused of espionage. In 1898 Zola published 'J'accuse' in *L'Aurore*. This was an open letter to the President of the Republic in support of Dreyfus. Accordingly Zola was prosecuted and ordered to pay 3,000 f. or go to gaol for a year. The issue divided the whole country.

10 Cabaner: According to Vollard, Cabaner was one of those who gathered at the Nouvelles Athènes in Paris. He was something of a poet, something of a philosopher and something of a musician (Vollard, op. cit., p.40).

11 Ibid., pp.41–2.

12 'Ce qu'il faut, c'est refaire le Poussin sur nature. Tout est là' (ibid., p.78).

13 The quotation reads: '"Ce Dominique est bougrement fort": puis, donnant un coup de pinceau et se reculant pour juger de l'effet: "mais il est bien em ..."' (ibid., p.94).

14 Ibid., p.87.

15 *Scène de plein air*: this is *Déjeuner sur l'Herbe* (1869–70), which Fry intended to include in *Vision and Design*; but it was overlooked and the illustration did not appear.

16 *Bathers resting*: (1875–6). Now in the Barnes Foundation, Philadelphia.

17 *Mme Cézanne in a greenhouse*: (*c.*1890). Now in New York, Metropolitan Museum of Art.

RENOIR

In 1920 Renoir died and Fry wrote 'The Last Words of Renoir', *Athenaeum*, 11 Jan. 1920, pp.771–2). This essay is based on 'Renoir' (*Athenaeum*, 20 Feb. 1920, p.247) with the passage 'More than any other ... reaction to life' added for *Vision and Design*.

1 'Pourquoi ... Batignolles.' I have been unable to find the source of this quotation.

2 Mornington Crescent: Sickert moved to 6 Mornington Crescent and set up a studio there in 1907.

3 *Les Parapluies*: painted 1881–6. Entered the National Gallery, London through the Lane Bequest in 1917.

4 Cosima or Cosimo Tura (1430–95). Ferrarese painter and late Gothic 'mannerist' with a highly individual style.

5 his celebrated saying: 'Tout dans la nature se modèle selon la sphère, le cône et le cylindre, il faut s'apprendre à peindre sur ces figures simples, on pourra ensuite faire tout ce qu'on voudra'. Emile Bernard, *Souvenirs sur Paul Cézanne* (Paris, 1912), p.35.

6 bas relief: sculpture with a minimum degree of projection from the background.

7 *Charpentier family*: in the Metropolitan Museum of Art, New York.

A POSSIBLE DOMESTIC ARCHITECTURE

First published as 'A Possible Domestic Architecture. A Challenge to Self-Conscious Picturesqueness', *Vogue*, 51 (March 1918), pp.40–1, 66, 68.

1 See note 2, p.214 above.

2 Mr Blow: Detmar Blow (1867–1939). He built 34, Queen Anne's Gate, 10 Carlton House Terrace and other London buildings; also Fonthill House, Bramham Park, Wilsford Manor, Heale House and Harewood House.

3 The house called 'Durbins' still stands in Chantrey Dean on the south side of Guildford.

4 On 8 April 1908 Fry wrote to his father Sir Edward Fry: 'I am thinking of taking a piece of land close to the Chantries at Guildford and building a house there. It seems clear that whatever happens the best chance for Helen [his wife] is to have a more or less country life without the excitement of London ... I find I can buy an acre of land on the edge of a chalk hill just outside Guildford (20 min. from the station). It faces S. and S.W. and is sheltered from N. and E. and has a lovely view. The land will cost £600 which is just the sum you kindly gave me lately and which I set aside for some such purpose. Having bought the land I could I find borrow the money for the building on mortgage. I have found that a home such as would fulfil our requirements would cost £1650 and that I could borrow this at 4%' (quoted Frances Spalding, *Roger Fry, Art and Life* (1980), p.112, from the Fry Papers, King's College, Cambridge).

5 The plate shows (from left to right): painting *Ka Cox* by Duncan Grant; painting in alcove, Florentine master; above mantelpiece, *Elephant Tray* by Duncan Grant; above door, picture *Maternity* by Vanessa Bell; right of door, altar-piece by Andrea di Giusti; in foreground, Omega embroidered chair-back and refectory table designed by Roger Fry.

JEAN MARCHAND

First published as 'Jean Marchand', *Athenaeum*, 11 April 1919, pp.178–9. Jean Hippolyte Marchand was born 1883 in Paris and had his first one-man show in London at the Carfax Gallery. In the introduction to the catalogue Clive Bell said that 'no living painter is more purely concerned with the creation of form, with the emotional significance of shapes and colours, than Marchand. ... He wants to create significant form, and all means to that end he finds good' (p.2). The exhibition was also favourably reviewed in *The Times*, 31 March 1919, p.15. In later life he reverted to naturalism and his pictures can be found in Paris, Chicago and the Tate Gallery, London.

1 André Derain (1880–1954).

2 'I feasted ... on the spectacle of ideal drawings, which I saw in the dark; all the work of my own hands: freely pencilled houses and trees, picturesque rocks and ruins, Cuyp-like groups of cattle, sweet paintings of butterflies hovering over unblown roses ... '(Charlotte Brontë, *Jane Eyre*, ed. J. Jack and M. Smith (Oxford, 1969), p.87).

3 Viollet-le-Duc (1814–79). Gothic revival architect and restorer. In 1845 he restored Notre Dame, Paris. He wrote voluminously on architectural building, restoration and history.

RETROSPECT

This essay was written for *Vision and Design* in 1920.

1 Balak called upon Balaam to curse the children of Israel, but God said, 'thou shalt not curse the people: for they are blessed' (Num. 22:12).

2 See note 8, p.213.

3 the 'Decorators': Fry is probably thinking of painters like Walter Crane, William Morris and Albert Moore.

4 Fry wrote an essay on Seurat in *Transformations* (1926).

5 On 27 September 1894 Fry wrote to his father, Sir Edward Fry, during the preparation of a set of lectures on Italian art: 'The more I study the Old Masters, the more terrible does the chaos of modern art seem to me' (see Introduction, p.xx).

6 Cézanne died in 1906. In 1904 a whole room in the Salon d'Automne had been set aside for his work.

7 'We confess to having been hitherto sceptical about Cézanne's genius but these two pieces [at the International Society exhibition] reveal a power which is entirely distinct and personal ...' (*Athenaeum*, 13 Jan. 1906, pp.56–7).

8 Fry favoured 'expressionists', but the journalist with whom he was discussing the problem disliked the term. So Fry said, 'Oh, let's just call them Post-Impressionists; at any rate, they came after the Impressionists' (see Desmond MacCarthy, 'The Art-Quake of 1910', *Listener*, 1 Feb. 1945). Fry's exhibition was called 'Manet and the Post-Impressionists' and one wonders to what extent the idea was influenced by an important history of painting by Théodore Duret, translated in 1910 as *Manet and the Impressionists*.

9 M. Lhote: In 1917 André Lhote defended the aims of synthetic cubism in *La Nouvelle Revue Française*. Its 'droit à la métaphore plastique ... pousse à la limite de la vraisemblance' (quoted in Katarina Ambrozić, *André Lhote et ses élèves jougoslaves* (Belgrade, 1974), p.42).

10 Tang: a Chinese dynasty which flourished between AD 618 and 906. It is best known for its ceramic tomb figures which appeared in Europe in 1909.
Ming: a Chinese dynasty 1368–1644.

11 Amico di Sandro: i.e. friend of Sandro Botticelli. A name given by Bernard Berenson to an artist he invented as the painter of several pictures which seemed to be between the styles of Botticelli and Filippino Lippi. Berenson later repudiated him and the pictures were reattributed.

12 Leo Tolstoy, *What is Art?*, trans. Aylmer Maude (1898).

13 These lectures are still unpublished and the manuscript is in the Fry Papers, King's College, Cambridge. They were given in 1909 and are summarised in Sutton, *Letters of Roger Fry*, p.315, note.

14 Clive Bell, *Art* (1914).

15 J.W. von Goethe, *Italian Journey*, trans. W.H. Auden and E. Mayer (1962), pp.431–2. The entry is for 25 Jan. 1787.

SELECT BIBLIOGRAPHY

✱

BIBLIOGRAPHY

Laing, Donald A., *Roger Fry. An Annotated Bibliography of The Published Writings* (New York and London, 1979).

BIOGRAPHY

Spalding, Frances, *Roger Fry, Art and Life* (London, 1980).

Sutton, Denys, ed., *Letters of Roger Fry*, 2 vols. (London, 1972).

Woolf, Virginia. *Roger Fry* (London, 1940, repr. Penguin Books, 1979).

CRITICAL WORKS

Bell, Clive, 'Roger Fry (1866–1934)', *Cornhill Magazine*, 166 (1952–3), pp.180–97.

Fishman, Solomon, *The Interpretation of Art* (Univ. of California Press, 1963).

Hannay, Howard, *Roger Fry, and Other Essays* (London, 1937).

Hough, Graham, 'Ruskin and Roger Fry: Two Aesthetic Theories', *Cambridge Journal*, 1 (1947–8), pp.14-27.

MacColl. D.S., 'A Note on Roger Fry', *Burlington Magazine*, 65 (Nov. 1934), pp. 231–5.

Nicolson, Benedict, 'Post-Impressionism and Roger Fry', *Burlington Magazine* 93 (Jan. 1951), pp.11–15.

Pevsner, Nikolaus, 'Ω', *Architectural Review*, 90 (1941), pp. 45–8.

Read, Herbert, 'Roger Fry as an Art Critic', *Listener*, 12 Oct. 1939, pp. 725–6.

Smart, Alistair, 'Roger Fry and Early Italian Art', *Apollo*, 33 (April 1966), pp. 262–71.

INDEX

✱

A CATALOG OF SELECTED

DOVER BOOKS

IN ALL FIELDS OF INTEREST

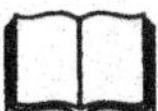

A CATALOG OF SELECTED DOVER BOOKS IN ALL FIELDS OF INTEREST

100 BEST-LOVED POEMS, Edited by Philip Smith. "The Passionate Shepherd to His Love," "Shall I compare thee to a summer's day?" "Death, be not proud," "The Raven," "The Road Not Taken," plus works by Blake, Wordsworth, Byron, Shelley, Keats, many others. 96pp. 5³⁄₁₆ x 8¼. 0-486-28553-7

100 SMALL HOUSES OF THE THIRTIES, Brown-Blodgett Company. Exterior photographs and floor plans for 100 charming structures. Illustrations of models accompanied by descriptions of interiors, color schemes, closet space, and other amenities. 200 illustrations. 112pp. 8⅜ x 11. 0-486-44131-8

1000 TURN-OF-THE-CENTURY HOUSES: With Illustrations and Floor Plans, Herbert C. Chivers. Reproduced from a rare edition, this showcase of homes ranges from cottages and bungalows to sprawling mansions. Each house is meticulously illustrated and accompanied by complete floor plans. 256pp. 9⅜ x 12¼. 0-486-45596-3

101 GREAT AMERICAN POEMS, Edited by The American Poetry & Literacy Project. Rich treasury of verse from the 19th and 20th centuries includes works by Edgar Allan Poe, Robert Frost, Walt Whitman, Langston Hughes, Emily Dickinson, T. S. Eliot, other notables. 96pp. 5³⁄₁₆ x 8¼. 0-486-40158-8

101 GREAT SAMURAI PRINTS, Utagawa Kuniyoshi. Kuniyoshi was a master of the warrior woodblock print — and these 18th-century illustrations represent the pinnacle of his craft. Full-color portraits of renowned Japanese samurais pulse with movement, passion, and remarkably fine detail. 112pp. 8⅜ x 11. 0-486-46523-3

ABC OF BALLET, Janet Grosser. Clearly worded, abundantly illustrated little guide defines basic ballet-related terms: arabesque, battement, pas de chat, relevé, sissonne, many others. Pronunciation guide included. Excellent primer. 48pp. 4⁵⁄₁₆ x 5¾. 0-486-40871-X

ACCESSORIES OF DRESS: An Illustrated Encyclopedia, Katherine Lester and Bess Viola Oerke. Illustrations of hats, veils, wigs, cravats, shawls, shoes, gloves, and other accessories enhance an engaging commentary that reveals the humor and charm of the many-sided story of accessorized apparel. 644 figures and 59 plates. 608pp. 6 ⅛ x 9¼. 0-486-43378-1

ADVENTURES OF HUCKLEBERRY FINN, Mark Twain. Join Huck and Jim as their boyhood adventures along the Mississippi River lead them into a world of excitement, danger, and self-discovery. Humorous narrative, lyrical descriptions of the Mississippi valley, and memorable characters. 224pp. 5³⁄₁₆ x 8¼. 0-486-28061-6

ALICE STARMORE'S BOOK OF FAIR ISLE KNITTING, Alice Starmore. A noted designer from the region of Scotland's Fair Isle explores the history and techniques of this distinctive, stranded-color knitting style and provides copious illustrated instructions for 14 original knitwear designs. 208pp. 8⅜ x 10⅞. 0-486-47218-3

CATALOG OF DOVER BOOKS

ALICE'S ADVENTURES IN WONDERLAND, Lewis Carroll. Beloved classic about a little girl lost in a topsy-turvy land and her encounters with the White Rabbit, March Hare, Mad Hatter, Cheshire Cat, and other delightfully improbable characters. 42 illustrations by Sir John Tenniel. 96pp. 5³⁄₁₆ x 8¼. 0-486-27543-4

AMERICA'S LIGHTHOUSES: An Illustrated History, Francis Ross Holland. Profusely illustrated fact-filled survey of American lighthouses since 1716. Over 200 stations — East, Gulf, and West coasts, Great Lakes, Hawaii, Alaska, Puerto Rico, the Virgin Islands, and the Mississippi and St. Lawrence Rivers. 240pp. 8 x 10¾. 0-486-25576-X

AN ENCYCLOPEDIA OF THE VIOLIN, Alberto Bachmann. Translated by Frederick H. Martens. Introduction by Eugene Ysaye. First published in 1925, this renowned reference remains unsurpassed as a source of essential information, from construction and evolution to repertoire and technique. Includes a glossary and 73 illustrations. 496pp. 6⅛ x 9¼. 0-486-46618-3

ANIMALS: 1,419 Copyright-Free Illustrations of Mammals, Birds, Fish, Insects, etc., Selected by Jim Harter. Selected for its visual impact and ease of use, this outstanding collection of wood engravings presents over 1,000 species of animals in extremely lifelike poses. Includes mammals, birds, reptiles, amphibians, fish, insects, and other invertebrates. 284pp. 9 x 12. 0-486-23766-4

THE ANNALS, Tacitus. Translated by Alfred John Church and William Jackson Brodribb. This vital chronicle of Imperial Rome, written by the era's great historian, spans A.D. 14-68 and paints incisive psychological portraits of major figures, from Tiberius to Nero. 416pp. 5³⁄₁₆ x 8¼. 0-486-45236-0

ANTIGONE, Sophocles. Filled with passionate speeches and sensitive probing of moral and philosophical issues, this powerful and often-performed Greek drama reveals the grim fate that befalls the children of Oedipus. Footnotes. 64pp. 5³⁄₁₆ x 8 ¼. 0-486-27804-2

ART DECO DECORATIVE PATTERNS IN FULL COLOR, Christian Stoll. Reprinted from a rare 1910 portfolio, 160 sensuous and exotic images depict a breathtaking array of florals, geometrics, and abstracts — all elegant in their stark simplicity. 64pp. 8⅜ x 11. 0-486-44862-2

THE ARTHUR RACKHAM TREASURY: 86 Full-Color Illustrations, Arthur Rackham. Selected and Edited by Jeff A. Menges. A stunning treasury of 86 full-page plates span the famed English artist's career, from *Rip Van Winkle* (1905) to masterworks such as *Undine, A Midsummer Night's Dream,* and *Wind in the Willows* (1939). 96pp. 8⅜ x 11. 0-486-44685-9

THE AUTHENTIC GILBERT & SULLIVAN SONGBOOK, W. S. Gilbert and A. S. Sullivan. The most comprehensive collection available, this songbook includes selections from every one of Gilbert and Sullivan's light operas. Ninety-two numbers are presented uncut and unedited, and in their original keys. 410pp. 9 x 12. 0-486-23482-7

THE AWAKENING, Kate Chopin. First published in 1899, this controversial novel of a New Orleans wife's search for love outside a stifling marriage shocked readers. Today, it remains a first-rate narrative with superb characterization. New introductory Note. 128pp. 5³⁄₁₆ x 8¼. 0-486-27786-0

BASIC DRAWING, Louis Priscilla. Beginning with perspective, this commonsense manual progresses to the figure in movement, light and shade, anatomy, drapery, composition, trees and landscape, and outdoor sketching. Black-and-white illustrations throughout. 128pp. 8⅜ x 11. 0-486-45815-6

THE BATTLES THAT CHANGED HISTORY, Fletcher Pratt. Historian profiles 16 crucial conflicts, ancient to modern, that changed the course of Western civilization. Gripping accounts of battles led by Alexander the Great, Joan of Arc, Ulysses S. Grant, other commanders. 27 maps. 352pp. 5⅜ x 8½. 0-486-41129-X

BEETHOVEN'S LETTERS, Ludwig van Beethoven. Edited by Dr. A. C. Kalischer. Features 457 letters to fellow musicians, friends, greats, patrons, and literary men. Reveals musical thoughts, quirks of personality, insights, and daily events. Includes 15 plates. 410pp. 5⅜ x 8½. 0-486-22769-3

BERNICE BOBS HER HAIR AND OTHER STORIES, F. Scott Fitzgerald. This brilliant anthology includes 6 of Fitzgerald's most popular stories: "The Diamond as Big as the Ritz," the title tale, "The Offshore Pirate," "The Ice Palace," "The Jelly Bean," and "May Day." 176pp. 5⅜ x 8½. 0-486-47049-0

BESLER'S BOOK OF FLOWERS AND PLANTS: 73 Full-Color Plates from Hortus Eystettensis, 1613, Basilius Besler. Here is a selection of magnificent plates from the *Hortus Eystettensis,* which vividly illustrated and identified the plants, flowers, and trees that thrived in the legendary German garden at Eichstätt. 80pp. 8⅜ x 11. 0-486-46005-3

THE BOOK OF KELLS, Edited by Blanche Cirker. Painstakingly reproduced from a rare facsimile edition, this volume contains full-page decorations, portraits, illustrations, plus a sampling of textual leaves with exquisite calligraphy and ornamentation. 32 full-color illustrations. 32pp. 9⅜ x 12¼. 0-486-24345-1

THE BOOK OF THE CROSSBOW: With an Additional Section on Catapults and Other Siege Engines, Ralph Payne-Gallwey. Fascinating study traces history and use of crossbow as military and sporting weapon, from Middle Ages to modern times. Also covers related weapons: balistas, catapults, Turkish bows, more. Over 240 illustrations. 400pp. 7¼ x 10⅛. 0-486-28720-3

THE BUNGALOW BOOK: Floor Plans and Photos of 112 Houses, 1910, Henry L. Wilson. Here are 112 of the most popular and economic blueprints of the early 20th century — plus an illustration or photograph of each completed house. A wonderful time capsule that still offers a wealth of valuable insights. 160pp. 8⅜ x 11. 0-486-45104-6

THE CALL OF THE WILD, Jack London. A classic novel of adventure, drawn from London's own experiences as a Klondike adventurer, relating the story of a heroic dog caught in the brutal life of the Alaska Gold Rush. Note. 64pp. 5$\frac{3}{16}$ x 8¼. 0-486-26472-6

CANDIDE, Voltaire. Edited by Francois-Marie Arouet. One of the world's great satires since its first publication in 1759. Witty, caustic skewering of romance, science, philosophy, religion, government — nearly all human ideals and institutions. 112pp. 5$\frac{3}{16}$ x 8¼. 0-486-26689-3

CELEBRATED IN THEIR TIME: Photographic Portraits from the George Grantham Bain Collection, Edited by Amy Pastan. With an Introduction by Michael Carlebach. Remarkable portrait gallery features 112 rare images of Albert Einstein, Charlie Chaplin, the Wright Brothers, Henry Ford, and other luminaries from the worlds of politics, art, entertainment, and industry. 128pp. 8⅜ x 11. 0-486-46754-6

CHARIOTS FOR APOLLO: The NASA History of Manned Lunar Spacecraft to 1969, Courtney G. Brooks, James M. Grimwood, and Loyd S. Swenson, Jr. This illustrated history by a trio of experts is the definitive reference on the Apollo spacecraft and lunar modules. It traces the vehicles' design, development, and operation in space. More than 100 photographs and illustrations. 576pp. 6¾ x 9¼. 0-486-46756-2

DOOMED SHIPS: Great Ocean Liner Disasters, William H. Miller, Jr. Nearly 200 photographs, many from private collections, highlight tales of some of the vessels whose pleasure cruises ended in catastrophe: the *Morro Castle, Normandie, Andrea Doria, Europa,* and many others. 128pp. 8⅞ x 11¾. 0-486-45366-9

THE DORÉ BIBLE ILLUSTRATIONS, Gustave Doré. Detailed plates from the Bible: the Creation scenes, Adam and Eve, horrifying visions of the Flood, the battle sequences with their monumental crowds, depictions of the life of Jesus, 241 plates in all. 241pp. 9 x 12. 0-486-23004-X

DRAWING DRAPERY FROM HEAD TO TOE, Cliff Young. Expert guidance on how to draw shirts, pants, skirts, gloves, hats, and coats on the human figure, including folds in relation to the body, pull and crush, action folds, creases, more. Over 200 drawings. 48pp. 8¼ x 11. 0-486-45591-2

DUBLINERS, James Joyce. A fine and accessible introduction to the work of one of the 20th century's most influential writers, this collection features 15 tales, including a masterpiece of the short-story genre, "The Dead." 160pp. 5³⁄₁₆ x 8¼. 0-486-26870-5

EASY-TO-MAKE POP-UPS, Joan Irvine. Illustrated by Barbara Reid. Dozens of wonderful ideas for three-dimensional paper fun — from holiday greeting cards with moving parts to a pop-up menagerie. Easy-to-follow, illustrated instructions for more than 30 projects. 299 black-and-white illustrations. 96pp. 8⅜ x 11. 0-486-44622-0

EASY-TO-MAKE STORYBOOK DOLLS: A "Novel" Approach to Cloth Dollmaking, Sherralyn St. Clair. Favorite fictional characters come alive in this unique beginner's dollmaking guide. Includes patterns for Pollyanna, Dorothy from *The Wonderful Wizard of Oz,* Mary of *The Secret Garden,* plus easy-to-follow instructions, 263 black-and-white illustrations, and an 8-page color insert. 112pp. 8¼ x 11. 0-486-47360-0

EINSTEIN'S ESSAYS IN SCIENCE, Albert Einstein. Speeches and essays in accessible, everyday language profile influential physicists such as Niels Bohr and Isaac Newton. They also explore areas of physics to which the author made major contributions. 128pp. 5 x 8. 0-486-47011-3

EL DORADO: Further Adventures of the Scarlet Pimpernel, Baroness Orczy. A popular sequel to *The Scarlet Pimpernel,* this suspenseful story recounts the Pimpernel's attempts to rescue the Dauphin from imprisonment during the French Revolution. An irresistible blend of intrigue, period detail, and vibrant characterizations. 352pp. 5³⁄₁₆ x 8¼. 0-486-44026-5

ELEGANT SMALL HOMES OF THE TWENTIES: 99 Designs from a Competition, Chicago Tribune. Nearly 100 designs for five- and six-room houses feature New England and Southern colonials, Normandy cottages, stately Italianate dwellings, and other fascinating snapshots of American domestic architecture of the 1920s. 112pp. 9 x 12. 0-486-46910-7

THE ELEMENTS OF STYLE: The Original Edition, William Strunk, Jr. This is the book that generations of writers have relied upon for timeless advice on grammar, diction, syntax, and other essentials. In concise terms, it identifies the principal requirements of proper style and common errors. 64pp. 5⅜ x 8½. 0-486-44798-7

THE ELUSIVE PIMPERNEL, Baroness Orczy. Robespierre's revolutionaries find their wicked schemes thwarted by the heroic Pimpernel — Sir Percival Blakeney. In this thrilling sequel, Chauvelin devises a plot to eliminate the Pimpernel and his wife. 272pp. 5³⁄₁₆ x 8¼. 0-486-45464-9

AN ENCYCLOPEDIA OF BATTLES: Accounts of Over 1,560 Battles from 1479 B.C. to the Present, David Eggenberger. Essential details of every major battle in recorded history from the first battle of Megiddo in 1479 B.C. to Grenada in 1984. List of battle maps. 99 illustrations. 544pp. 6½ x 9¼. 0-486-24913-1

ENCYCLOPEDIA OF EMBROIDERY STITCHES, INCLUDING CREWEL, Marion Nichols. Precise explanations and instructions, clearly illustrated, on how to work chain, back, cross, knotted, woven stitches, and many more — 178 in all, including Cable Outline, Whipped Satin, and Eyelet Buttonhole. Over 1400 illustrations. 219pp. 8⅜ x 11¼. 0-486-22929-7

ENTER JEEVES: 15 Early Stories, P. G. Wodehouse. Splendid collection contains first 8 stories featuring Bertie Wooster, the deliciously dim aristocrat and Jeeves, his brainy, imperturbable manservant. Also, the complete Reggie Pepper (Bertie's prototype) series. 288pp. 5⅜ x 8½. 0-486-29717-9

ERIC SLOANE'S AMERICA: Paintings in Oil, Michael Wigley. With a Foreword by Mimi Sloane. Eric Sloane's evocative oils of America's landscape and material culture shimmer with immense historical and nostalgic appeal. This original hardcover collection gathers nearly a hundred of his finest paintings, with subjects ranging from New England to the American Southwest. 128pp. 10⅝ x 9. 0-486-46525-X

ETHAN FROME, Edith Wharton. Classic story of wasted lives, set against a bleak New England background. Superbly delineated characters in a hauntingly grim tale of thwarted love. Considered by many to be Wharton's masterpiece. 96pp. 5³⁄₁₆ x 8 ¼. 0-486-26690-7

THE EVERLASTING MAN, G. K. Chesterton. Chesterton's view of Christianity — as a blend of philosophy and mythology, satisfying intellect and spirit — applies to his brilliant book, which appeals to readers' heads as well as their hearts. 288pp. 5⅜ x 8½. 0-486-46036-3

THE FIELD AND FOREST HANDY BOOK, Daniel Beard. Written by a co-founder of the Boy Scouts, this appealing guide offers illustrated instructions for building kites, birdhouses, boats, igloos, and other fun projects, plus numerous helpful tips for campers. 448pp. 5³⁄₁₆ x 8¼. 0-486-46191-2

FINDING YOUR WAY WITHOUT MAP OR COMPASS, Harold Gatty. Useful, instructive manual shows would-be explorers, hikers, bikers, scouts, sailors, and survivalists how to find their way outdoors by observing animals, weather patterns, shifting sands, and other elements of nature. 288pp. 5⅜ x 8½. 0-486-40613-X

FIRST FRENCH READER: A Beginner's Dual-Language Book, Edited and Translated by Stanley Appelbaum. This anthology introduces 50 legendary writers — Voltaire, Balzac, Baudelaire, Proust, more — through passages from *The Red and the Black, Les Misérables, Madame Bovary,* and other classics. Original French text plus English translation on facing pages. 240pp. 5⅜ x 8½. 0-486-46178-5

FIRST GERMAN READER: A Beginner's Dual-Language Book, Edited by Harry Steinhauer. Specially chosen for their power to evoke German life and culture, these short, simple readings include poems, stories, essays, and anecdotes by Goethe, Hesse, Heine, Schiller, and others. 224pp. 5⅜ x 8½. 0-486-46179-3

FIRST SPANISH READER: A Beginner's Dual-Language Book, Angel Flores. Delightful stories, other material based on works of Don Juan Manuel, Luis Taboada, Ricardo Palma, other noted writers. Complete faithful English translations on facing pages. Exercises. 176pp. 5⅜ x 8½. 0-486-25810-6